10 00/0

D1197846

MUSIC IN THE HISTORY
OF
THE WESTERN CHURCH

BY EDWARD DICKINSON

THE SPIRIT OF MUSIC

MUSIC IN THE HISTORY OF THE WESTERN CHURCH

THE STUDY OF THE HISTORY OF MUSIC

THE EDUCATION OF A MUSIC LOVER

MUSIC AND THE HIGHER EDUCATION

CHARLES SCRIBNER'S SONS

MUSIC IN THE HISTORY

OF THE WESTERN CHURCH

WITH AN INTRODUCTION

ON RELIGIOUS MUSIC AMONG PRIMITIVE AND

ANCIENT PEOPLES

BY

EDWARD DICKINSON

Professor of the History of Music, in the Conservatory of Music,
Oberlin College

ST. JOSEPH'S UNIVERSITY

STX

ML3000.D65 1970
Music in the history of the Western chur

3 9353 00124 6394

ML
3000
D65
1970

NEW YORK

CHARLES SCRIBNER'S SONS

Republished by
Scholarly Press, 22929 Industrial East, St. Clair Shores, Michigan 48080

125829

COPYRIGHT, 1902, BY
CHARLES SCRIBNER'S SONS

Printed in the United States of America

*All rights reserved. No part of this book
may be reproduced in any form without
the permission of Charles Scribner's Sons*

This edition is printed on a high-quality,
acid-free paper that meets specification
requirements for fine book paper referred
to as "300-year" paper

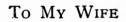

To My Wife

PREFACE

THE practical administration of music in public worship is one of the most interesting of the secondary problems with which the Christian Church has been called upon to deal. Song has proved such a universal necessity in worship that it may almost be said, no music no Church. The endless diversity of musical forms and styles involves the perennial question, How shall music contribute most effectually to the ends which church worship has in view without renouncing those attributes upon which its freedom as fine art depends?

The present volume is an attempt to show how this problem has been treated by different confessions and in different nations and times; how music, in issuing from the bosom of the Church, has been moulded under the influence of varying ideals of devotion, liturgic usages, national temperaments, and types and methods of expression current in secular art. It is the author's chief purpose and hope to arouse in the minds of ministers and non-professional lovers of music, as well as of church musicians, an interest in this branch of art such as they cannot feel so long as its history is unknown to them.

A knowledge of history always tends to promote humility and reverence, and to check the spread of capricious perversions of judgment. Even a feeble sense of the grandeur and beauty of the forms which ecclesiastical music has taken, and the vital relation which it has always held in organized worship, will serve to convince a devoted servant of the Church that its proper administration is as much a matter of concern to-day as it ever has been in the past.

A few of the chapters in this work have appeared in somewhat modified form in the *American Catholic Quarterly Review*, the *Bibliotheca Sacra*, and *Music*. The author acknowledges the permission given by the editors of these magazines to use this material in its present form.

CONTENTS

MUSIC IN THE HISTORY OF THE WESTERN CHURCH

CHAPTER I

PRIMITIVE AND ANCIENT RELIGIOUS MUSIC

LEON GAUTIER, in opening his history of the epic poetry of France, ascribes the primitive poetic utterance of mankind to a religious impulse. "Represent to yourselves," he says, "the first man at the moment when he issues from the hand of God, when his vision rests for the first time upon his new empire. Imagine, if it be possible, the exceeding vividness of his impressions when the magnificence of the world is reflected in the mirror of his soul. Intoxicated, almost mad with admiration, gratitude, and love, he raises his eyes to heaven, not satisfied with the spectacle of the earth; then discovering God in the heavens, and attributing to him all the honor of this magnificence and of the harmonies of creation, he opens his mouth, the first stammerings of speech escape his lips — he speaks; ah, no, he sings, and the first song of the lord of creation will be a hymn to God his creator."

If the language of poetical extravagance may be admitted into serious historical composition, we may

1   1

accept this theatrical picture as an allegorized image of
a truth. Although we speak no longer of a "first man,"
and although we have the best reasons to suppose that
the earliest vocal efforts of our anthropoid progenitors
were a softly modulated love call or a strident battle cry
rather than a *sursum corda;* yet taking for our point of
departure that stage in human development when art
properly begins, when the unpremeditated responses
to simple sensation are supplemented by the more stable
and organized expression of a soul life become self-
conscious, then we certainly do find that the earliest
attempts at song are occasioned by motives that must
in strictness be called religious. The savage is a
very religious being. In all the relations of his simple
life he is hedged about by a stiff code of regulations
whose sanction depends upon his recognition of the
presence of invisible powers and his duties to them.
He divines a mysterious presence as pervasive as the
atmosphere he breathes, which takes in his childish
fancy diverse shapes, as of ghosts, deified ancestors,
anthropomorphic gods, embodied influences of sun and
cloud. In whatever guise these conceptions may clothe
themselves, he experiences a feeling of awe which sometimes appears as abject fear, sometimes as reverence and
love. The emotions which the primitive man feels
under the pressure of these ideas are the most profound
and persistent of which he is capable, and as they involve notions which are held in common by all the
members of the tribe (for there are no sceptics or non-
conformists in the savage community), they are formulated in elaborate schemes of ceremony. The religious

2

sentiment inevitably seeks expression in the assembly —
"the means," as Professor Brinton says, "by which
that most potent agent in religious life, collective suggestion, is brought to bear upon the mind " — the liturgy,
the festival, and the sacrifice.[1] By virtue of certain
laws of the human mind which are evident everywhere,
in the highest civilized condition as in the savage, the
religious emotion, intensified by collective suggestion in
the assembly, will find expression not in the ordinary
manner of thought communication, but in those rhythmic and inflected movements and cadences which are the
natural outlet of strong mental excitement when thrown
back upon itself. These gestures and vocal inflections
become regulated and systematized in order that they
may be permanently retained, and serve in their reaction
to stimulate anew the mental states by which they were
occasioned. Singing, dancing, and pantomime compose
the means by which uncivilized man throughout the
world gives expression to his controlling ideas. The
needed uniformity in movement and accent is most
easily effected by rhythmical beats; and as these beats
are more distinctly heard, and also blend more agreeably
with the tones of the voice if they are musical sounds,
a rude form of instrumental music arises. Here we have
elements of public religious ceremony as they exist in
the most highly organized and spiritualized worships,
— the assemblage, where common motives produce common action and react to produce a common mood, the
ritual with its instrumental music, and the resulting
sense on the part of the participant of detachment from

---

[1] Brinton, *The Religions of Ancient Peoples.*

3

material interests and of personal communion with the unseen powers.

The symbolic dance and the choral chant are among the most primitive, probably the most primitive, forms of art. Out of their union came music, poetry, and dramatic action. Sculpture, painting, and architecture were stimulated if not actually created under the same auspices. "The festival," says Prof. Baldwin Brown, "creates the artist."[1] Festivals among primitive races, as among ancient cultured peoples, are all distinctly religious. Singing and dancing are inseparable. Vocal music is a sort of chant, adopted because of its nerve-exciting property, and also for the sake of enabling a mass of participants to utter the words in unison where intelligible words are used. A separation of caste between priesthood and laity is effected in very early times. The ritual becomes a form of magical incantation; the utterance of the wizard, prophet, or priest consists of phrases of mysterious meaning or incoherent ejaculations.

The prime feature in the earlier forms of worship is the dance. It held also a prominent place in the rites of the ancient cultured nations, and lingers in dim reminiscence in the processions and altar ceremonies of modern liturgical worship. Its function was as important as that of music in the modern Church, and its effect was in many ways closely analogous. When connected with worship, the dance is employed to produce that condition of mental exhilaration which accompanies the expenditure of surplus physical energy, or as a mode

[1] Brown, *The Fine Arts*.

4

of symbolic, semi-dramatic expression of definite reli·
gious ideas. "The audible and visible manifestations
of joy," says Herbert Spencer, "which culminate in
singing and dancing, have their roots in instinctive
actions like those of lively children who, on seeing in
the distance some indulgent relative, run up to him,
joining one another in screams of delight and breaking
their run with leaps; and when, instead of an indulgent
relative met by joyful children, we have a conquering
chief or king met by groups of his people, there will
almost certainly occur saltatory and vocal expressions
of elated feeling, and these must become by implication
signs of respect and loyalty, — ascriptions of worth
which, raised to a higher power, become worship." [1]
Illustrations of such motives in the sacred dance are
found in the festive procession of women, led by
Miriam, after the overthrow of the Egyptians, the
dance of David before the ark, and the dance of the boy
Sophocles around the trophies of Salamis. But the
sacred dance is by no means confined to the discharge
of physical energy under the promptings of joy. The
funeral dance is one of the most frequent of such observances, and dread of divine wrath and the hope of propitiation by means of rites pleasing to the offended
power form a frequent occasion for rhythmic evolution
and violent bodily demonstration.

Far more commonly, however, does the sacred dance
assume a representative character and become a rudimentary drama, either imitative or emblematic. It
depicts the doings of the gods, often under the supposi-

[1] Spencer, *Professional Institutions : Dancer and Musician.*

tion that the divinities are aided by the sympathetic efforts of their devotees. Certain mysteries, known only to the initiated, are symbolized in bodily movement. The fact that the dance was symbolic and instructive, like the sacrificial rite itself, enables us to understand why dancing should have held such prominence in the worship of nations so grave and intelligent as the Egyptians, Hebrews, and Greeks. Representations of religious processions and dances are found upon the monuments of Egypt and Assyria. The Egyptian peasant, when gathering his harvest, sacrificed the first fruits, and danced to testify his thankfulness to the gods. The priests represented in their dances the course of the stars and scenes from the histories of Osiris and Isis. The dance of the Israelites in the desert around the golden calf was probably a reproduction of features of the Egyptian Apis worship. The myths of many ancient nations represent the gods as dancing, and supposed imitations of such august examples had a place in the ceremonies devoted to their honor. The dance was always an index of the higher or lower nature of the religious conceptions which fostered it. Among the purer and more elevated worships it was full of grace and dignity. In the sensuous cults of Phœnicia and Lydia, and among the later Greek votaries of Cybele and Dionysus, the dance reflected the fears and passions that issued in bloody, obscene, and frenzied rites, and degenerated into almost incredible spectacles of wantonness and riot.

It was among the Greeks, however, that the religious dance developed its highest possibilities of expressive-

6

ness and beauty, and became raised to the dignity of a fine art. The admiration of the Greeks for the human form, their unceasing effort to develop its symmetry, strength, and grace, led them early to perceive that it was in itself an efficient means for the expression of the soul, and that its movements and attitudes could work sympathetically upon the fancy. The dance was therefore cultivated as a coequal with music and poetry; educators inculcated it as indispensable to the higher discipline of youth; it was commended by philosophers and celebrated by poets. It held a prominent place in the public games, in processions and celebrations, in the mysteries, and in public religious ceremonies. Every form of worship, from the frantic orgies of the drunken devotees of Dionysus to the pure and tranquil adoration offered to Phœbus Apollo, consisted to a large extent of dancing. Andrew Lang's remark in regard to the connection between dancing and religious solemnity among savages would apply also to the Hellenic sacred dance, that "to dance this or that means to be acquainted with this or that myth, which is represented in a dance or *ballet d'action*." [1] Among the favorite subjects for pantomimic representation, united with choral singing, were the combat between Apollo and the dragon and the sorrows of Dionysus, the commemoration of the latter forming the origin of the splendid Athenian drama. The ancient dance, it must be remembered, had as its motive the expression of a wide range of emotion, and could be employed to symbolize sentiments of wonder, love, and gratitude. Regularly

[1] Lang, *Myth, Ritual, and Religion.*

7

ordered movements, often accompanied by gesture, could well have a place in religious ceremony, as the gods and their relations to mankind were then conceived; and moreover, at a time when music was in a crude state, rhythmic evolutions and expressive gestures, refined and moderated by the exquisite sense of proportion native to the Greek mind, undoubtedly had a solemnizing effect upon the participants and beholders not unlike that of music in modern Christian worship. Cultivated as an art under the name of *orchestik*, the mimic dance reached a degree of elegance and emotional significance to which modern times afford no proper parallel. It was not unworthy of the place it held in the society of poetry and music, with which it combined to form that composite art which filled so high a station in Greek culture in the golden age.

The Hellenic dance, both religious and theatric, was adopted by the Romans, but, like so much that was noble in Greek art, only to be degraded in the transfer. It passed over into the Christian Church, like many other ceremonial practices of heathenism, but modified and by no means of general observance. It appeared on occasions of thanksgiving and celebrations of important events in the Church's history. The priest would often lead the dance around the altar on Sundays and festal days. The Christians sometimes gathered about the church doors at night and danced and sang songs. There is nothing in these facts derogatory to the piety of the early Christians. They simply expressed their joy according to the universal fashion of the age; and especially on those occasions which, as for instance Christmas, were adaptations of old pagan festivals, they naturally imitated many of the time-honored observances. The Christian dance, however, finally degenerated; certain features, such as the nocturnal festivities, gave rise to scandal; the church authorities began to condemn them, and the rising spirit of asceticism drove them into disfavor. The dance was a dangerous reminder of the heathen worship with all its abominations; and since many pagan beliefs and customs, with attendant immoralities, lingered for centuries as a seductive snare to the weaker brethren, the Church bestirred itself to eliminate all perilous associations from religious ceremony and to arouse a love for an absorbed and spiritual worship. During the Middle Age, and even in comparatively recent times in Spain and Spanish America, we find survivals of the ancient religious dance in the Christian Church, but in the more enlightened countries it has practically ceased to exist. The Christian religion is more truly joyful than the Greek; yet the Christian devotee, even in his most confident moments, no longer feels inclined to give vent to his happiness in physical movements, for there is mingled with his rapture a sentiment of awe and submission which bids him adore but be still. Religious processions are frequent in Christian countries, but the participants do not, like the Egyptians and Greeks, dance as they go. We find even in ancient times isolated opinions that public dancing is indecorous. Only in a naïve and childlike stage of society will dancing as a feature of worship seem appropriate and innocent. As reflection increases, the unrestrained and conspicuous manifestation of feeling in shouts and violent bodily movements is deemed unworthy; a more spiritual conception of the nature of the heavenly power and man's relation to it requires that forms of worship should become more refined and moderate. Even the secular dance has lost much of its ancient dignity from somewhat similar reasons, partly also because the differentiation and high development of music, taking the place of dancing as a social art, has relegated the latter to the realm of things outgrown, which no longer minister to man's intellectual necessities.

As we turn to the subject of music in ancient religious rites, we find that where the dance had already reached a high degree of artistic development, music was still in dependent infancy. The only promise of its splendid future was in the reverence already accorded to it, and the universality of its use in prayer and praise. On its vocal side it was used to add solemnity to the words of the officiating priest, forming the intonation, or ecclesiastical accent, which has been an inseparable feature of liturgical worship in all periods. So far as the people had a share in religious functions, vocal music was employed by them in hymns to the gods, or in responsive refrains. In its instrumental form it was used to assist the singers to preserve the correct pitch and rhythm, to regulate the steps of the dance, or, in an independent capacity, to act upon the nerves of the worshipers and increase their sense of awe in the presence of the deity. It is the nervous excitement produced by certain kinds of musical performance that accounts for the fact that incantations, exorcisms, and

10

the ceremonies of demon worship among savages and barbarians are accompanied by harsh-sounding instruments; that tortures, executions, and human sacrifices, such as those of the ancient Phœnicians and Mexicans, were attended by the clamor of drums, trumpets, and cymbals. Even in the Hebrew temple service the blasts of horns and trumpets could have had no other purpose than that of intensifying emotions of awe and dread.

Still another office of music in ancient ceremony, perhaps still more valued, was that of suggesting definite ideas by means of an associated symbolism. In certain occult observances, such as those of the Egyptians and Hindus, relationships were imagined between instruments or melodies and religious or moral conceptions, so that the melody or random tone of the instrument indicated to the initiate the associated principle, and thus came to have an imputed sanctity of its own. This symbolism could be employed to recall to the mind ethical precepts or religious tenets at solemn moments, and tone could become a doubly powerful agent by uniting the effect of vivid ideas to its inherent property of nerve excitement.

Our knowledge of the uses of music among the most ancient nations is chiefly confined to its function in religious ceremony. All ancient worship was ritualistic and administered by a priesthood, and the liturgies and ceremonial rites were intimately associated with music. The oldest literatures that have survived contain hymns to the gods, and upon the most ancient monuments are traced representations of instruments and players. Among the literary records discovered on the site of

Nineveh are collections of hymns, prayers, and penitential psalms, addressed to the Assyrian deities, designed,
as expressly stated, for public worship, and which Professor Sayce compares to the English Book of Common
Prayer. On the Assyrian monuments are carved reliefs
of instrumental players, sometimes single, sometimes in
groups of considerable numbers. Allusions in the
Bible indicate that the Assyrians employed music on
festal occasions, that hymns to the gods were sung at
banquets and dirges at funerals. The kings maintained bands at their courts, and provided a considerable
variety of instruments for use in the idol worship.[1]

There is abundant evidence that music was an important factor in the religious rites of Egypt. The testimony of carved and painted walls of tombs and
temples, the papyrus records, the accounts of visitors,
inform us that music was in Egypt preëminently a
sacred art, as it must needs have been in a land in
which, as Ranke says, there was nothing secular.
Music was in the care of the priests, who jealously
guarded the sacred hymns and melodies from innovation
and foreign intrusion.[2] In musical science, knowledge
of the divisions of the monochord, systems of keys,
notation, etc., the Egyptians were probably in advance

[1] A full account of ancient Assyrian music, so far as known, may be
found in Engel's *Music of the Most Ancient Nations.*

[2] "Long ago they [the Egyptians] appear to have recognized the principle that their young citizens must be habituated to forms and strains of
virtue. These they fixed, and exhibited the patterns of them in their
temples; and no painter or artist is allowed to innovate upon them, or to
leave the traditional forms and invent new ones. To this day no alteration is allowed either in these arts, or in music at all." — Plato, *Laws,*
Book II., Jowett's translation.

of all other nations. The Greeks certainly derived much of their musical practice from the dwellers on the Nile. They possessed an extensive variety of instruments, from the little tinkling sistrum up to the profusely ornamented harp of twelve or thirteen strings, which towered above the performer. From such an instrument as the latter it would seem as though some kind of harmony must have been produced, especially since the player is represented as using both hands. But if such were the case, the harmony could not have been reduced to a scientific system, since otherwise a usage so remarkable would not have escaped the attention of the Greek musicians who derived so much of their art from Egypt. Music never failed at public or private festivity, religious ceremony, or funeral rite. As in all ancient religions, processions to the temples, carrying images of the gods and offerings, were attended by dances and vocal and instrumental performances. Lyrical poems, containing the praises of gods and heroes, were sung at public ceremonies; hymns were addressed to the rising and setting sun, to Ammon and the other gods. According to Chappell, the custom of carolling or singing without words, like birds, to the gods existed among the Egyptians, — a practice which was imitated by the Greeks, from whom the custom was transferred to the Western Church.[1] The chief instrument of the temple worship was the sistrum, and connected with all the temples in the time of the New Empire were companies of female sistrum players who stood in symbolic relations to the god as inmates of his

[1] Chappell, *History of Music.*

13

harem, holding various degrees of rank. These women received high honors, often of a political nature.[1]

In spite of the simplicity and frequent coarseness of ancient music, the older nations ascribed to it an influence over the moral nature which the modern music lover would never think of attributing to his highly developed art. They referred its invention to the gods, and imputed to it thaumaturgical properties. The Hebrews were the only ancient cultivated nation that did not assign to music a superhuman source. The Greek myths of Orpheus, Amphion, and Arion are but samples of hundreds of marvellous tales of musical effect that have place in primitive legends. This belief in the magical power of music was connected with the equally universal opinion that music in itself could express and arouse definite notions and passions, and could exert a direct moral or immoral influence. The importance ascribed by the Greeks to music in the education of youth, as emphatically affirmed by philosophers and law-givers, is based upon this belief. Not only particular melodies, but the different modes or keys were held by the Greeks to exert a positive influence upon character. The Dorian mode was considered bold and manly, inspiring valor and fortitude; the Lydian, weak and enervating. Plato, in the second book of the *Laws*, condemns as "intolerable and blasphemous" the opinion that the purpose of music is to give pleasure. He finds a direct relation between morality and certain forms of music, and would have musicians constrained to compose only such melodies

[1] Erman, *Life in Ancient Egypt*, translated by Tirard.

14

and rhythms as would turn the plastic mind toward virtue. Plutarch, in his discourse concerning music in his *Morals*, says: "The ancient Greeks deemed it requisite by the assistance of music to form and compose the minds of youth to what was decent, sober, and virtuous; believing the use of music beneficially efficacious to incite to all serious actions." He even goes so far as to say that "the right moulding of ingenuous manners and civil conduct lies in a well-grounded musical education." Assumptions of direct moral, intellectual, and even pathological action on the part of music, as distinct from an æsthetic appeal, are so abundant in ancient writings that we cannot dismiss them as mere fanciful hyperbole, but must admit that music really possessed a power over the emotions and volitions which has been lost in its later evolution. The explanation of this apparent anomaly probably lies, first, in the fact that music in antiquity was not a free independent art, and that when the philosophers speak of music they think of it in its associations with poetry, religious and patriotic observances, moral and legal precepts, historic relations, etc. Music, on its vocal side, was mere emphasized speech inflection; it was a slave to poetry; it had no rhythmical laws of its own. The melody did not convey æsthetic charm in itself alone, but simply heightened the sensuous effect of measured speech and vivified the thought. Mr. Spencer's well-known expression that "cadence is the comment of the emotion upon the propositions of the intellect" would apply very accurately to the musical theories of the ancients. Certain modes (that is, keys), on account of convenience of

15

pitch, were employed for certain kinds of poetical expression; and as a poem was always chanted in the mode that was first assigned to it, particular classes of ideas would come to be identified with particular modes. Associations of race character would lead to similar interpretation. The Dorian mode would seem to partake of the sternness and vigor of the warlike Dorian Spartans; the Lydian mode and its melodies would hint of Lydian effeminacy.[1] Instrumental music also was equally restricted to definite meanings through association. It was an accompaniment to poetry, bound up with the symbolic dance, subordinated to formal social observances; it produced not the artistic effect of melody, harmony, and form, but the nervous stimulation of crude unorganized tone, acting upon recipients who had never learned to consider music as anything but a direct emotional excitant or an intensifier of previously conceived ideas.

Another explanation of the ancient view of music as possessing a controlling power over emotion, thought, and conduct lies in the fact that music existed only in its rude primal elements; antiquity in its conception and use of music never passed far beyond that point where tone was the outcome of simple emotional states, and to which notions of precise intellectual significance still clung. · Whatever theory of the origin of music may finally prevail, there can be no question that music in its primitive condition is more directly the outcome of clearly realized feeling than it is when developed into a free, intellectualized, and heterogeneous

---

[1] See Plato, *Republic*, book iii.

art form. Music, the more it rises into an art, the more it exerts a purely æsthetic effect through its action upon intelligences that delight in form, organization, and ideal motion, loses in equal proportion the emotional definiteness that exists in simple and spontaneous tone inflections. The earliest reasoning on the rationale of musical effects always takes for granted that music's purpose is to convey exact ideas, or at least express definite emotion. Music did not advance so far among the ancients that they were able to escape from this naturalistic conception. They could conceive of no higher purpose in music than to move the mind in definite directions, and so they maintained that it always did so. Even in modern life numberless instances prove that the music which exerts the greatest effect over the impulses is not the mature and complex art of the masters, but the simple strains which emanate from the people and bring up recollections which in themselves alone have power to stir the heart. The song that melts a congregation to tears, the patriotic air that fires the enthusiasm of an assembly on the eve of a political crisis, the strain that nerves an army to desperate endeavor, is not an elaborate work of art, but a simple and obvious tune, which finds its real force in association. All this is especially true of music employed for religious ends, and we find in such facts a reason why it could make no progress in ancient times, certainly none where it was under the control of an organized social caste. For the priestly order is always conservative, and in antiquity this conservatism petrified melody, at the same time with the rites to which it adhered, into

2   17

stereotyped formulas. Where music is bound up with a ritual, innovation in the one is discountenanced as tending to loosen the traditional strictness of the other.

I have laid stress upon this point because this attempt of the religious authorities in antiquity to repress music in worship to a subsidiary function was the sign of a conception of music which has always been more or less active in the Church, down even to our own day. As soon as musical art reaches a certain stage of development it strives to emancipate itself from the thraldom of word and visible action, and to exalt itself for its own undivided glory. Strict religionists have always looked upon this tendency with suspicion, and have often strenuously opposed it, seeing in the sensuous fascinations of the art an obstacle to complete absorption in spiritual concerns. The conflict between the devotional and the æsthetic principles, which has been so active in the history of worship music in modern times, never appeared in antiquity except in the later period of Greek art. Since this outbreak of the spirit of rebellion occurred only when Hellenic religion was no longer a force in civilization, its results were felt only in the sphere of secular music; but no progress resulted, for musical culture was soon assumed everywhere by the Christian Church, which for a thousand years succeeded in restraining music within the antique conception of bondage to liturgy and ceremony.

Partly as a result of this subjection of music by its allied powers, partly, perhaps, as a cause, a science of harmony was never developed in ancient times. That music was always performed in unison and octaves, as has been generally believed, is, however, not probable. In view of the fact that the Egyptians possessed harps over six feet in height, having twelve or thirteen strings, and played with both hands, and that the monuments of Assyria and Egypt and the records of musical practice among the Hebrews, Greeks, and other nations show us a large variety of instruments grouped in bands of considerable size, we are justified in supposing that combinations of different sounds were often produced. But the absence from the ancient treatises of any but the most vague and obscure allusions to the production of accordant tones, and the conclusive evidence in respect to the general lack of freedom and development in musical art, is proof positive that, whatever concords of sounds may have been occasionally produced, nothing comparable to our present contrapuntal and harmonic system existed. The music so extravagantly praised in antiquity was, vocally, chant, or recitative, ordinarily in a single part; instrumental music was rude and unsystematized sound, partly a mechanical aid to the voice and the dance step, partly a means of nervous exhilaration. The modern conception of music as a free, self-assertive art, subject only to its own laws, lifting the soul into regions of pure contemplation, where all temporal relations are lost in a tide of self-forgetful rapture, — this was a conception unknown to the mind of antiquity.

The student of the music of the Christian Church naturally turns with curiosity to that one of the ancient nations whose religion was the antecedent of the Christian, and whose sacred literature has furnished the worship of the Church with the loftiest expression of its trust and aspiration. The music of the Hebrews, as Ambros says, "was divine service, not art."[1] Many modern writers have assumed a high degree of perfection in ancient Hebrew music, but only on sentimental grounds, not because there is any evidence to support such an opinion. There is no reason to suppose that music was further developed among the Hebrews than among the most cultivated of their neighbors. Their music, like that of the ancient nations generally, was entirely subsidiary to poetic recitation and dancing; it was unharmonic, simple, and inclined to be coarse and noisy. Although in general use, music never attained so great honor among them as it did among the Greeks. We find in the Scriptures no praises of music as a nourisher of morality, rarely a trace of an ascription of magical properties. Although it had a place in military operations and at feasts, private merry-makings, etc., its chief value lay in its availability for religious purposes. To the Hebrews the arts obtained significance only as they could be used to adorn the courts of Jehovah, or could be employed in the ascription of praise to him. Music was to them an efficient agent to excite emotions of awe, or to carry more directly to the heart the rhapsodies and searching admonitions of psalmists and prophets.

No authentic melodies have come down to us from the time of the Israelitish residence in Palestine. No treatise on Hebrew musical theory or practice, if any such

---

[1] Ambros, *Geschichte der Musik.*

ever existed, has been preserved. No definite light is thrown upon the Hebrew musical system by the Bible or any other ancient book. We may be certain that if the Hebrews had possessed anything distinctive, or far in advance of the practice of their contemporaries, some testimony to that effect would be found. All evidence and analogy indicate that the Hebrew song was a unison chant or cantillation, more or less melodious, and sufficiently definite to be perpetuated by tradition, but entirely subordinate to poetry, in rhythm following the accent and metre of the text.

We are not so much in the dark in respect to the use and nature of Hebrew instruments, although we know as little of the style of music that was performed upon them. Our knowledge of the instruments themselves is derived from those represented upon the monuments of Assyria and Egypt, which were evidently similar to those used by the Hebrews. The Hebrews never invented a musical instrument. Not one in use among them but had its equivalent among nations older in civilization. And so we may infer that the entire musical practice of the Hebrews was derived first from their early neighbors the Chaldeans, and later from the Egyptians; although we may suppose that some modifications may have arisen after they became an independent nation. The first mention of musical instruments in the Bible is in Gen. iv. 21, where Jubal is spoken of as "the father of all such as handle the *kinnor* and *ugab*" (translated in the revised version "harp and pipe"). The word *kinnor* appears frequently in the later books, and is applied to the instrument used by David. This *kinnor* of David and the psalmists was a small portable instrument and might properly be called a lyre. Stringed instruments are usually the last to be developed by primitive peoples, and the use of the *kinnor* implies a considerable degree of musical advancement among the remote ancestors of the Hebrew race in their primeval Chaldean home. The word *ugab* may signify either a single tube like the flute or oboe, or a connected series of pipes like the Pan's pipes or syrinx of the Greeks. There is only one other mention of instruments before the Exodus, *viz.*, in connection with the episode of Laban and Jacob, where the former asks his son-in-law reproachfully, "Wherefore didst thou flee secretly, and steal away from me; and didst not tell me, that I might have sent thee away with mirth and with songs, with *toph* and *kinnor*?"[1] — the *toph* being a sort of small hand drum or tambourine.

After the Exodus other instruments, perhaps derived from Egypt, make their appearance: the *shophar*, or curved tube of metal or ram's horn, heard amid the smoke and thunderings of Mt. Sinai,[2] and to whose sound the walls of Jericho were overthrown;[3] the *hazozerah*, or long silver tube, used in the desert for announcing the time for breaking camp,[4] and employed later by the priests in religious service,[5] popular gatherings, and sometimes in war.[6] The *nebel* was either a harp somewhat larger than the *kinnor*, or possibly a sort of guitar. The *chalil*, translated in the English version

[1] Gen. xxxi. 27.
[2] Ex. xix.
[3] Jos. vi.

[4] Num. x. 2–8.
[5] 2 Chron. v. 12, 13 ; xxix. 26–28.
[6] 2 Chron. xiii. 12, 14.

"pipe," may have been a sort of oboe or flageolet. The band of prophets met by Saul advanced to the sound of *nebel*, *toph*, *chalil*, and *kinnor*.[1] The word "psaltery," which frequently appears in the English version of the psalms, is sometimes the *nebel*, sometimes the *kinnor*, sometimes the *asor*, which was a species of *nebel*. The "instrument of ten strings" was also the *nebel* or *asor*. Percussion instruments, such as the drum, cymbals, bell, and the Egyptian sistrum (which consisted of a small frame of bronze into which three or four metal bars were loosely inserted, producing a jingling noise when shaken), were also in common use. In the Old Testament there are about thirteen instruments mentioned as known to the Hebrews, not including those mentioned in Dan. iii., whose names, according to Chappell, are not derived from Hebrew roots.[2] All of these were simple and rude, yet considerably varied in character, representing the three classes into which instruments, the world over, are divided, *viz.*, stringed instruments, wind instruments, and instruments of percussion.[3]

Although instruments of music had a prominent place in public festivities, social gatherings, and private recreation, far more important was their use in connection with religious ceremony. As the Hebrew nation increased in power, and as their conquests became permanently secured, so the arts of peace developed in

[1] 1 Sam. x. 5.

[2] Chappell, *History of Music*, Introduction.

[3] For extended descriptions of ancient musical instruments the reader is referred to Chappell, *History of Music;* Engel, *The Music of the Most Ancient Nations;* and Stainer, *The Music of the Bible.*

greater profusion and refinement, and with them the embellishments of the liturgical worship became more highly organized. With the capture of Jerusalem and the establishment of the royal residence within its ramparts, the worship of Jehovah increased in splendor; the love of pomp and display, which was characteristic of David, and still more of his luxurious son Solomon, was manifest in the imposing rites and ceremonies that were organized to the honor of the people's God. The epoch of these two rulers was that in which the national force was in the flower of its youthful vigor, the national pride had been stimulated by continual triumphs, the long period of struggle and fear had been succeeded by glorious peace. The barbaric splendor of religious service and festal pageant was the natural expression of popular joy and self-confidence. In all these ebullitions of national feeling, choral and instrumental music on the most brilliant and massive scale held a conspicuous place. The description of the long series of public rejoicings, culminating in the dedication of Solomon's temple, begins with the transportation of the ark of the Lord from Gibeah, when "David and all the house of Israel played before the Lord with all manner of instruments made of fir-wood, and with harps (*kinnor*), and with psalteries (*nebel*), and with timbrels (*toph*), with castanets (*sistrum*), and with cymbals (*tzeltzelim*)." [1] And again, when the ark was brought from the house of Obed-edom into the city of David, the king danced "with all his might," and the ark was brought up "with shouting and with the sound of a trumpet." [2] Singers

[1] 2 Sam. vi. 5.   [2] 2 Sam. vi. 14, 15.

were marshalled under leaders and supported by bands of instruments. The ode ascribed to David was given to Asaph as chief of the choir of Levites; Asaph beat the time with cymbals, and the royal pæan was chanted by masses of chosen singers to the accompaniment of harps, lyres, and trumpets.[1] In the organization of the temple service no detail received more careful attention than the vocal and instrumental music. We read that four thousand Levites were appointed to praise the Lord with instruments.[2] There were also two hundred and eighty-eight skilled singers who sang to instrumental accompaniment beside the altar.[3]

The function performed by instruments in the temple service is also indicated in the account of the reëstablishment of the worship of Jehovah by Hezekiah according to the institutions of David and Solomon. With the burnt offering the song of praise was uplifted to the accompaniment of the "instruments of David," the singers intoned the psalm and the trumpets sounded, and this continued until the sacrifice was consumed. When the rite was ended a hymn of praise was sung by the Levites, while the king and the people bowed themselves.[4]

With the erection of the second temple after the return from the Babylonian exile, the liturgical service was restored, although not with its pristine magnificence. Ezra narrates: "When the builders laid the

---

[1] 1 Chron. xvi. 5, 6.
[2] 1 Chron. xxiii. 5.
[3] 1 Chron. xxv.; 2 Chron. v. 12. See also 2 Chron. v. 11–14.
[4] 2 Chron. xxix. 25–30.

foundation of the temple of the Lord, they set the priests in their apparel with trumpets, and the Levites the sons of Asaph with cymbals, to praise the Lord, after the order of David king of Israel. And they sang one to another in praising and giving thanks unto the Lord, saying, For he is good, for his mercy endureth forever toward Israel." [1] And at the dedication of the wall of Jerusalem, as recorded by Nehemiah, instrumentalists and singers assembled in large numbers, to lead the multitude in rendering praise and thanks to Jehovah. [2] Instruments were evidently employed in independent flourishes and signals, as well as in accompanying the singers. The trumpets were used only in the interludes; the pipes and stringed instruments strengthened the voice parts; the cymbals were used by the leader of the chorus to mark the rhythm.

Notwithstanding the prominence of instruments in all observances of public and private life, they were always looked upon as accessory to song. Dramatic poetry was known to the Hebrews, as indicated by such compositions as the Book of Job and the Song of Songs. No complete epic has come down to us, but certain allusions in the Pentateuch, such as the mention in Numbers xxi. 14 of the "book of the wars of Jehovah," would tend to show that this people possessed a collection of ballads which, taken together, would properly constitute a national epic. But whether lyric, epic, or dramatic, the Hebrew poetry was delivered, according to the universal custom of ancient nations, not in the speaking voice, but in musical tone. The minstrel poet,

[1] Ezra iii. 10, 11.   [2] Neh. xii.

it has been said, was the type of the race. Lyric poetry may be divided into two classes: first, that which is the expression of individual, subjective feeling, the poet communing with himself alone, imparting to his thought a color derived solely from his personal inward experience; and second, that which utters sentiments that are shared by an organization, community, or race, the poet serving as the mouthpiece of a mass actuated by common experiences and motives. The second class is more characteristic of a people in the earlier stages of culture, when the individual is lost in the community, before the tendency towards specialization of interests gives rise to an expression that is distinctly personal. In all the world's literature the Hebrew psalms are the most splendid examples of this second order of lyric poetry; and although we find in them many instances in which an isolated, purely subjective experience finds a voice, yet in all of them the same view of the universe, the same conception of the relation of man to his Creator, the same broad and distinctively national consciousness, control their thought and their diction. And there are very few even of the first class which a Hebrew of earnest piety, searching his own heart, could not adopt as the fitting declaration of his need and assurance.

All patriotic songs and religious poems properly called hymns belong in the second division of lyrics; and in the Hebrew psalms devotional feeling, touched here and there with a patriot's hopes and fears, has once for all projected itself in forms of speech which seem to exhaust the capabilities of sublimity in language. These psalms were set to music, and presuppose music in their thought and their technical structure. A text most appropriate for musical rendering must be free from all subtleties of meaning and over-refinements of phraseology; it must be forcible in movement, its metaphors those that touch upon general observation, its ideas those that appeal to the common consciousness and sympathy. These qualities the psalms possess in the highest degree, and in addition they have a sublimity of thought, a magnificence of imagery, a majesty and strength of movement, that evoke the loftiest energies of a musical genius that ventures to ally itself with them. In every nation of Christendom they have been made the foundation of the musical service of the Church; and although many of the greatest masters of the harmonic art have lavished upon them the richest treasures of their invention, they have but skimmed the surface of their unfathomable suggestion.

Of the manner in which the psalms were rendered in the ancient Hebrew worship we know little. The present methods of singing in the synagogues give us little help, for there is no record by which they can be traced back beyond the definite establishment of the synagogue worship. It is inferred from the structure of the Hebrew poetry, as well as unbroken usage from the beginning of the Christian era, that the psalms were chanted antiphonally or responsively. That form of verse known as parallelism — the repetition of a thought in different words, or the juxtaposition of two contrasted thoughts forming an antithesis — pervades a large amount of the Hebrew poetry, and may be called its technical principle. It is, we might say, a rhythm of thought, an assonance of feeling. This parallelism is more frequently double, sometimes triple. We find this peculiar structure as far back as the address of Lamech to his wives in Gen. iv. 23, 24, in Moses' song after the passage of the Red Sea, in the triumphal ode of Deborah and Barak, in the greeting of the Israelitish women to Saul and David returning from the slaughter of the Philistines, in the Book of Job, in a large proportion of the rhythmical imaginative utterances of the psalmists and prophets. The Oriental Christians sang the psalms responsively; this method was passed on to Milan in the fourth century, to Rome very soon afterward, and has been perpetuated in the liturgical churches of modern Christendom. Whether, in the ancient temple service, this twofold utterance was divided between separate portions of the choir, or between a precentor and the whole singing body, there are no grounds for stating, — both methods have been employed in modern times. It is not even certain that the psalms were sung in alternate half-verses, for in the Jewish Church at the present day the more frequent usage is to divide at the end of a verse. It is evident that the singing was not congregational, and that the share of the people, where they participated at all, was confined to short responses, as in the Christian Church in the time next succeeding the apostolic age. The female voice, although much prized in secular music, according to the Talmud was not permitted in the temple service. There is nothing in the Old Testament that contradicts this except, as some suppose, the reference to the three daughters of Heman in 1 Chron.

xxv. 5, where we read: "And God gave to Heman fourteen sons and three daughters;" and in verse 6: "All these were under the hands of their father for song in the house of the Lord." It is probable, however, that the mention of the daughters is incidental, not intended as an assertion that they were actual members of the temple chorus, for we cannot conceive why an exception should have been made in their behalf. Certainly the whole implication from the descriptions of the temple service and the enumeration of the singers and players is to the effect that only the male voice was utilized in the liturgical worship. There are many allusions to "women singers" in the Scriptures, but they plainly apply only to domestic song, or to processions and celebrations outside the sacred enclosure. It is certainly noteworthy that the exclusion of the female voice, which has obtained in the Catholic Church throughout the Middle Age, in the Eastern Church, in the German Protestant Church, and in the cathedral service of the Anglican Church, was also enforced in the temple worship of Israel. The conviction has widely prevailed among the stricter custodians of religious ceremony in all ages that there is something sensuous and passionate (I use these words in their simpler original meaning) in the female voice — something at variance with the austerity of ideal which should prevail in the music of worship. Perhaps, also, the association of men and women in the sympathy of so emotional an office as that of song is felt to be prejudicial to the complete absorption of the mind which the sacred function demands. Both these reasons have undoubtedly combined in so many historic epochs to keep all the offices of ministry in the house of God in the hands of the male sex. On the other hand, in the more sensuous cults of paganism no such prohibition has existed.

There is difference of opinion in regard to the style of melody employed in the delivery of the psalms in the worship of the temple at Jerusalem. Was it a mere intoned declamation, essentially a monotone with very slight changes of pitch, like the "ecclesiastical accent" of the Catholic Church? Or was it a freer, more melodious rendering, as in the more ornate members of the Catholic Plain Song? The modern Jews incline to the latter opinion, that the song was true melody, obeying, indeed, the universal principle of chant as a species of vocalism subordinated in rhythm to the text, yet with abundant movement and possessing a distinctly tuneful character. It has been supposed that certain inscriptions at the head of some of the psalms are the titles of well-known tunes, perhaps secular folk-songs, to which the psalms were sung. We find, *e. g.*, at the head of Ps. xxii. the inscription, "After the song beginning, Hind of the Dawn." Ps. lvi. has, "After the song, The silent Dove in far-off Lands." Others have, "After lilies" (Ps. xlv. and lxix.), and "Destroy not" (Ps. lvii.–lix.). We cannot on *a priori* principles reject the supposition that many psalms were sung to secular melodies, for we shall find, as we trace the history of music in the Christian era, that musicians have over and over again borrowed profane airs for the hymns of the Church. In fact, there is hardly a branch of the Christian Church that has not at some time done so, and even the rigid Jews in modern times have employed the same means to increase their store of religious melodies.

That the psalms were sung with the help of instruments seems indicated by superscriptions, such as " With stringed instruments," and " To the flutes," although objections have been raised to these translations. No such indications are needed, however, to prove the point, for the descriptions of worship contained in the Old Testament seem explicit. The instruments were used to accompany the voices, and also for preludes and interludes. The word " Selah," so often occurring at the end of a psalm verse, is understood by many authorities to signify an instrumental interlude or flourish, while the singers were for a moment silent. One writer says that at this point the people bowed in prayer.[1]

Such, generally speaking, is the most that can definitely be stated regarding the office performed by music in the worship of Israel in the time of its glory. With the rupture of the nation, its gradual political decline, the inroads of idolatry, the exile in Babylon, the conquest by the Romans, the disappearance of poetic and musical inspiration with the substitution of formality and routine in place of the pristine national sincerity and fervor, it would inevitably follow that the great musical traditions would fade away, until at the time of the birth of Christ but little would remain of the elaborate ritual once committed to the guardianship of

[1] *Synagogue Music*, by F. L. Cohen, in *Papers read at the Anglo-Jewish Historical Exhibition*, London, 1887.

cohorts of priests and Levites. The sorrowing exiles
who hung their harps on the willows of Babylon and
refused to sing the songs of Zion in a strange land certainly never forgot the airs consecrated by such sweet
and bitter memories; but in the course of centuries they
became lost among the strange peoples with whom the
scattered Israelites found their home. Many were for a
time preserved in the synagogues, which, in the later
years of Jewish residence in Palestine, were established in large numbers in all the towns and villages.
The service of the synagogue was a liturgical service,
consisting of benedictions, chanting of psalms and other
Scripture passages, with responses by the people, lessons from the law and the prophets, and sermons. The
instrumental music of the temple and the first synagogues eventually disappeared, and the greater part, if
not the whole, of the ancient psalm melodies vanished
also with the dispersion of the Levites, who were their
especial curators. Many details of ancient ritual and
custom must have survived in spite of vicissitude, but
the final catastrophe, which drove a desolate, heart-
broken remnant of the children of Judah into alien lands,
must inevitably have destroyed all but the merest fragment of the fair residue of national art by sweeping
away all the conditions by which a national art can live.

Does anything remain of the rich musical service
which for fifteen hundred years went up daily from
tabernacle and temple to the throne of the God of
Israel? A question often asked, but without a positive
answer. Perhaps a few notes of an ancient melody, or
a horn signal identical with one blown in the camp or

in the temple court, may survive in the synagogue to-day, a splinter from a mighty edifice which has been submerged by the tide of centuries. As would be presumed of a people so tenacious of time-honored usages, the voice of tradition declares that the intonations of the ritual chant used in the synagogue are survivals of forms employed in the temple at Jerusalem. These intonations are certainly Oriental in character and very ancient, but that they date back to the time of David cannot be proved or disproved. A style of singing like the well-known "cantillation" might easily be preserved, a complete melody possibly, but the presumption is against an antiquity so great as the Jews, with pardonable pride, claim for some of their weird, archaic strains.

With the possible exception of scanty fragments, nothing remains of the songs so much loved by this devoted people in their early home. We may speculate upon the imagined beauty of that music; it is natural to do so. *Omne ignotum pro magnifico.* We know that it often shook the hearts of those that heard it; but our knowledge of the comparative rudeness of all Oriental music, ancient and modern, teaches us that its effect was essentially that of simple unison successions of tones wedded to poetry of singular exaltation and vehemence, and associated with liturgical actions calculated to impress the beholder with an overpowering sense of awe. The interest which all must feel in the religious music of the Hebrews is not due to its importance in the history of art, but to its place in the history of culture. Certainly the art of music was never more highly honored, its efficacy as an agent in arousing the heart to the most ardent spiritual experiences was never more convincingly demonstrated, than when the seers and psalmists of Israel found in it an indispensable auxiliary of those appeals, confessions, praises, and pious raptures in which the whole after-world has seen the highest attainment of language under the impulse of religious ecstasy. Taking "the harp the monarch minstrel swept" as a symbol of Hebrew devotional song at large, Byron's words are true:

> " It softened men of iron mould,
>   It gave them virtues not their own;
> No ear so dull, no soul so cold,
>   That felt not, fired not to the tone,
>   Till David's lyre grew mightier than his throne."

This music foreshadowed the completer expression of Christian art of which it became the type. Inspired by the grandest of traditions, provided with credentials as, on equal terms with poetry, valid in the expression of man's consciousness of his needs and his infinite privilege, — thus consecrated for its future mission, the soul of music passed from Hebrew priests to apostles and Christian fathers, and so on to the saints and hierarchs, who laid the foundation of the sublime structure of the worship music of a later day.

CHAPTER II

RITUAL AND SONG IN THE EARLY CHRISTIAN CHURCH
A.D. 50–600

THE epoch of the apostles and their immediate successors is that around which the most vigorous controversies have been waged ever since modern criticism recognized the supreme importance of that epoch in the history of doctrine and ecclesiastical government. Hardly a form of belief or polity but has sought to obtain its sanction from the teaching and usages of those churches that received their systems most directly from the personal disciples of the Founder. A curiosity less productive of contention, but hardly less persistent, attaches to the forms and methods of worship practised by the Christian congregations. The rise of liturgies, rites, and ceremonies, the origin and use of hymns, the foundation of the liturgical chant, the degree of participation enjoyed by the laity in the offices of praise and prayer, — these and many other closely related subjects of inquiry possess far more than an antiquarian interest; they are bound up with the history of that remarkable transition from the homogenous, more democratic system of the apostolic age, to the hierarchical organization which became matured and consolidated under the Western popes and Eastern patriarchs. Associated with this administrative development and related in its causes, an elaborate system of rites and ceremonies arose, partly an evolution from within, partly an inheritance of ancient habits and predispositions, which at last became formulated into unvarying types of devotional expression. Music participated in this ritualistic movement; it rapidly became liturgical and clerical, the laity ceased to share in the worship of song and resigned this office to a chorus drawn from the minor clergy, and a highly organized body of chants, applied to every moment of the service, became almost the entire substance of worship music, and remained so for a thousand years.

In the very nature of the case a new energy must enter the art of music when enlisted in the ministry of the religion of Christ. A new motive, a new spirit, unknown to Greek or Roman or even to Hebrew, had taken possession of the religious consciousness. To the adoration of the same Supreme Power, before whom the Jew bowed in awe-stricken reverence, was added the recognition of a gift which the Jew still dimly hoped for; and this gift brought with it an assurance, and hence a felicity, which were never granted to the religionist of the old dispensation.

The Christian felt himself the chosen joint-heir of a risen and ascended Lord, who by his death and resurrection had brought life and immortality to light. The devotion to a personal, ever-living Saviour transcended and often supplanted all other loyalty whatsoever, — to country, parents, husband, wife, or child. This religion was, therefore, emphatically one of joy, — a joy so absorbing, so completely satisfying, so founded on the loftiest hopes that the human mind is able to entertain, that even the ecstatic worship of Apollo or Dionysus seems melancholy and hopeless in comparison. Yet it was not a joy that was prone to expend itself in noisy demonstrations. It was mingled with such a profound sense of personal unworthiness and the most solemn responsibilities, tempered with sentiments of awe and wonder in the presence of unfathomable mysteries, that the manifestations of it must be subdued to moderation, expressed in forms that could appropriately typify spiritual and eternal relationships. And so, as sculpture was the art which most adequately embodied the humanistic conceptions of Greek theology, poetry and music became the arts in which Christianity found a vehicle of expression most suited to her genius. These two arts, therefore, when acted upon by ideas so sublime and penetrating as those of the Gospel, must at last become transformed, and exhibit signs of a renewed and aspiring activity. The very essence of the divine revelation in Jesus Christ must strike a more thrilling note than tone and emotional speech had ever sounded before. The genius of Christianity, opening up new soul depths, and quickening, as no other religion could, the higher possibilities of holiness in man, was especially adapted to evoke larger manifestations of musical invention. The religion of Jesus revealed God in the universality of his fatherhood, and his omnipresence in nature and in the human conscience. God must be worshipped in spirit and in truth, as one who draws men into communion with him by his immediate action upon the heart. This

38

religion made an appeal that could only be met by the purification of the heart, and by reconciliation and union with God through the merits of the crucified Son. The believer felt the possibility of direct and loving communion with the Infinite Power as the stirring of the very bases of his being. This new consciousness must declare itself in forms of expression hardly glimpsed by antiquity, and literature and art undergo re-birth. Music particularly, the art which seems peculiarly capable of reflecting the most urgent longings of the spirit, felt the animating force of Christianity as the power which was to emancipate it from its ancient thraldom and lead it forth into a boundless sphere of action.

Not at once, however, could musical art spring up full grown and responsive to these novel demands. An art, to come to perfection, requires more than a motive. The motive, the vision, the emotion yearning to realize itself, may be there, but beyond this is the mastery of material and form, and such mastery is of slow and tedious growth. Especially is this true in respect to the art of music; musical forms, having no models in nature like painting and sculpture, no associative symbolism like poetry, no guidance from considerations of utility like architecture, must be the result, so far as any human work can be such, of actual free creation. And yet this creation is a progressive creation; its forms evolve from forms preëxisting as demands for expression arise to which the old are inadequate. Models must be found, but in the nature of the case the art can never go outside of itself for its suggestion. And although Christian music must be a development and not the sudden product of an exceptional inspiration, yet we must not suppose that the early Church was compelled to work out its melodies from those crude elements in which anthropology discovers the first stage of musical progress in primitive man. The Christian fathers, like the founders of every historic system of religious music, drew their suggestion and perhaps some of their actual material from both religious and secular sources. The principle of ancient music, to which the early Christian music conformed, was that of the subordination of music to poetry and the dance-figure. Harmony was virtually unknown in antiquity, and without a knowledge of part-writing no independent art of music is possible. The song of antiquity was the most restricted of all melodic styles, *viz.*, the chant or recitative. The essential feature of both chant and recitative is that the tones are made to conform to the metre and accent of the text, the words of which are never repeated or prosodically modified out of deference to melodic phrases and periods. In true song, on the contrary, the words are subordinated to the exigencies of musical laws of structure, and the musical phrase, not the word, is the ruling power. The principle adopted by the Christian fathers was that of the chant, and Christian music could not begin to move in the direction of modern artistic attainment until, in the course of time, a new technical principle, and a new conception of the relation between music and poetry, could be introduced.

In theory, style, usage, and probably to some extent in actual melodies also, the music of the primitive Church forms an unbroken line with the music of pre-

Christian antiquity. The relative proportion contributed by Jewish and Greek musical practice cannot be known. There was at the beginning no formal break with the ancient Jewish Church; the disciples assembled regularly in the temple for devotional exercises; worship in their private gatherings was modelled upon that of the synagogue which Christ himself had implicitly sanctioned. The synagogical code was modified by the Christians by the introduction of the eucharistic service, the Lord's Prayer, the baptismal formula, and other institutions occasioned by the new doctrines and the "spiritual gifts." At Christ's last supper with his disciples, when the chief liturgical rite of the Church was instituted, the company sang a hymn which was unquestionably the "great Hallel" of the Jewish Passover celebration.[1] The Jewish Christians clung with an inherited reverence to the venerable forms of their fathers' worship; they observed the Sabbath, the three daily hours of prayer, and much of the Mosaic ritual. In respect to musical usages, the most distinct intimation in early records of the continuation of ancient forms is found in the occasional reference to the habit of antiphonal or responsive chanting of the psalms. Fixed forms of prayer were also used in the apostolic Church, which were to a considerable extent modelled upon the psalms and the benedictions of the synagogue ritual. That the Hebrew melodies were borrowed at the same time cannot be demonstrated, but it may be assumed as a necessary inference.

[1] Ps. cxiii–cxviii.

With the spread of the Gospel among the Gentiles, the increasing hostility between Christians and Jews, the dismemberment of the Jewish nationality, and the overthrow of Jewish institutions to which the Hebrew Christians had maintained a certain degree of attachment, dependence upon the Jewish ritual was loosened, and the worship of the Church came under the influence of Hellenic systems and traditions. Greek philosophy and Greek art, although both in decadence, were dominant in the intellectual life of the East, and it was impossible that the doctrine, worship, and government of the Church should not be gradually leavened by them. St. Paul wrote in the Greek language; the earliest liturgies are in Greek. The sentiment of prayer and praise was, of course, Hebraic; the psalms formed the basis of all lyric expression, and the hymns and liturgies were to a large extent colored by their phraseology and spirit. The shapeliness and flexibility of Greek art, the inward fervor of Hebrew aspiration, the love of ceremonial and symbolism, which was not confined to any single nation but was a universal characteristic of the time, all contributed to build up the composite and imposing structure of the later worship of the Eastern and Western churches.

The singing of psalms formed a part of the Christian worship from the beginning, and certain special psalms were early appointed for particular days and occasions. At what time hymns of contemporary origin were added we have no means of knowing. Evidently during the life of St. Paul, for we find him encouraging the Ephesians and Colossians to the use of "psalms, hymns, and spiritual songs."[1] To be sure he is not specifically alluding to public worship in these exhortations (in the first instance "speaking to yourselves" and "singing and making melody in your hearts," in the second "teaching and admonishing one another"), but it is hardly to be supposed that the spiritual exercise of which he speaks would be excluded from the religious services which at that time were of daily observance. The injunction to teach and admonish by means of songs also agrees with other evidences that a prime motive for hymn singing in many of the churches was instruction in the doctrines of the faith. It would appear that among the early Christians, as with the Greeks and other ancient nations, moral precepts and instruction in religious mysteries were often thrown into poetic and musical form, as being by this means more impressive and more easily remembered.

It is to be noticed that St. Paul, in each of the passages cited above, alludes to religious songs under three distinct terms, *viz.*: ψαλμοί, ὕμνοι, and ᾠδαὶ πνευματικαί. The usual supposition is that the terms are not synonymous, that they refer to a threefold classification of the songs of the early Church into: 1, the ancient Hebrew psalms properly so called; 2, hymns taken from the Old Testament and not included in the psalter and since called canticles, such as the thanksgiving of Hannah, the song of Moses, the Psalm of the Three Children from the continuation of the Book of Daniel, the vision of Habakkuk, etc.; and, 3, songs composed by the Christians themselves. The last of these three classes

[1] Eph. v. 19; Col. iii. 16.

points us to the birth time of Christian hymnody. The lyric inspiration, which has never failed from that day to this, began to move the instant the proselyting work of the Church began. In the freedom and informality of the religious assembly as it existed among the Hellenic Christians, it became the practice for the believers to contribute impassioned outbursts, which might be called songs in a rudimentary state. In moments of highly charged devotional ecstasy this spontaneous utterance took the form of broken, incoherent, unintelligible ejaculations, probably in cadenced, half-rhythmic tone, expressive of rapture and mystical illumination. This was the "glossolalia," or "gift of tongues" alluded to by St. Paul in the first epistle to the Corinthians as a practice to be approved, under certain limitations, as edifying to the believers.[1]

Dr. Schaff defines the gift of tongues as "an utterance proceeding from a state of unconscious ecstasy in the speaker, and unintelligible to the hearer unless interpreted. The speaking with tongues is an involuntary, psalm-like prayer or song uttered from a spiritual trance, in a peculiar language inspired by the Holy Spirit. The soul is almost entirely passive, an instrument on which the Spirit plays his heavenly melodies." "It is emotional rather than intellectual, the language of excited imagination, not of cool reflection."[2] St. Paul was himself an adept in this singular form of worship, as he himself declares in 1 Cor. xiv. 18; but with his habitual coolness of judgment he warns the

[1] 1 Cor. xii. and xiv.

[2] Schaff, *History of the Christian Church,* I. p. 234 f.; p. 435.

excitable Corinthian Christians that sober instruction is more profitable, that the proper end of all utterance in common public worship is edification, and enjoins as an effective restraint that "if any man speaketh in a tongue, let one interpret; but if there be no interpreter, let him keep silence in the Church; and let him speak to himself and to God."[1]   With the regulation of the worship in stated liturgic form this extemporaneous ebullition of feeling was done away, but if it was analogous, as it probably was, to the practice so common in Oriental vocal music, both ancient and modern, of delivering long wordless tonal flourishes as an expression of joy, then it has in a certain sense survived in the "jubilations" of the Catholic liturgical chant, which in the early Middle Age were more extended than now. Chappell finds traces of a practice somewhat similar to the "jubilations" existing in ancient Egypt.   "This practice of carolling or singing without words, like birds, to the gods, was copied by the Greeks, who seem to have carolled on four vowels.   The vowels had probably, in both cases, some recognized meaning attached to them, as substitutes for certain words of praise — as was the case when the custom was transferred to the Western Church."[2]   This may or may not throw light upon the obscure nature of the glossolalia, but it is not to be supposed that the Corinthian Christians invented this custom, since we find traces of it in the worship of the ancient pagan nations; and so far as it was the unrestrained outburst of emotion, it must have been to

[1] 1 Cor. xiv. 27, 28.
[2] Chappell. *History of Music.*

some extent musical, and only needed regulation and the application of a definite key-system to become, like the mediæval Sequence under somewhat similar conditions, an established order of sacred song.

Out of a musical impulse, of which the glossolalia was one of many tokens, united with the spirit of prophecy or instruction, grew the hymns of the infant Church, dim outlines of which begin to appear in the twilight of this obscure period. The worshipers of Christ could not remain content with the Hebrew psalms, for, in spite of their inspiriting and edifying character, they were not concerned with the facts on which the new faith was based, except as they might be interpreted as prefiguring the later dispensation. Hymns were required in which Christ was directly celebrated, and the apprehension of his infinite gifts embodied in language which would both fortify the believers and act as a converting agency. It would be contrary to all analogy and to the universal facts of human nature if such were not the case, and we may suppose that a Christian folk-song, such as the post-apostolic age reveals to us, began to appear in the first century. Some scholars believe that certain of these primitive hymns, or fragments of them, are embalmed in the Epistles of St. Paul and the Book of the Revelation.[1] The magnificent description of the worship of God and the Lamb in the Apocalypse has been supposed by some to have been suggested by the manner of worship, already become liturgical, in the

[1] Among such supposed quotations are: Eph. v. 14 ; 1 Tim. iii. 16 ; 2 Tim. ii. 11; Rev. iv. 11 ; v. 9–13 ; xi. 15–18 ; xv. 3, 4.

Eastern churches. Certainly there is a manifest resemblance between the picture of one sitting upon the
throne with the twenty-four elders and a multitude of
angels surrounding him, as set forth in the Apocalypse,
and the account given in the second book of the Constitutions of the Apostles of the throne of the bishop in the
middle of the church edifice, with the presbyters and
deacons on each side and the laity beyond. In this
second book of the Constitutions, belonging, of course,
to a later date than the apostolic period, there is no
mention of hymn singing. The share of the people is
confined to responses at the end of the verses of the
psalms, which are sung by some one appointed to this
office.[1] The sacerdotal and liturgical movement had
already excluded from the chief acts of worship the
independent song of the people. Those who assume
that the office of song in the early Church was freely
committed to the general body of believers have some
ground for their assumption; but if we are able to distinguish between the private and public worship, and
could know how early it was that set forms and liturgies were adopted, it would appear that at the longest
the time was very brief when the laity were allowed a
share in any but the subordinate offices. The earliest
testimony that can be called definite is contained in the
celebrated letter of the younger Pliny from Bithynia
to the Emperor Trajan, in the year 112, in which the
Christians are described as coming together before
daylight and singing hymns alternately (invicem) to
Christ. This may with some reason be held to refer

[1] *Constitutions of the Apostles,* book. ii. chap. 57.

47

to responsive or antiphonal singing, similar to that described by Philo in his account of the worship of the Jewish sect of the Therapeutæ in the first century. The tradition was long preserved in the Church that Ignatius, bishop of Antioch in the second century, introduced antiphonal chanting into the churches of that city, having been moved thereto by a vision of angels singing in that manner. But we have only to go back to the worship of the ancient Hebrews for the suggestion of this practice. This alternate singing appears to have been most prevalent in the Syrian churches, and was carried thence to Milan and Rome, and through the usage in these cities was established in the permanent habit of the Western Church.

Although the singing of psalms and hymns by the body of worshipers was, therefore, undoubtedly the custom of the churches while still in their primitive condition as informal assemblies of believers for mutual counsel and edification, the steady progress of ritualism and the growth of sacerdotal ideas inevitably deprived the people of all initiative in the worship, and concentrated the offices of public devotion, including that of song, exclusively in the hands of the clergy. By the middle of the fourth century, if not earlier, the change was complete. The simple organization of the apostolic age had developed by logical gradations into a compact hierarchy of patriarchs, bishops, priests, and deacons. The clergy were no longer the servants or representatives of the people, but held a mediatorial position as the channels through which divine grace was transmitted to the faithful. The great Eastern liturgies, such as those which bear the names of St. James and St. Mark, if not yet fully formulated and committed to writing, were in all essentials complete and adopted as the substance of the public worship. The principal service was divided into two parts, from the second of which, the eucharistic service proper, the catechumens and penitents were excluded. The prayers, readings, and chanted sentences, of which the liturgy mainly consisted, were delivered by priests, deacons, and an officially constituted choir of singers, the congregation uniting only in a few responses and ejaculations. In the liturgy of St. Mark, which was the Alexandrian, used in Egypt and neighboring countries, we find allotted to the people a number of responses: "Amen," "Kyrie eleison," "And to thy spirit" (in response to the priest's "Peace be to all"); "We lift them up to the Lord" (in response to the priest's "Let us lift up our hearts"); and "In the name of the Lord; Holy God, holy mighty, holy immortal," after the Trisagion; "And from the Holy Spirit was he made flesh," after the prayer of oblation; "Holy, holy, holy Lord," before the consecration; "Our Father, who art in heaven," etc.; before the communion, "One Father holy, one Son holy, one Spirit holy, in the unity of the Holy Spirit, Amen;" at the dismissal, "Amen, blessed be the name of the Lord."

In the liturgy of St. James, the liturgy of the Jerusalem Church, a very similar share, in many instances with identical words, is assigned to the people; but a far more frequent mention is made of the choir of singers who render the Trisagion hymn, which, in St.

Mark's liturgy, is given by the people: besides the "Allelulia," the hymn to the Virgin Mother, "O taste and see that the Lord is good," and "The Holy Ghost shall come upon thee, and the power of the Highest shall overshadow thee."

A large portion of the service, as indicated by these liturgies, was occupied by prayers, during which the people kept silence. In the matter of responses the congregation had more direct share than in the Catholic Church to-day, for now the chancel choir acts as their representatives, while the Kyrie eleison has become one of the choral portions of the Mass, and the Thrice Holy has been merged in the choral Sanctus. But in the liturgical worship, whatever may have been the case in non-liturgical observances, the share of the people was confined to these few brief ejaculations and prescribed sentences, and nothing corresponding to the congregational song of the Protestant Church can be found. Still earlier than this final issue of the ritualistic movement the singing of the people was limited to psalms and canticles, a restriction justified and perhaps occasioned by the ease with which doctrinal vagaries and mystical extravagances could be instilled into the minds of the converts by means of this very subtle and persuasive agent. The conflict of the orthodox churches with the Gnostics and Arians showed clearly the danger of unlimited license in the production and singing of hymns, for these formidable heretics drew large numbers away from the faith of the apostles by means of the choral songs which they employed everywhere for proselyting purposes. The Council of Laodicea (held

50

between 343 and 381) decreed in its 13th Canon: "Besides the appointed singers, who mount the ambo and sing from the book, others shall not sing in the church."[1] The exact meaning of this prohibition has not been determined, for the participation of the people in the church song did not entirely cease at this time. How generally representative this council was, or how extensive its authority, is not known; but the importance of this decree has been exaggerated by historians of music, for, at most, it serves only as a register of a fact which was an inevitable consequence of the universal hierarchical and ritualistic tendencies of the time.

The history of the music of the Christian Church properly begins with the establishment of the priestly liturgic chant, which had apparently supplanted the popular song in the public worship as early as the fourth century. Of the character of the chant melodies at this period in the Eastern Church, or of their sources, we have no positive information. Much vain conjecture has been expended on this question. Some are persuaded that the strong infusion of Hebraic feeling and phraseology into the earliest hymns, and the adoption of the Hebrew psalter into the service, necessarily implies the inheritance of the ancient temple and synagogue melodies also. Others assume that the allusion of St. Augustine to the usage at Alexandria under St. Athanasius, which was "more like speaking than singing,"[2] was an example of the practice of the Oriental and Roman churches generally, and that the later chant

---

[1] Hefele, *History of the Councils of the Church*, translated by Oxenham.
[2] St. Augustine, *Confessions.*

developed out of this vague song-speech. Others, like Kiesewetter, exaggerating the antipathy of the Christians to everything identified with Judaism and paganism, conceive the primitive Christian melodies as entirely an original invention, a true Christian folk-song.[1] None of these suppositions, however, could have more than a local and temporary application; the Jewish Christian congregations in Jerusalem and neighboring cities doubtless transferred a few of their ancestral melodies to the new worship; a prejudice against highly developed tune as suggesting the sensuous cults of paganism may have existed among the more austere; here and there new melodies may have sprung up to clothe the extemporized lyrics that became perpetuated in the Church. But the weight of evidence and analogy inclines to the belief that the liturgic song of the Church, both of the East and West, was drawn partly in form and almost wholly in spirit and complexion from the Greek and Greco-Roman musical practice.

But scanty knowledge of Christian archæology and liturgics is necessary to show that much of form, ceremony, and decoration in the worship of the Church was the adaptation of features anciently existing in the faiths and customs which the new religion supplanted. The practical genius which adopted Greek metres for Christian hymns, and modified the styles of basilikas, scholæ, and domestic architecture in effecting a suitable form of church building, would not cavil at the melodies and vocal methods which seemed so well suited to be a musical garb for the liturgies. Greek music was,

[1] Kiesewetter, *Geschichte der europäisch-abendländischen Musik.*

indeed, in some of its phases, in decadence at this period. It had gained nothing in purity by passing into the hands of Roman voluptuaries. The age of the virtuosos, aiming at brilliancy and sensationalism, had succeeded to the classic traditions of austerity and reserve. This change was felt, however, in instrumental music chiefly, and this the Christian churches disdained to touch. It was the residue of what was pure and reverend, drawn from the tradition of Apollo's temple and the Athenian tragic theatre; it was the form of vocalism which austere philosophers like Plutarch praised that was drafted into the service of the Gospel. Perhaps even this was reduced to simple terms in the Christian practice; certainly the oldest chants that can be traced are the plainest, and the earliest scale system of the Italian Church would appear to allow but a very narrow compass to melody. We can form our most accurate notion of the nature of the early Christian music, therefore, by studying the records of Greek practice and Greek views of music's nature and function in the time of the flowering of Greek poetry, for certainly the Christian fathers did not attempt to go beyond that; and perhaps, in their zeal to avoid all that was meretricious in tonal art, they adopted as their standard those phases which could most easily be made to coalesce with the inward and humble type of piety inculcated by the faith of the Gospel. This hypothesis does not imply a note-for-note borrowing of Greek and Roman melodies, but only their adaptation. As Luther and the other founders of the music of the German Protestant Church took

melodies from the Catholic chant and the German and
Bohemian religious and secular folk-song, and recast
them to fit the metres of their hymns, so the early
Christian choristers would naturally be moved to do
with the melodies which they desired to transplant.
Much modification was necessary, for while the Greek
and Roman songs were metrical, the Christian psalms,
antiphons, prayers, responses, etc., were unmetrical;
and while the pagan melodies were always sung to an
instrumental accompaniment, the church chant was
exclusively vocal. Through the influence of this
double change of technical and æsthetic basis, the liturgic song was at once more free, aspiring, and varied than
its prototype, taking on that rhythmic flexibility and
delicate shading in which also the unique charm of the
Catholic chant of the present day so largely consists.

In view of the controversies over the use of instrumental music in worship, which have been so violent in
the British and American Protestant churches, it is an
interesting question whether instruments were employed
by the primitive Christians. We know that instruments
performed an important function in the Hebrew temple
service and in the ceremonies of the Greeks. At this
point, however, a break was made with all previous
practice, and although the lyre and flute were sometimes employed by the Greek converts, as a general rule
the use of instruments in worship was condemned.
Many of the fathers, speaking of religious song, make
no mention of instruments; others, like Clement of
Alexandria and St. Chrysostom, refer to them only to
denounce them. Clement says: " Only one instrument

do we use, *viz.*, the word of peace wherewith we honor God, no longer the old psaltery, trumpet, drum, and flute." Chrysostom exclaims: "David formerly sang in psalms, also we sing to-day with him; he had a lyre with lifeless strings, the Church has a lyre with living strings. Our tongues are the strings of the lyre, with a different tone, indeed, but with a more accordant piety." St. Ambrose expresses his scorn for those who would play the lyre and psaltery instead of singing hymns and psalms; and St. Augustine adjures believers not to turn their hearts to theatrical instruments. The religious guides of the early Christians felt that there would be an incongruity, and even profanity, in the use of the sensuous nerve-exciting effects of instrumental sound in their mystical, spiritual worship. Their high religious and moral enthusiasm needed no aid from external stimulus; the pure vocal utterance was the more proper expression of their faith. This prejudice against instrumental music, which was drawn from the very nature of its æsthetic impression, was fortified by the associations of instruments with superstitious pagan rites, and especially with the corrupting scenes habitually represented in the degenerate theatre and circus. "A Christian maiden," says St. Jerome, "ought not even to know what a lyre or a flute is, or what it is used for." No further justification for such prohibitions is needed than the shameless performances common upon the stage in the time of the Roman empire, as portrayed in the pages of Apuleius and other delineators of the manners of the time. Those who assumed the guardianship of the morals of the little Christian communities were compelled to employ the strictest measures to prevent their charges from breathing the moral pestilence which circulated without check in the places of public amusement; most of all must they insist that every reminder of these corruptions, be it an otherwise innocent harp or flute, should be excluded from the common acts of religion.

The transfer of the office of song from the general congregation to an official choir involved no cessation of the production of hymns for popular use, for the distinction must always be kept in mind between liturgical and non-liturgical song, and it was only in the former that the people were commanded to abstain from participation in all but the prescribed responses. On the other hand, as ceremonies multiplied and festivals increased in number, hymnody was stimulated, and lyric songs for private and social edification, for the hours of prayer, and for use in processions, pilgrimages, dedications, and other occasional celebrations, were rapidly produced. As has been shown, the Christians had their hymns from the very beginning, but with the exception of one or two short lyrics, a few fragments, and the great liturgical hymns which were also adopted by the Western Church, they have been lost. Clement of Alexandria, third century, is often spoken of as the first known Christian hymn writer; but the single poem, the song of praise to the Logos, which has gained him this title, is not, strictly speaking, a hymn at all. From the fourth century onward the tide of Oriental hymnody steadily rose, reaching its culmination in the eighth and ninth centuries. The Eastern hymns are divided into two schools — the Syrian and the Greek. Of the group of Syrian poets the most celebrated are Synesius, born about 375, and Ephraem, who died at Edessa in 378. Ephraem was the greatest teacher of his time in the Syrian Church, and her most prolific and able hymnist. He is best remembered as the opponent of the followers of Bardasanes and Harmonius, who had beguiled many into their Gnostic errors by the charm of their hymns and melodies. Ephraem met these schismatics on their own ground, and composed a large number of songs in the spirit of orthodoxy, which he gave to choirs of his followers to be sung on Sundays and festal days. The hymns of Ephraem were greatly beloved by the Syrian Church, and are still valued by the Maronite Christians. The Syrian school of hymnody died out in the fifth century, and poetic inspiration in the Eastern Church found its channel in the Greek tongue.

Before the age of the Greek Christian poets whose names have passed into history, the great anonymous unmetrical hymns appeared which still hold an eminent place in the liturgies of the Catholic and Protestant Churches as well as of the Eastern Church. The best known of these are the two Glorias — the Gloria Patri and the Gloria in excelsis; the Ter Sanctus or Cherubic hymn, heard by Isaiah in vision; and the Te Deum. The Magnificat or thanksgiving of Mary, and the Benedicite or Song of the Three Children, were early adopted by the Eastern Church. The Kyrie eleison appears as a response by the people in the liturgies of St. Mark and St. James. It was adopted into the Roman liturgy at a very early date; the addition of the

Christe eleison is said to have been made by Gregory the Great. The Gloria in excelsis, the "greater doxology," with the possible exception of the Te Deum the noblest of the early Christian hymns, is the angelic song given in Luke ii. 14, with additions which were made not later than the fourth century. "Begun in heaven, finished on earth." It was first used in the Eastern Church as a morning hymn. The Te Deum laudamus has often been given a Western origin, St. Ambrose and St. Augustine, according to a popular legend, having been inspired to improvise it in alternate verses at the baptism of St. Augustine by the bishop of Milan. Another tradition ascribes the authorship to St. Hilary in the fourth century. Its original form is unknown, but it is generally believed to have been formed by accretions upon a Greek original. Certain phrases contained in it are also in the earlier liturgies. The present form of the hymn is probably as old as the fifth century.[1]

Of the very few brief anonymous songs and fragments which have come down to us from this dim period the most perfect is a Greek hymn, which was sometimes sung in private worship at the lighting of the lamps. It has been made known to many English readers through Longfellow's beautiful translation in "The Golden Legend:"

> "O gladsome light
> Of the Father immortal,
> And of the celestial
> Sacred and blessed

[1] For an exhaustive discussion of the history of the To Deum see Julian's *Dictionary of Hymnology.*

> Jesus, our Saviour !
> Now to the sunset
> Again hast thou brought us ;
> And seeing the evening
> Twilight, we bless thee,
> Praise thee, adore thee
> Father omnipotent !
> Son, the Life-giver !
> Spirit, the Comforter !
> Worthy at all times
> Of worship and wonder ! "

Overlapping the epoch of the great anonymous hymns and continuing beyond it is the era of the Greek hymnists whose names and works are known, and who contributed a vast store of lyrics to the offices of the Eastern Church. Eighteen quarto volumes, says Dr. J. M. Neale, are occupied by this huge store of religious poetry. Dr. Neale, to whom the English-speaking world is chiefly indebted for what slight knowledge it has of these hymns, divides them into three epochs :

1. "That of formation, when this poetry was gradually throwing off the bondage of classical metres, and inventing and perfecting its various styles; this period ends about A. D. 726."

2. "That of perfection, which nearly coincides with the period of the iconoclastic controversy, 726–820."

3. "That of decadence, when the effeteness of an effeminate court and the dissolution of a decaying empire reduced ecclesiastical poetry, by slow degrees, to a stilted bombast, giving great words to little meaning, heaping up epithet upon epithet, tricking out commonplaces in diction more and more gorgeous, till

59

sense and simplicity are alike sought in vain; 820-1400." [1]

The centres of Greek hymnody in its most brilliant period were Sicily, Constantinople, and Jerusalem and its neighborhood, particularly St. Sabba's monastery, where lived St. Cosmas and St. John Damascene, the two greatest of the Greek Christian poets. The hymnists of this epoch preserved much of the narrative style and objectivity of the earlier writers, especially in the hymns written to celebrate the Nativity, the Epiphany, and other events in the life of Christ. In others a more reflective and introspective quality is found. The fierce struggles, hatreds, and persecutions of the iconoclastic controversy also left their plain mark upon many of them in a frequent tendency to magnify temptations and perils, in a profound sense of sin, a consciousness of the necessity of penitential discipline for the attainment of salvation, and a certain fearful looking-for of judgment. This attitude, so different from the peace and confidence of the earlier time, attains its most striking manifestation in the sombre and powerful funeral dirge ascribed to St. John Damascene ("Take the last kiss") and the Judgment hymn of St. Theodore of the Studium. In the latter the poet strikes with trembling hand the tone which four hundred years later was sounded with such imposing majesty in the Dies Iræ of St. Thomas of Celano.

The Catholic hymnody, so far at least as concerns the usage of the ritual, belongs properly to a later

[1] *Hymns of the Eastern Church*, translated, with notes and an introduction by J. M. Neale, D.D.

period. The hymns of St. Hilary, St. Damasus, St. Augustine, St. Ambrose, Prudentius, Fortunatus, and St. Gregory, which afterward so beautified the Divine Office, were originally designed for private devotion and for accessory ceremonies, since it was not until the tenth or eleventh century that hymns were introduced into the office at Rome, following a tendency that was first authoritatively recognized by the Council of Toledo in the seventh century.

The history of Christian poetry and music in the East ends with the separation of the Eastern and Western Churches. From that time onward a chilling blight rested upon the soil which the apostles had cultivated with such zeal and for a time with such grand result. The fatal controversy over icons, the check inflicted by the conquests of the Mohammedan power, the crushing weight of Byzantine luxury and tyranny, and that insidious apathy which seems to dwell in the very atmosphere of the Orient, sooner or later entering into every high endeavor, relaxing and corrupting—all this sapped the spiritual life of the Eastern Church. The pristine enthusiasm was succeeded by fanaticism, and out of fanaticism, in its turn, issued formalism, bigotry, stagnation. It was only among the nations that were to rear a new civilization in Western Europe on the foundations laid by the Roman empire that political and social conditions could be created which would give free scope for the expansion of the divine life of Christianity. It was only in the West, also, that the motives that were adequate to inspire a Christian art, after a long struggle against Byzantine formalism and

61

convention, could issue in a prophetic artistic progress. The attempted reconciliation of Christian ideas and traditional pagan method formed the basis of Christian art, but the new insight into spiritual things, and the profounder emotions that resulted, demanded new ideals and principles as well as new subjects. The nature and destiny of the soul, the beauty and significance that lie in secret self-scrutiny and aspiration kindled by a new hope, this, rather than the loveliness of outward shape, became the object of contemplation and the endless theme of art. Architecture and sculpture became symbolic, painting the presentation of ideas designed to stimulate new life in the soul, poetry and music the direct witness and the immediate manifestation of the soul itself.

With the edicts of Constantine early in the fourth century, which practically made Christianity the dominant religious system of the empire, the swift dilation of the pent-up energy of the Church inaugurated an era in which ritualistic splendor kept pace with the rapid acquisition of temporal power. The hierarchical developments had already traversed a course parallel to those of the East, and now that the Church was free to work out that genius for organization of which it had already become definitely conscious, it went one step farther than the Oriental system in the establishment of the papacy as the single head from which the subordinate members derived legality. This was not a time when a democratic form of church government could endure. There was no place for such in the ideas of that age. In the furious tempests that overwhelmed the Roman empire, in the readjustment of political and social conditions all over Europe, with the convulsions and frequent triumphs of savagery that inevitably attended them, it was necessary that the Church, as the sole champion and preserver of civilization and righteousness, should concentrate all her forces, and become in doctrine, worship, and government a single, compact, unified, spiritual state. The dogmas of the Church must be formulated, preserved, and guarded by an official class, and the ignorant and fickle mass of the common people must be taught to yield a reverent, unquestioning obedience to the rule of their spiritual lords. The exposition of theology, the doctrine of the ever-renewed sacrifice of Christ upon the altar, the theory of the sacraments generally, all involved the conception of a mediatorial priesthood deriving its authority by direct transmission from the apostles. Out of such conditions and tendencies proceeded also the elaborate and awe-inspiring rites, the fixed liturgies embalming the central dogmas of the faith, and the whole machinery of a worship which was itself viewed as of an objective efficacy, inspired by the Holy Spirit, and designed both for the edification of the believer and as an offering of the Church to its Redeemer. In the development of the outward observances of worship, with their elaborate symbolic ceremonialism, the student is often struck with surprise to see how lavishly the Church drew its forms and decorations from paganism and Judaism. But there is nothing in this that need excite wonder, nothing that was not inevitable under the conditions of the times. Says Lanciani: "In accepting rites and customs which were not offensive to her principles and morality, the Church showed equal tact and foresight, and contributed to the peaceful accomplishment of the transformation."[1] The pagan or Jewish convert was not obliged to part with all his ancestral notions of the nature of worship. He found his love of pomp and splendor gratified by the ceremonies of a religion which knew how to make many of the fair features of earthly life accessory to the inculcation of spiritual truth. And so it was that symbolism and the appeal to the senses aided in commending Christianity to a world which was not yet prepared for a faith which should require only a silent, unobtrusive experience. Instruction must come to the populace in forms which would satisfy their inherited predispositions. The Church, therefore, establishing itself amidst heathenism, adopted a large number of rites and customs from classical antiquity; and in the externals of its worship, as well as of its government, assumed forms which were contributions from without, as well as evolutions from within. These acquisitions, however, did not by any means remain a meaningless or incongruous residuum of dead superstitions. An instructive symbolism was imparted to them; they were moulded with marvellous art into the whole vesture with which the Church clothed herself for her temporal and spiritual office, and were made to become conscious witnesses to the truth and beauty of the new faith.

The commemoration of martyrs and confessors passed

[1] Lanciani, *Pagan and Christian Rome.*

into invocations for their aid as intercessors with Christ. They became the patron saints of individuals and orders, and honors were paid to them at particular places and on particular days, involving a multitude of special ritual observances. Festivals were multiplied and took the place in popular regard of the old Roman Lupercalia and Saturnalia and the mystic rites of heathenism. As among the cultivated nations of antiquity, so in Christian Rome the festival, calling into requisition every available means of decoration, became the basis of a rapid development of art. Under all these conditions the music of the Church in Italy became a liturgic music, and, as in the East, the laity resigned the main offices of song to a choir consisting of subordinate clergy and appointed by clerical authority. The method of singing was undoubtedly not indigenous, but derived, as already suggested, directly or indirectly from Eastern practice. Milman asserts that the liturgy of the Roman Church for the first three centuries was Greek. However this may have been, we know that both Syriac and Greek influences were strong at that time in the Italian Church. A number of the popes in the seventh century were Greeks. Until the cleavage of the Church into its final Eastern and Western divisions the interaction was strong between the two sections, and much in the way of custom and art was common to both. The conquests of the Moslem power in the seventh century drove many Syrian monks into Italy, and their liturgic practice, half Greek, half Semitic, could not fail to make itself felt among their adopted brethren.

A notable instance of the transference of Oriental

65

custom into the Italian Church is to be found in the establishment of antiphonal chanting in the Church of Milan, at the instance of St. Ambrose, bishop of that city. St. Augustine, the pupil and friend of St. Ambrose, has given an account of this event, of which he had personal knowledge. "It was about a year, or not much more," he relates, "since Justina, the mother of the boy-emperor Justinian, persecuted thy servant Ambrose in the interest of her heresy, to which she had been seduced by the Arians." [This persecution was to induce St. Ambrose to surrender some of the churches of the city to the Arians.] "The pious people kept guard in the church, prepared to die with their bishop, thy servant. At this time it was instituted that, after the manner of the Eastern Church, hymns and psalms should be sung, lest the people should pine away in the tediousness of sorrow, which custom, retained from then till now, is imitated by many — yea, by almost all of thy congregations throughout the rest of the world." [1]

The conflict of St. Ambrose with the Arians occurred in 386. Before the introduction of the antiphonal chant the psalms were probably rendered in a semimusical recitation, similar to the usage mentioned by St. Augustine as prevailing at Alexandria under St. Athanasius, "more speaking than singing." That a more elaborate and emotional style was in use at Milan in St. Augustine's time is proved by the very interesting passage in the tenth book of the *Confessions*, in which he analyzes the effect upon himself of the music

[1] St. Augustine, *Confessions*, book ix. chap. 7.

of the Church, fearing lest its charm had beguiled him from pious absorption in the sacred words into a purely æsthetic gratification. He did not fail, however, to render the just meed of honor to the music that so touched him: "How I wept at thy hymns and canticles, pierced to the quick by the voices of thy melodious Church! Those voices flowed into my ears, and the truth distilled into my heart, and thence there streamed forth a devout emotion, and my tears ran down, and happy was I therein." [1]

Antiphonal psalmody, after the pattern of that employed at Milan, was introduced into the divine office at Rome by Pope Celestine, who reigned 422–432. It is at about this time that we find indications of the more systematic development of the liturgic priestly chant. The history of the papal choir goes back as far as the fifth century. Leo I., who died in 461, gave a durable organization to the divine office by establishing a community of monks to be especially devoted to the service of the canonical hours. In the year 580 the monks of Monte Cassino, founded by St. Benedict, suddenly appeared in Rome and announced the destruction of their monastery by the Lombards. Pope Pelagius received them hospitably, and gave them a dwelling near the Lateran basilica. This cloister became a means of providing the papal chapel with singers. In connection with the college of men singers, who held the clerical title of sub-deacon, stood an establishment for boys, who were to be trained for service in the pope's choir, and who were also given instruction in

---

[1] St. Augustine, *Confessions*, book ix. chap. 6.

other branches.   This school received pupils from the wealthiest and most distinguished families, and a number of the early popes, including Gregory II. and Paul I., received instruction within its walls.

By the middle or latter part of the sixth century, the mediæval epoch of church music had become fairly inaugurated. A large body of liturgic chants had been classified and systematized, and the teaching of their form and the tradition of their rendering given into the hands of members of the clergy especially detailed for their culture.   The liturgy, essentially completed during or shortly before the reign of Gregory the Great (590–604), was given a musical setting throughout, and this liturgic chant was made the law of the Church equally with the liturgy itself, and the first steps were taken to impose one uniform ritual and one uniform chant upon all the congregations of the West.

It was, therefore, in the first six centuries, when the Church was organizing and drilling her forces for her victorious conflicts, that the final direction of her music, as of all her art, was consciously taken.   In rejecting the support of instruments and developing for the first time an exclusively vocal art, and in breaking loose from the restrictions of antique metre which in Greek and Greco-Roman music had forced melody to keep step with strict prosodic measure, Christian music parted company with pagan art, threw the burden of expression not, like Greek music, upon rhythm, but upon melody, and found in this absolute vocal melody a new art principle of which all the worship music of modern Christendom is the natural fruit. More vital still than these special forms and principles, comprehending and necessitating them, was the true ideal of music, proclaimed once for all by the fathers of the liturgy. This ideal is found in the distinction of the church style from the secular style, the expression of the universal mood of prayer, rather than the expression of individual, fluctuating, passionate emotion with which secular music deals — that rapt, pervasive, exalted tone which makes no attempt at detailed painting of events or superficial mental states, but seems rather to symbolize the fundamental sentiments of humility, awe, hope, and love which mingle all particular experiences in the common offering that surges upward from the heart of the Church to its Lord and Master. In this avoidance of an impassioned emphasis of details in favor of an expression drawn from the large spirit of worship, church music evades the peril of introducing an alien dramatic element into the holy ceremony, and asserts its nobler power of creating an atmosphere from which all worldly custom and association disappear. This grand conception was early injected into the mind of the Church, and has been the parent of all that has been most noble and edifying in the creations of ecclesiastical music.

CHAPTER III

THERE is no derogation of the honor due to the Catholic Church in the assertion that a large element in the extraordinary spell which she has always exercised upon the minds of men is to be found in the beauty of her liturgy, the solemn magnificence of her forms of worship, and the glorious products of artistic genius with which those forms have been embellished. Every one who has accustomed himself to frequent places of Catholic worship at High Mass, especially the cathedrals of the old world, whether he is in sympathy with the idea of that worship or not, must have been impressed with something peculiarly majestic, elevating, and moving in the spectacle; he must have felt as if drawn by some irresistible fascination out of his accustomed range of thought, borne by a spiritual tide that sets toward regions unexplored. The music which pervades the mystic ceremony is perhaps the chief agent of this mental reaction through the peculiar spell which the very nature of music enables it to exert upon the emotion. Music in the Catholic ritual seems to act almost in excess of its normal efficacy. It may, without impropriety, be compared to the music of the dramatic

70

stage in the aid it derives from accessories and poetic association. The music is such a vital constituent of the whole act of devotion that the impressions drawn from the liturgy, ceremony, architecture, decoration, and the sublime memories of a venerable past are all insensibly invoked to lend to the tones of priest and choir and organ a grandeur not their own. This is the reason why Catholic music, even when it is tawdry and sensational, or indifferently performed, has a certain air of nobility. The ceremony is always imposing, and the music which enfolds the act of worship like an atmosphere must inevitably absorb somewhat of the dignity of the rite to which it ministers. And when the music in itself is the product of the highest genius and is rendered with reverence and skill, the effect upon a sensitive mind is more solemnizing than that obtained from any other variety of musical experience.

This secret of association and artistic setting must always be taken into account if we would measure the peculiar power of the music of the Catholic Church. We must observe that music is only one of many means of impression, and is made to act not alone, but in union with reinforcing agencies. These agencies — which include all the elements of the ceremony that affect the eye and the imagination — are intended to supplement and enhance each other; and in analyzing the attractive force which the Catholic Church has always exercised upon minds vastly diverse in culture, we cannot fail to admire the consummate skill with which she has made her appeal to the universal susceptibility to ideas of beauty and grandeur and mystery as

71

embodied in sound and form. The union of the arts for the sake of an immediate and undivided effect, of which we have heard so much in recent years, was achieved by the Catholic Church centuries ago. She rears the most sumptuous edifices, decorates their walls with masterpieces of painting, fills every sightly nook with sculptures in wood and stone, devises a ritual of ingenious variety and lavish splendor, pours over this ritual music that alternately subdues and excites, adjusts all these means so that each shall heighten the effect of the others and seize upon the perceptions at the same moment. In employing these artistic agencies the Church has taken cognizance of every degree of enlightenment and variety of temper. For the vulgar she has garish display, for the superstitious wonder and concealment; for the refined and reflective she clothes her doctrines in the fairest guise and makes worship an æsthetic delight. Her worship centres in a mystery — the Real Presence — and this mystery she embellishes with every allurement that can startle, delight, and enthrall.

Symbolism and artistic decoration — in the use of which the Catholic Church has exceeded all other religious institutions except her sister Church of the East — are not mere extraneous additions, as though they might be cut off without essential loss ; they are the natural outgrowth of her very spirit and genius, the proper outward manifestation of the idea which pervades her culture and her worship. Minds that need no external quickening, but love to rise above ceremonial observances and seek immediate contact with the divine source of life, are comparatively rare. Mysticism is not for the multitude; the majority of mankind require that spiritual influences shall come to them in the guise of that which is tangible; a certain nervous thrill is needed to shock them out of their accustomed material habitudes. Recognizing this fact, and having taken up into her system a vast number of ideas which inevitably require objective representation in order that they may be realized and operative, the Catholic Church has even incurred the charge of idolatry on account of the extreme use she has made of images and symbols. But it may be that in this she has shown greater wisdom than those who censure her. She knows that the externals of religious observance must be endowed with a large measure of sensuous charm if they would seize hold upon the affections of the bulk of mankind. She knows that spiritual aspiration and the excitement of the senses can never be entirely separated in actual public worship, and she would run the risk of subordinating the first to the second rather than offer a service of bare intellectuality empty of those persuasions which artistic genius offers, and which are so potent to bend the heart in reverence and submission.

In the study of the Catholic system of rites and ceremonies, together with their motive and development, the great problem of the relation of religion and art meets us squarely. The Catholic Church has not been satisfied to prescribe fixed forms and actions for every devotional impulse—she has aimed to make those forms and actions beautiful. There has been no phase of art which could be devoted to this object that has not offered to her the choicest of its achievements. And not for decoration merely, not simply to subjugate the spirit by fascinating the senses, but rather impelled by an inner necessity which has effected a logical alliance of the special powers of art with the aims and needs of the Church. Whatever may be the attitude toward the claims of this great institution, no one of sensibility can deny that the world has never seen, and is never likely to see, anything fairer or more majestic than that sublime structure, compounded of architecture, sculpture, and painting, and informed by poetry and music, which the Church created in the Middle Age, and fixed in enduring mould for the wondering admiration of all succeeding time. Every one who studies it with a view to searching its motive is compelled to admit that it was a work of sincere conviction. It came from no "vain or shallow thought;" it testifies to something in the heart of Catholicism that has never failed to stir the most passionate affection, and call forth the loftiest efforts of artistic skill. This marvellous product of Catholic art, immeasurable in its variety, has gathered around the rites and ordinances of the Church, and taken from them its spirit, its forms, and its tendencies; — architecture to erect a suitable enclosure for worship, and to symbolize the conception of the visible kingdom of Christ in time and of the eternal kingdom of Christ in heaven; sculpture to adorn this sanctuary, and standing like the sacred edifice itself in closest relation to the centre of churchly life and deriving from that its purpose and norm; painting performing a like function, and also more definitely acting for instruction, vividly illustrating the doctrines and traditions of the faith, directing the thought of the believer more intently to their moral purport and ideal beauty; poetry and music, the very breath of the liturgy itself, acting immediately upon the heart, kindling the latent sentiment of reverence into lively emotions of joy and love. In the employment of rites and ceremonies with their sumptuous artistic setting, in the large stress that is laid upon prescribed forms and external acts of worship, the Catholic Church has been actuated by a conviction from which she has never for an instant swerved. This conviction is twofold: first, that the believer is aided thereby in the offering of an absorbed, fervent, and sincere worship; and second, that it is not only fitting, but a duty, that all that is most precious, the product of the highest development of the powers that God has given to man, should be offered as a witness of man's love and adoration, — that the expenditure of wealth in the erection and decoration of God's sanctuaries, and the tribute of the highest artistic skill in the creation of forms of beauty, are worthy of his immeasurable glory and of ourselves as his dependent children. Says Cardinal Gibbons: "The ceremonies of the Church not only render the divine service more solemn, but they also rivet and captivate our attention and lift it up to God. Our mind is so active, so volatile, and full of distractions, our imagination is so fickle, that we have need of some external objects on which to fix our thoughts. True devotion must be interior and come from the heart; but we are not to infer that exterior worship is to be condemned because interior worship is prescribed as essential. On the contrary, the rites and ceremonies which are enjoined in the worship of God and in the administration of the sacraments are dictated by right reason, and are sanctioned by Almighty God in the old law, and by Christ and his apostles in the new."[1] "Not by the human understanding," says a writer in the *Cæcilien Kalendar*, "was the ritual devised, man knows not whence it came. Its origin lies outside the inventions of man, like the ideas which it presents. The liturgy arose with the faith, as speech with thought. What the body is for the soul, such is the liturgy for religion. Everything in the uses of the Church, from the mysterious ceremonies of the Mass and of Good Friday, to the summons of the evening bell to prayer, is nothing else than the eloquent expression of the content of the redemption of the Son of God."[2]

Since the ritual is prayer, the offering of the Church to God through commemoration and representation as well as through direct appeal, so the whole ceremonial, act as well as word, blends with this conception of prayer, not as embellishment merely but as constituent factor. Hence the large use of symbolism, and even of semi-dramatic representation. "When I speak of the dramatic form of our ceremonies," says Cardinal Wiseman, "I make no reference whatever to outward display; and I choose that epithet for the reason that the poverty of language affords me no other for my meaning. The object and power of dramatic poetry consist

---

[1] Gibbons, *The Faith of our Fathers*, chap. 24.
[2] *Cæcilien Kalendar* (Regensburg), 1879.

in its being not merely descriptive but representative.
Its character is to bear away the imagination and soul
to the view of what others witnessed, and excite in us,
through their words, such impressions as we might
have felt on the occasion. The service of the Church
is eminently poetical, the dramatic power runs through
the service in a most marked manner, and must be kept
in view for its right understanding. Thus, for example,
the entire service for the dead, office, exequies, and
Mass, refers to the moment of death, and bears the
imagination to the awful crisis of separation of soul
and body." "In like manner the Church prepares us
during Advent for the commemoration of our dear
Redeemer's birth, as though it were really yet to take
place. As the festival approaches, the same ideal return to the very moment and circumstances of our
divine Redeemer's birth is expressed; all the glories
of the day are represented to the soul as if actually
occurring." "This principle, which will be found to
animate the church service of every other season, rules
most remarkably that of Holy Week, and gives it life
and soul. It is not intended to be merely commemora-
tive or historical; it is, strictly speaking, representative." [1] "The traditions and rules of church art," says
Jakob, "are by no means arbitrary, they are not an
external accretion, but they proceed from within outward, they have grown organically from the guiding
spirit of the Church, out of the requirements of her
worship. Therein lies the justification of symbolism

[1] Wiseman, *Four Lectures on the Offices and Ceremonies of Holy
Week as performed in the Papal Chapels, delivered in Rome, 1837.*

and symbolic representation in ecclesiastical art. The church of stone must be a speaking image of the living Church and her mysteries; the pictures on the walls and on the altars are not mere ornament for the eye, but for the heart a book full of instruction, a sermon full of truth. And thereby is art raised to be a partici- pant in the work of edifying the believers; it becomes a profound teacher of thousands, a bearer and preserver of great ideas for the centuries." [1] " Our Holy Church," says a German priest, " which completely understands the nature and the needs of humanity, presents to us divine truth and grace in sensible form, in order that by this means they may be more easily grasped and more securely appropriated by us. The law of sense perception, which constitutes so important a factor in human education, forms also a fundamental law in the action of Holy Church, whereby she seeks to raise us out of this earthly material life into the supernatural life of grace. She therefore confers upon us redemp- tive grace in the holy sacraments in connection with external signs, through which the inner grace is shadowed forth and accomplished, as for instance the inward washing of the soul from sin in baptism through the outward washing of the body. In like manner the eye of the instructed Catholic sees in the symbolic ceremonies of the holy sacrifice of the Mass the thrill- ing representation of the fall of man, our redemption, and finally our glorification at the second coming of our Lord. Out of this ground law of presentation to the senses has arisen the whole liturgy of the Church,

[1] Jakob, *Die Kunst im Dienste der Kirche.*

i. e., the sum of all religious actions and prayers to
the honor of God and the communication of his grace
to us, and this whole expressive liturgy forms at once
the solemn ceremonial in the sanctuary of the Heavenly
King, in which he receives our adoration and bestows
upon us the most plentiful tokens of his favor." [1]

These citations sufficiently indicate the mind of the
Catholic Church in respect to the uses of ritual and
symbolic ceremony.   The prime intention is the instruction and edification of the believer, but it is evident that a necessary element in this edification is the
thought that the rite is one composite act of worship,
a prayer, an offering to Almighty God.   This is the
theory of Catholic art, the view which pious churchmen have always entertained of the function of artistic
forms in worship.   That all the products of religious
art in Catholic communities have been actuated by this
motive alone would be too much to say.   The principle
of "art for art's sake," precisely antagonistic to the
traditional ecclesiastical principle, has often made itself
felt in periods of relapsed zeal, and artists have employed traditional subjects out of habit or policy, finding them as good as any others as bases for experiments
in the achievement of sensuous charm in form, texture,
and color.   But so far as changeless dogma, liturgic
unity, and consistent tradition have controlled artistic
effort, individual determination has been allowed enough
play to save art from petrifying into a hieratic formalism, but not enough to endanger the faith, morals,

[1] Sermon by Dr. Leonhard Kuhn, published in the *Kirchenmusikalisches
Jahrbuch* (Regensburg), 1892.

or loyalty of the flock. He therefore who would know the spirit of Catholicism must give a large portion of his study to its art. From the central genius of this institution, displayed not merely in its doctrines and traditions, but also in its sublime faith in its own divine ordination and guidance, and in its ideals of holiness, have issued its liturgy, its ceremonial, and the infinitely varied manifestations of its symbolic, historic, and devotional art. The Catholic Church has aimed to rear on earth a visible type of the spiritual kingdom of God, and to build for her disciples a home, suggestive in its splendor of the glory prepared for those who keep the faith.

All Catholic art, in so far as it may in the strict use of language be called church art, separates itself from the larger and more indefinite category of religious art, and derives its character not from the personal determination of individual artists, but from conceptions and models that have become traditional and canonical. These traditional laws and forms have developed organically out of the needs of the Catholic worship; they derive their sanction and to a large extent their style from the doctrine and also from the ceremonial. The centre of the whole churchly life is the altar, with the great offices of worship there performed. Architecture, painting, decoration, music, — all are comprehended in a unity of impression through the liturgy which they serve. Ecclesiastical art has evolved from within the Church itself, and has drawn its vitality from those ideas which have found their permanent and most terse embodiment in the liturgy. Upon the liturgy and the ceremonial functions attending it must be based all study of the system of artistic expression officially sanctioned by the Catholic Church.

The Catholic liturgy, or text of the Mass, is not the work of any individual or conference. It is a growth, an evolution. Set forms of prayer began to come into use as soon as the first Christian congregations were founded by the apostles. The dogma of the eucharist was the chief factor in giving the liturgy its final shape. By a logical process of selection and integration, certain prayers, Scripture lessons, hymns, and responses were woven together, until the whole became shaped into what may be called a religious poem, in which was expressed the conceived relation of Christ to the Church, and the emotional attitude of the Church in view of his perpetual presence as both paschal victim and high priest. This great prayer of the Catholic Church is mainly composed of contributions made by the Eastern Church during the first four centuries. Its essential features were adopted and transferred to Latin by the Church of Rome, and after a process of sifting and rearranging, with some additions, its form was completed by the end of the sixth century essentially as it stands to-day. The liturgy is, therefore, the voice of the Church, weighted with her tradition, resounding with the commanding tone of her apostolic authority, eloquent with the longing and the assurance of innumerable martyrs and confessors, the mystic testimony to the commission which the Church believes to have been laid upon her by the Holy Spirit. It is not surprising, therefore, that devout Catholics have come to

6   81

consider this liturgy as divinely inspired, raised above all mere human speech, the language of saints and angels, a truly celestial poem ; and that Catholic writers have well-nigh exhausted the vocabulary of enthusiasm in expounding its spiritual significance.

The insistence upon the use of one unvarying language in the Mass and all the other offices of the Catholic Church is necessarily involved in the very conception of catholicity and immutability. A universal Church must have a universal form of speech ; national languages imply national churches ; the adoption of the vernacular would be the first step toward disintegration. The Catholic, into whatever strange land he may wander, is everywhere at home the moment he enters a sanctuary of his faith, for he hears the same worship, in the same tongue, accompanied with the same ceremonies, that has been familiar to him from childhood. This universal language must inevitably be the Latin. Unlike all living languages it is never subject to change, and hence there is no danger that any misunderstanding of refined points of doctrine or observance will creep in through alteration in the connotation of words. Latin is the original language of the Catholic Church, the language of scholarship and diplomacy in the period of ecclesiastical formation, the tongue to which were committed the ritual, articles of faith, legal enactments, the writings of the fathers of the Church, ancient conciliar decrees, etc. The only exceptions to the rule which prescribes Latin as the liturgical speech are to be found among certain Oriental congregations, where, for local reasons, other languages are permitted, *viz.*, Greek, Syriac, Chaldaic, Slavonic, Wal-lachian, Armenian, Coptic, and Ethiopic. In each of these instances, however, the liturgic speech is not the vernacular, but the ancient form which has passed out of use in other relations.[1]

The Mass is the most solemn rite among the offices of the Catholic Church, and embodies the fundamental doctrine upon which the Catholic system of worship mainly rests. It is the chief sacrament, the permanent channel of grace ever kept open between God and his Church. It is an elaborate development of the last supper of Christ with his disciples, and is the fulfilment of the perpetual injunction laid by the Master upon his followers. Developed under the control of the idea of sacrifice, which was drawn from the central conception of the old Jewish dispensation and imbedded in the tradition of the Church at a very early period, the office of the Mass became not a mere memorial of the atone-ment upon Calvary, but a perpetual renewal of it upon the altar through the power committed to the priesthood by the Holy Spirit. To the Protestant, Christ was offered once for all upon the cross, and the believer par-takes through repentance and faith in the benefits con-ferred by that transcendent act; but to the Catholic this sacrifice is repeated whenever the eucharistic ele-ments of bread and wine are presented at the altar with certain prayers and formulas. The renewal of the atoning process is effected through the recurring miracle of transubstantiation, by which the bread and wine are transmuted into the very body and blood of

[1] O'Brien, *History of the Mass.*

Christ. It is in this way that the Catholic Church literally interprets the words of Jesus: " This is my body;
this is my blood; whoso eateth my flesh and drinketh my
blood hath eternal life." When the miraculous transformation has taken place at the repetition by the priest of
Christ's words of institution, the consecrated host and
chalice are offered to God by the priest in the name and
for the sake of the believers, both present and absent,
for whom prayer is made and who share through faith in
the benefits of this sacrificial act. " The sacrifice of the
Mass," says Cardinal Gibbons, " is identical with that of
the cross, both having the same victim and high priest
— Jesus Christ. The only difference consists in the
manner of the oblation. Christ was offered upon the
cross in a bloody manner; in the Mass he is offered up
in an unbloody manner. On the cross he purchased our
ransom, and in the eucharistic sacrifice the price of that
ransom is applied to our souls." [1] This conception
is the keystone of the whole structure of Catholic
faith, the super-essential dogma, repeated from century
to century in declarations of prelates, theologians, and
synods, reasserted once for all in terms of binding definition by the Council of Trent. All, therefore, who
assist in this mystic ceremony, either as celebrants and
ministers or as indirect participants through faith, share
in its supernatural efficacy. It is to them a sacrifice of
praise, of supplication, and of propitiation.

The whole elaborate ceremony of the Mass, which is
such an enigma to the uninstructed, is nowhere vain or
repetitious. Every word has its fitting relation to the

[1] Gibbons, *The Faith of our Fathers.*

whole ; every gesture and genuflection, every change of vestments, has its symbolic significance. All the elements of the rite are merged into a unity under the sway of this central act of consecration and oblation. All the lessons, prayers, responses, and hymns are designed to lead up to it, to prepare the officers and people to share in it, and to impress upon them its meaning and effect. The architectural, sculptural, and decorative beauty of altar, chancel, and apse finds its justification as a worthy setting for the august ceremony, and as a fitting shrine to harbor the very presence of the Lord. The display of lights and vestments, the spicy clouds of incense, the solemnity of priestly chant, and the pomp of choral music, are contrived solely to enhance the impression of the rite, and to compel the mind into a becoming mood of adoration.

There are several kinds of Masses, differing in certain details, or in manner of performance, or in respect to the occasions to which they are appropriated, such as the High Mass, Solemn High Mass, Low Mass, Requiem Mass or Mass for the Dead, Mass of the Presanctified, Nuptial Mass, Votive Mass, etc. The widest departure from the ordinary Mass form is in the Requiem Mass, where the Gloria and Credo are omitted, and their places supplied by the mediæval judgment hymn, Dies Irae, together with certain special prayers for departed souls. In respect to the customary service on Sundays, festal, and ferial days there is no difference in the words of the High Mass, Solemn High Mass, and Low Mass, but only in the manner of performance and the degree of embellishment. The Low Mass is said in a low tone of voice and in the manner of ordinary speech, the usual marks of solemnity being dispensed with ; there is no chanting and no choir music. The High Mass is given in musical tones throughout by celebrant and choir. The Solemn High Mass is performed with still greater ritualistic display, and with deacon, sub-deacon, and a full corps of inferior ministers.

The prayers, portions of Scripture, hymns, and responses which compose the Catholic liturgy consist both of parts that are unalterably the same and of parts that change each day of the year. Those portions that are invariable constitute what is known as the Ordinary of the Mass. The changeable or " proper " parts include the Introits, Collects, Epistles and Lessons, Graduals, Tracts, Gospels, Offertories, Secrets, Prefaces, Communions, and Post-Communions. Every day of the year has its special and distinctive form, according as it commemorates some event in the life of our Lord or is devoted to the memory of some saint, martyr, or confessor.[1] Mass may be celebrated on any day of the year except Good Friday, the great mourning day of the Church.

[1] The musical composition commonly called a Mass — such, for instance as the Imperial Mass of Haydn, the Mass in C by Beethoven, the St. Cecilia Mass by Gounod — is a musical setting of those portions of the office of the Mass that are invariable and that are sung by a choir. These portions are the Kyrie, Gloria, Credo, Sanctus and Benedictus, and Agnus Dei. The musical composition called Requiem, or Mass for the Dead, consists of the Introit — Requiem æternam and Te decet hymnus, Kyrie eleison, Dies Iræ, Offertory (Domine Jesu Christe), Communion — Lux æterna, and sometimes with the addition of Libera me Domine. These choral Masses must always be distinguished from the larger office of the Mass of which they form a part.

The outline of the Mass ceremony that follows relates to the High Mass, which may be taken as the type of the Mass in general. It must be borne in mind that the entire office is chanted or sung.

After the entrance of the officiating priest and his attendants the celebrant pronounces the words : " In the name of the Father, and of the Son, and of the Holy Spirit, Amen ; " and then recites the 42d psalm (43d in the Protestant version). Next follows the confession of sin and prayer for pardon. After a few brief prayers and responses the Introit — a short Scripture selection, usually from a psalm — is chanted. Then the choir sings the Kyrie eleison, Christe eleison. The first of these ejaculations was used in the Eastern Church in the earliest ages as a response by the people. It was adopted into the liturgies of the Western Church at a very early period, and is one of the two instances of the survival in the Latin office of phrases of the original Greek liturgies. The Christe eleison was added a little later.

The Kyrie is immediately followed by the singing by the choir of the Gloria in excelsis Deo. This hymn, also called the greater doxology, is of Greek origin, and is the angelic song given in chapter ii. of Luke's Gospel, with additions which were made not later than the fourth century. It was adopted into the Roman liturgy at least as early as the latter part of the sixth century, since it appears, connected with certain restrictions, in the sacramentary of Pope Gregory the Great.

Next are recited the Collects — short prayers appropriate to the day, imploring God's blessing. Then comes the reading of the Epistle, a psalm verse called the Gradual, the Alleluia, or, when that is omitted, the Tractus (which is also usually a psalm verse), and at certain festivals a hymn called Sequence. Next is recited the Gospel appointed for the day. If a sermon is preached its place is next after the Gospel.

The confession of faith — Credo — is then sung by the choir. This symbol is based on the creed adopted by the council of Nicæa in 325 and modified by the council of Constantinople in 381, but it is not strictly identical with either the Nicene or the Constantinople creed. The most important difference between the Constantinople creed and the present Roman consists in the addition in the Roman creed of the words " and from the Son " (filioque) in the declaration concerning the procession of the Holy Ghost. The present creed has been in use in Spain since 589, and according to what seems good authority was adopted into the Roman liturgy in 1014.

After a sentence usually taken from a psalm and called the Offertory, the most solemn portion of the Mass begins with the Oblation of the Host, the ceremonial preparation of the elements of bread and wine, with prayers, incensings, and ablutions.

All being now ready for the consummation of the sacrificial act, the ascription of thanksgiving and praise called the Preface is offered, which varies with the season, but closes with the Sanctus and Benedictus, sung by the choir.

The Sanctus, also called Trisagion or Thrice Holy,

is the cherubic hymn heard by Isaiah in vision, as described in Is. vi. 3. The Benedictus is the shout of acclamation by the concourse who met Christ on his entry into Jerusalem. There is a poetic significance in the union of these two passages. The blessed one, who cometh in the name of the Lord, is the Lord himself, the God of Sabaoth, of whose glory heaven and earth are full.

The Canon of the Mass now opens with prayers that the holy sacrifice may be accepted of God, and may redound to the benefit of those present. The act of consecration is performed by pronouncing Christ's words of institution, and the sacred host and chalice, now become objects of the most rapt and absorbed devotion, are elevated before the kneeling worshipers, and committed to the acceptance of God with the most impressive vows and invocations.[1]

[1] As an illustration of the nobility of thought and beauty of diction that are found in the Catholic offices, the prayer immediately following the consecration of the chalice may be quoted :

" Wherefore, O Lord, we thy servants, as also thy holy people, calling to mind the blessed passion of the same Christ thy Son our Lord, his resurrection from the dead, and admirable ascension into heaven, offer unto thy most excellent Majesty of the gifts bestowed upon us a pure Host, a holy Host, an unspotted Host, the holy bread of eternal life, and chalice of everlasting salvation.

"Upon which vouchsafe to look, with a propitious and serene countenance, and to accept them, as thou wert graciously pleased to accept the gifts of thy just servant Abel, and the sacrifice of our patriarch Abraham, and that which thy high priest Melchisedech offered to thee, a holy sacrifice and unspotted victim.

" We most humbly beseech thee, Almighty God, command these things to be carried by the hands of thy holy angels to thy altar on high, in the sight of thy divine Majesty, that as many as shall partake of the most sacred body and blood of thy Son at this altar, may be filled with every heavenly grace and blessing."

In the midst of the series of prayers following the consecration the choir sings the Agnus Dei, a short hymn which was introduced into the Roman liturgy at a very early date. The priest then communicates, and those of the congregation who have been prepared for the exalted privilege by confession and absolution kneel at the sanctuary rail and receive from the celebrant's hands the consecrated wafer. The Post-Communion, which is a brief prayer for protection and grace, the dismissal [1] and benediction, and the reading of the first fourteen verses of the Gospel according to St. John close the ceremony.

Interspersed with the prayers, lessons, responses, hymns, etc., which constitute the liturgy are a great number of crossings, obeisances, incensings, changing of vestments, and other liturgic actions, all an enigma to the uninitiated, yet not arbitrary or meaningless, for each has a symbolic significance, designed not merely to impress the congregation, but still more to enforce upon the ministers themselves a sense of the magnitude of the work in which they are engaged. The complexity of the ceremonial, the rapidity of utterance and the frequent inaudibility of the words of the priest, together with the fact that the text is in a dead language, are not inconsistent with the purpose for which the Mass is conceived. For it is not considered as proceeding from the people, but it is an ordinance performed for them and in their name by a priesthood,

---

[1] It is worthy of note, as a singular instance of the exaltation of a comparatively unimportant word, that the word Mass, Lat. Missa, is taken from the ancient formula of dismissal, Ite, missa est.

whose function is that of representing the Church in its mediatorial capacity. The Mass is not simply a prayer, but also a semi-dramatic action, — an action which possesses in itself an efficacy *ex opere operato.* This idea renders it unnecessary that the worshipers should follow the office in detail; it is enough that they coöperate with the celebrant in faith and pious sympathy. High authorities declare that the most profitable reception of the rite consists in simply watching the action of the officiating priest at the altar, and yielding the spirit unreservedly to the holy emotions which are excited by a complete self-abandonment to the contemplation of the adorable mystery. The sacramental theory of the Mass as a vehicle by which grace is communicated from above to the believing recipient, also leaves him free to carry on private devotion during the progress of the ceremony. When the worshipers are seen kneeling in the pews or before an altar at the side wall, fingering rosaries or with eyes intent upon prayer-books, it is not the words of the Mass that they are repeating. The Mass is the prayer of the Church at large, but it does not emanate from the congregation. The theory of the Mass does not even require the presence of the laity, and as a matter of practice private and solitary Masses, although rare, are in no way contrary to the discipline of the Catholic Church.

CHAPTER IV

THE RITUAL CHANT OF THE CATHOLIC CHURCH

In reading the words of the Catholic liturgy from the Missal we must remember that they were written to be sung, and in a certain limited degree acted, and that we cannot receive their real force except when musically rendered and in connection with the ceremonies appropriated to them. For the Catholic liturgy is in conception and history a musical liturgy; word and tone are inseparably bound together. The immediate action of music upon the emotion supplements and reinforces the action of the text and the dogmatic teaching upon the understanding, and the ceremony at the altar makes the impression still more direct by means of visible representation. All the faculties are therefore held in the grasp of this composite agency of language, music, and bodily motion; neither is at any point independent of the others, for they are all alike constituent parts of the poetic whole, in which action becomes prayer and prayer becomes action.

The music of the Catholic Church as it exists to-day is the result of a long process of evolution. Although this process has been continuous, it has three times culminated in special forms, all of them coincident with three comprehensive ideas of musical expression which have succeeded each other chronologically, and which divide the whole history of modern music into clearly marked epochs. These epochs are those (1) of the unison chant, (2) of unaccompanied chorus music, and (3) of mixed solo and chorus with instrumental accompaniment.

(1) The period in which the unison chant was the only form of church music extends from the founding of the congregation of Rome to about the year 1100, and coincides with the centuries of missionary labor among the Northern and Western nations, when the Roman liturgy was triumphantly asserting its authority over the various local uses.

(2) The period of the unaccompanied contrapuntal chorus, based on the mediæval key and melodic systems, covers the era of the European sovereignty of the Catholic Church, including also the period of the Counter-Reformation of the sixteenth century. This phase of art, culminating in the works of Palestrina in Rome, Orlandus Lassus in Munich, and the Gabrielis in Venice, suffered no decline, and gave way at last to a style in sharp contrast with it only when it had gained an impregnable historic position.

(3) The style now dominant in the choir music of the Catholic Church, *viz.*, mixed solo and chorus music with free instrumental accompaniment, based on the modern transposing scales, arose in the seventeenth century as an outcome of the Renaissance secularization of art. It was taken up by the Catholic, Lutheran, and Anglican Churches, and was moulded into its

present types under the influence of new demands upon musical expression which had already brought forth the dramatic and concert styles.

The unison chant, although confined in the vast majority of congregations to the portions of the liturgy that are sung by the priest, is still the one officially recognized form of liturgic music. Although in the historic development of musical art representatives of the later phases of music have been admitted into the Church, they exist there only, we might say, by sufferance, — the chant still remains the legal basis of the whole scheme of worship music. The chant melodies are no mere musical accompaniment; they are the very life breath of the words. The text is so exalted in diction and import, partaking of the sanctity of the sacrificial function to which it ministers, that it must be uttered in tones especially consecrated to it. So intimate is this reciprocal relation of tone and language that in process of time these two elements have become amalgamated into a union so complete that no dissolution is possible even in thought. There is no question that the chant melodies as they exist to-day are only modifications, in most cases but slight modifications, of those that were originally associated with the several portions of the liturgy. At the moment when any form of words was given a place in the Missal or Breviary, its proper melody was then and there wedded to it. This fact makes the Catholic liturgic chant a distinctive church song in a special and peculiar sense. It is not, like most other church music, the artistic creation of individuals, enriching the service with contributions from without, and imparting to them a quality drawn from the composer's personal feeling and artistic methods. It is rather a sort of religious folk-song, proceeding from the inner shrine of religion. It is abstract, impersonal; its style is strictly ecclesiastical, both in its inherent solemnity and its ancient association, and it bears, like the ritual itself, the sanction of unimpeachable authority. The reverence paid by the Church to the liturgic chant as a peculiarly sacred form of utterance is plainly indicated by the fact that while there is no restraint upon the license of choice on the part of the choir, no other form of song has ever been heard, or can ever be permitted to be heard, from the priest in the performance of his ministrations at the altar.

If we enter a Catholic church during High Mass or Vespers we notice that the words of the priest are delivered in musical tones. This song at once strikes us as different in many respects from any other form of music with which we are acquainted. At first it seems monotonous, strange, almost barbaric, but when we have become accustomed to it the effect is very solemn and impressive. Many who are not instructed in the matter imagine that the priest extemporizes these cadences, but nothing could be further from the truth. Certain portions of this chant are very plain, long series of words being recited on a single note, introduced and ended with very simple melodic inflections; other portions are florid, of wider compass than the simple chant, often with many notes to a syllable. Sometimes the priest sings alone, without response or accompaniment; sometimes his utterances are answered by a choir of boys in the chancel or a mixed choir in the gallery; in certain portions of the service the organ supports the chant with harmonies which seem to be based on a different principle of key and scale from that which ordinarily obtains in modern chord progression. In its freedom of rhythm it bears some resemblance to dramatic recitative, yet it is far less dramatic or characteristic in color and expression, and at the same time both more severe and more flexible. To one who understands the whole conception and spirit of the Catholic worship there is a singular appropriateness in the employment of this manner of utterance, and when properly rendered it blends most efficiently with the architectural splendors of altar and sanctuary, with incense, lights, vestments, ceremonial action, and all the embellishments that lend distinction and solemnity to the Catholic ritual. This is the celebrated liturgic chant, also called Gregorian chant, Plain Song, or Choral, and is the special and peculiar form of song in which the Catholic Church has clothed its liturgy for certainly fifteen hundred years.

This peculiar and solemn form of song is the musical speech in which the entire ritual of the Catholic Church was originally rendered, and to which a large portion of the ritual is confined at the present day. It is always sung in unison, with or without instrumental accompaniment. It is unmetrical though not unrhythmical; it follows the phrasing, the emphasis, and the natural inflections of the voice in reciting the text, at the same time that it idealizes them. It is a sort of

heightened form of speech, a musical declamation, having for its object the intensifying of the emotional
powers of ordinary spoken language. It stands to true
song or tune in much the same relation as prose to
verse, less impassioned, more reflective, yet capable of
moving the heart like eloquence.

The chant appears to be the natural and fundamental
form of music employed in all liturgical systems the
world over, ancient and modern. The sacrificial song
of the Egyptians, the Hebrews, and the Greeks was
a chant, and this is the form of music adopted by the
Eastern Church, the Anglican, and every system in
which worship is offered in common and prescribed
forms. The chant form is chosen because it does not
make an independent artistic impression, but can be
held in strict subordination to the sacred words; its
sole function is to carry the text over with greater force
upon the attention and the emotions. It is in this
relationship of text and tone that the chant differs from
true melody. The latter obeys musical laws of structure and rhythm; the music is paramount and the text
accessory, and in order that the musical flow may not
be hampered, the words are often extended or repeated,
and may be compared to a flexible framework on which
the tonal decoration is displayed. In the chant, on the
other hand, this relation of text and tone is reversed;
there is no repetition of words, the laws of structure
and rhythm are rhetorical laws, and the music never
asserts itself to the concealment or subjugation of the
meaning of the text. The " jubilations " or " melismas,"
which are frequent in the choral portions of the Plain

7   97

Song system, particularly in the richer melodies of the Mass, would seem at first thought to contradict this principle ; in these florid melodic phrases the singer would appear to abandon himself to a sort of inspired rapture, giving vent to the emotions aroused in him by the sacred words. Here musical utterance seems for the moment to be set free from dependence upon word and symbol and to assert its own special prerogatives of expression, adopting the conception that underlies modern figurate music. These occasional ebullitions of feeling permitted in the chant are, however, only momentary; they relieve what would otherwise be an unvaried austerity not contemplated in the spirit of Catholic art; they do not violate the general principle of universality and objectiveness as opposed to individual subjective expression, — subordination to word and rite rather than purely musical self-assertion, — which is the theoretic basis of the liturgic chant system.

Chant is speech-song, probably the earliest form of vocal music ; it proceeds from the modulations of impassioned speech ; it results from the need of regulating and perpetuating these modulations when certain exigencies require a common and impressive form of utterance, as in religious rites, public rejoicing or mourning, etc. The necessity of filling large spaces almost inevitably involves the use of balanced cadences. Poetic recitation among ancient and primitive peoples is never recited in the ordinary level pitch of voice in speech, but always in musical inflections, controlled by some principle of order. Under the authority of a permanent corporate institution these inflections are reduced to a system, and are imposed upon all whose office it is to administer the public ceremonies of worship. This is the origin of the liturgic chant of ancient peoples, and also, by historic continuation, of the Gregorian melody. The Catholic chant is a projection into modern art of the altar song of Greece, Judæa, and Egypt, and through these nations reaches back to that epoch of unknown remoteness when mankind first began to conceive of invisible powers to be invoked or appeased. A large measure of the impressiveness of the liturgic chant, therefore, is due to its historic religious associations. It forms a connecting link between ancient religion and the Christian, and perpetuates to our own day an ideal of sacred music which is as old as religious music itself. It is a striking fact that only within the last six hundred or seven hundred years, and only within the bounds of Christendom, has an artificial form of worship music arisen in which musical forms have become emancipated from subjection to the rhetorical laws of speech, and been built up under the shaping force of inherent musical laws, gaining a more or less free play for the creative impulses of an independent art. The conception which is realized in the Gregorian chant, and which exclusively prevailed until the rise of the modern polyphonic system, is that of music in subjection to rite and liturgy, its own charms merged and, so far as conscious intention goes, lost in the paramount significance of text and action. It is for this reason, together with the historic relation of chant and liturgy, that the rulers of the Catholic Church have always labored so strenuously for uniformity in the liturgic chant as well as for its perpetuity. There are even churchmen at the present time who urge the abandonment of all the modern forms of harmonized music and the restoration of the unison chant to every detail of the service. A notion so ascetic and monastic can never prevail, but one who has fully entered into the spirit of the Plain Song melodies can at least sympathize with the reverence which such a reactionary attitude implies. There is a solemn unearthly sweetness in these tones which appeals irresistibly to those who have become habituated to them. They have maintained for centuries the inevitable comparison with every other form of melody, religious and secular, and there is reason to believe that they will continue to sustain all possible rivalry, until they at last outlive every other form of music now existing.

No one can obtain any proper conception of this magnificent Plain Song system from the examples which one ordinarily hears in Catholic churches, for only a minute part of it is commonly employed at the present day. Only in certain convents and a few churches where monastic ideas prevail, and where priests and choristers are enthusiastic students of the ancient liturgic song, can we hear musical performances which afford us a revelation of the true affluence of this mediæval treasure. What we customarily hear is only the simpler intonings of the priest at his ministrations, and the eight " psalm tones " sung alternately by priest and choir. These " psalm tones " or " Gregorian tones " are plain melodic formulas, with variable endings, and are appointed to be sung to the Latin psalms and can-

ticles. When properly delivered, and supported by an
organist who knows the secret of accompanying them,
they are exceedingly beautiful. They are but a hint,
however, of the rich store of melodies, some of them
very elaborate and highly organized, which the chant-
books contain, and which are known only to special
students. To this great compendium belong the chants
anciently assigned to those portions of the liturgy which
are now usually sung in modern settings, — the Kyrie,
Gloria, Credo, Sanctus, Benedictus, Agnus Dei, and the
variable portions of the Mass, such as the Introits,
Graduals, Prefaces, Offertories, Sequences, etc., besides
the hymns sung at Vespers and the other canonical
hours. Few have ever explored the bulky volumes
which contain this unique bequest of the Middle Age ;
but one who has even made a beginning of such study,
or who has heard the florid chants worthily performed
in the traditional style, can easily understand the enthusiasm which these strains arouse in the minds of those
who love to penetrate to the innermost shrines of
Catholic devotional expression.

EXAMPLE OF GREGORIAN TONES. FIRST TONE WITH ITS ENDINGS.

Ma - gni - ficat anima me - a Do - mi - num.

Et ex - ulta - vit Spi - ritus me - us;

in Deo salu - ta - ri me - o. . .

2 Anima me - a Do - minum.

3 Anima me - a Do - mi - num.

4 Anima me - a Domi - num . .

5 Anima me - a Domi - num. . . . .

EXAMPLE OF A FLORID CHANT.

Ky - - - ri - e e - - lei - son.

Chri - ste . . . . e - lei - - son.

Ky - ri - e e - lei - - - son.

The theory and practice of the liturgic chant is a science of large dimensions and much difficulty. In the course of centuries a vast store of chant melodies has been accumulated, and in the nature of the case many variants of the older melodies — those composed before the development of a precise system of notation — have arisen, so that the verification of texts, comparison of authorities, and the application of methods of rendering to the needs of the complex ceremonial make this subject a very important branch of liturgical science.

The Plain Song may be divided into the simple and the ornate chants. In the first class the melodies are to a large extent syllabic (one note to a syllable), rarely with more than two notes to a syllable. The simplest of all are the tones employed in the delivery of certain prayers, the Epistle, Prophecy, and Gospel, technically known as " accents," which vary but little from monotone. The most important of the more melodious simple chants are the " Gregorian tones " already mentioned. The inflections sung to the versicles and responses are also included among the simple chants.

The ornate chants differ greatly in length, compass, and degree of elaboration. Some of these melodies are exceedingly florid and many are of great beauty. They constitute the original settings for all the portions of the Mass not enumerated among the simple chants, *viz.*, the Kyrie, Gloria, Introit, Prefaces, Communion, etc., besides the Sequences and hymns. Certain of these chants are so elaborate that they may almost be said to belong to a separate class. Examination of many of these extended melodies will often disclose a decided approach to regularity of form through the recurrence of certain definite melodic figures. "In the Middle Age," says P. Wagner, "nothing was known of an accompaniment; there was not the slightest need of one. The substance of the musical content, which we to-day commit to interpretation through harmony, the old musicians laid upon melody. The latter accomplished in itself the complete utterance of the artistically aroused fantasy. In this particular the melismas, which carry the extensions of the tones of the melody, are a necessary means of presentation in mediæval art; they proceed logically out of the principle of the unison melody." "Text repetition is virtually unknown in the unison music of the Middle Age. While modern singers repeat an especially emphatic thought or word, the old melodists repeat a melody or phrase which expresses the ground mood of the text in a striking manner. And they not only repeat it, but they make it unfold, and draw out of it new tones of melody. This method is certainly not less artistic than the later text repetition; it comes nearer, also, to the natural expression of the devotionally inspired heart." [1]

The ritual chant has its special laws of execution which involve long study on the part of one who wishes to master it. Large attention is given in the best seminaries to the purest manner of delivering the chant, and countless treatises have been written upon the subject. The first desideratum is an accurate pronunciation of the Latin, and a facile and distinct articulation. The notes have no fixed and measurable value,

[1] Wagner, *Einführung in die Gregorianischen Melodien.*

104

and are not intended to give the duration of the tones, but only to guide the modulation of the voice. The length of each tone is determined only by the proper length of the syllable. In this principle lies the very essence of Gregorian chant, and it is the point at which it stands in exact contradiction to the theory of modern measured music. The divisions of the chant are given solely by the text. The rhythm, therefore, is that of speech, of the prose text to which the chant tones are set. The rhythm is a natural rhythm, a succession of syllables combined into expressive groups by means of accent, varied pitch, and prolongations of tone. The fundamental rule for chanting is: "Sing the words with notes as you would speak them without notes." This does not imply that the utterance is stiff and mechanical as in ordinary conversation; there is a heightening of the natural inflection and a grouping of notes, as in impassioned speech or the most refined declamation. Like the notes and divisions, the pauses also are unequal and immeasurable, and are determined only by the sense of the words and the necessity of taking breath.

In the long florid passages often occurring on a single vowel analogous rules are involved. The text and the laws of natural recitation must predominate over melody. The jubilations are not to be conceived simply as musical embellishments, but, on the contrary, their beauty depends upon the melodic accents to which they are joined in a subordinate position. These florid passages are never introduced thoughtlessly or without meaning, but they are strictly for emphasizing the thought with which they are connected; " they make the soul in singing fathom the deeper sense of the words, and to taste of the mysteries hidden within them." [1] The particular figures must be kept apart and distinguished from each other, and brought into union with each other, like the words, clauses, and sentences of an oration. Even these florid passages are dependent upon the influence of the words and their character of prayer.

The principles above cited concern the rhythm of the chant. Other elements of expression must also be taken into account, such as prolonging and shortening tones, crescendos and diminuendos, subtle changes of quality of voice or tone color to suit different sentiments. The manner of singing is also affected by the conditions of time and place, such as the degree of the solemnity of the occasion, and the dimensions and acoustic properties of the edifice in which the ceremony is held.

In the singing of the mediæval hymn melodies, many beautiful examples of which abound in the Catholic office books, the above rules of rhythm and expression are modified as befits the more regular metrical character which the melodies derive from the verse. They are not so rigid, however, as would be indicated by the bar lines of modern notation, and follow the same laws of rhythm that would obtain in spoken recitation.

The liturgic chant of the Catholic Church has already been alluded to under its more popular title of "Gregorian." Throughout the Middle Age and down to

[1] Sauter, *Choral und Liturgie.*

our own day nothing in history has been more generally received as beyond question than that the Catholic chant is entitled to this appellation from the work performed in its behalf by Pope Gregory I., called the Great. This eminent man, who reigned from 590 to 604, was the ablest of the succession of early pontiffs who formulated the line of policy which converted the barbarians of the North and West, brought about the spiritual and political autonomy of the Roman See, and confirmed its supremacy over all the churches of the West.

In addition to these genuine services historians have generally concurred in ascribing to him a final shaping influence upon the liturgic chant, with which, however, he probably had very little to do. His supposed work in this department has been divided into the following four details:

(1) He freed the church song from the fetters of Greek prosody.

(2) He collected the chants previously existing, added others, provided them with a system of notation, and wrote them down in a book which was afterwards called the Antiphonary of St. Gregory, which he fastened to the altar of St. Peter's Church, in order that it might serve as an authoritative standard in all cases of doubt in regard to the true form of chant.

(3) He established a singing school in which he gave instruction.

(4) He added four new scales to the four previously existing, thus completing the tonal system of the Church.

The prime authority for these statements is the biography of Gregory I., written by John the Deacon about 872. Detached allusions to this pope as the founder of the liturgic chant appear before John's day, the earliest being in a manuscript addressed by Pope Hadrian I. to Charlemagne in the latter part of the eighth century, nearly two hundred years after Gregory's death. The evidences which tend to show that Gregory I. could not have had anything to do with this important work of sifting, arranging, and noting the liturgic melodies become strong as soon as they are impartially examined. In Gregory's very voluminous correspondence, which covers every known phase of his restless activity, there is no allusion to any such work in respect to the music of the Church, as there almost certainly would have been if he had undertaken to bring about uniformity in the musical practice of all the churches under his administration. The assertions of John the Deacon are not confirmed by any anterior document. No epitaph of Gregory, no contemporary records, no ancient panegyrics of the pope, touch upon the question. Isidor of Seville, a contemporary of Gregory, and the Venerable Bede in the next century, were especially interested in the liturgic chant and wrote upon it, yet they make no mention of Gregory in connection with it. The documents upon which John bases his assertion, the so-called Gregorian Antiphonary, do not agree with the ecclesiastical calendar of the actual time of Gregory I.

In reply to these objections and others that might be given there is no answer but legend, which John the Deacon incorporated in his work, and which was generally accepted toward the close of the eleventh century. That this legend should have arisen is not strange. It is no uncommon thing in an uncritical age for the achievement of many minds in a whole epoch to be attributed to the most commanding personality in that epoch, and such a personality in the sixth and seventh centuries was Gregory the Great.

What, then, is the origin of the so-called Gregorian chant? There is hardly a more interesting question in the whole history of music, for this chant is the basis of the whole magnificent structure of mediæval church song, and in a certain sense of all modern music, and it can be traced back unbroken to the earliest years of the Christian Church, the most persistent and fruitful form of art that the modern world has known. The most exhaustive study that has been devoted to this obscure subject has been undertaken by Gevaert, director of the Brussels Conservatory of Music, who has brought forward strong representation to show that the musical system of the early Church of Rome was largely derived from the secular forms of music practised in the private and social life of the Romans in the time of the empire, and which were brought to Rome from Greece after the conquest of that country B.C. 146. "No one to-day doubts," says Gevaert, "that the modes and melodies of the Catholic liturgy are a precious remains of antique art." "The Christian chant took its modal scales to the number of four, and its melodic themes, from the musical practice of the Roman empire, and particularly from the song given to the accompaniment of the kithara, the special style of music cultivated in private life. The most ancient monuments of the liturgic chant go back to the boundary of the fourth and fifth centuries, when the forms of worship began to be arrested in their present shape. Like the Latin language, the Greco-Roman music entered in like manner into the Catholic Church. Vocabulary and syntax are the same with the pagan Symmachus and his contemporary St. Ambrose; modes and rules of musical composition are identical in the hymns which Mesomedes addresses to the divinities of paganism and in the cantilenas of the Christian singers." " The compilation and composition of the liturgic songs, which was traditionally ascribed to St. Gregory I., is in truth a work of the Hellenic popes at the end of the seventh and the beginning of the eighth centuries. The Antiphonarium Missarum received its definitive form between 682 and 715; the Antiphonarium Officii was already fixed under Pope Agathon (678–681)." In the fourth century, according to Gevaert, antiphons were already known in the East. St. Ambrose is said to have transplanted them into the West. Pope Celestine I. (422–472) has been called the founder of the antiphonal song in the Roman Church. Leo the Great (440–461) gave the song permanence by the establishment of a singing school in the neighborhood of St. Peter's. Thus from the fifth century to the latter part of the seventh grew the treasure of melody, together with the unfolding of the liturgy. The four authentic modes were adaptations of four modes employed by the Greeks. The oldest chants

are the simplest, and of those now in existence the
antiphons of the Divine Office can be traced farthest
back to the transition point from the Greco-Roman
practice to that of the Christian Church. The florid
chants were of later introduction, and were probably
the contribution of the Greek and Syrian Churches.[1]

The Christian chants were, however, no mere repro-
ductions of profane melodies. The groundwork of the
chant is allied to the Greek melody ; the Christian song
is of a much richer melodic movement, bearing in all
its forms the evidence of the exuberant spiritual life of
which it is the chosen expression. The pagan melody
was sung to an instrument; the Christian was unaccompanied, and was therefore free to develop a special
rhythmical and melodic character unconditioned by any
laws except those involved in pure vocal expression.
The fact also that the Christian melodies were set to
unmetrical texts, while the Greek melody was wholly
confined to verse, marked the emancipation of the liturgic song from the bondage of strict prosody, and gave
a wider field to melodic and rhythmic development.

It would be too much to say that Gevaert has completely made out his case. The impossibility of verify-
ing the exact primitive form of the oldest chants, and
the almost complete disappearance of the Greco-Roman

---

[1] Gevaert first announced his conclusions in a discourse pronounced at
a public session of the class in fine arts of the Academy of Belgium at
Brussels, and which was published in 1890, under the title of *Les Origines
du Chant liturgique de l'Église latine.* This essay was amplified five
years later into a volume of 446 pages, entitled *La Mélopée antique dans
le Chant de l'Église latine.* These works are published by Ad. Hoste
Ghent.

melodies which are supposed to be the antecedent or the suggestion of the early Christian tone formulas, make a positive demonstration in such a case out of the question. Gevaert seems to rely mainly upon the identity of modes or keys which exists between the most ancient church melodies and those most in use in the kithara song. Other explanations, more or less plausible, have been advanced, and it is not impossible that the simpler melodies may have arisen in an idealization of the natural speech accent, with a view to procuring measured and agreeable cadences. Both methods — actual adaptations of older tunes and the spontaneous enunciation of more obvious melodic formulas — may have been allied in the production of the earlier liturgic chants. The laws that have been found valid in the development of all art would make the derivation of the ecclesiastical melodies from elements existing in the environment of the early Church a logical and reasonable supposition, even in the absence of documentary evidence.

There is no proof of the existence of a definite system of notation before the seventh century. The chanters, priests, deacons, and monks, in applying melodies to the text of the office, composed by aid of their memories, and their melodies were transmitted by memory, although probably with the help of arbitrary mnemonic signs. The possibility of this will readily be granted when we consider that special orders of monks made it their sole business to preserve, sing, and teach these melodies. In the confusion and misery following the downfall of the kingdom of the Goths in the middle of the sixth century the Church became a sanctuary of refuge from the evils of the time. With the revival of religious zeal and the accession of strength the Church flourished, basilicas and convents were multiplied, solemnities increased in number and splendor, and with other liturgic elements the chant. expanded. A number of popes in the seventh century were enthusiastic lovers of Church music, and gave it the full benefit of their authority. Among these were Gregory II. and Gregory III., one of whom may have inadvertently given his name to the chant.

The system of tonality upon which the music of the Middle Age was based was the modal or diatonic. The modern system of transposing scales, each major or minor scale containing the same succession of steps and half steps as each of its fellows, dates no further back than the first half of the seventeenth century. The mediæval system comprises theoretically fourteen, in actual use twelve, distinct modes or keys, known as the ecclesiastical modes or Gregorian modes. These modes are divided into two classes — the " authentic " and " plagal." The compass of each of the authentic modes lies between the keynote, called the " final," and the octave above, and includes the notes represented by the white keys of the pianoforte, excluding sharps and flats. The first authentic mode begins on D, the second on E, and so on. Every authentic mode is connected with a mode known as its plagal, which consists of the last four notes of the authentic mode transposed an octave below, and followed by the first five notes of the authentic, the " final " being the same in the two modes. The modes are sometimes transposed a fifth lower or a fourth higher by means of flatting the B. During the epoch of the foundation of the liturgic chant only the first eight modes (four authentic and four plagal) were in use. The first four authentic modes were popularly attributed to St. Ambrose, bishop of Milan in the fourth century, and the first four plagal to St. Gregory, but there is no historic basis for this tradition. The last two modes are a later addition to the system. The Greek names are those by which the modes are popularly known, and indicate a hypothetical connection with the ancient Greek scale system.

AUTHENTIC MODES.   PLAGAL MODES.

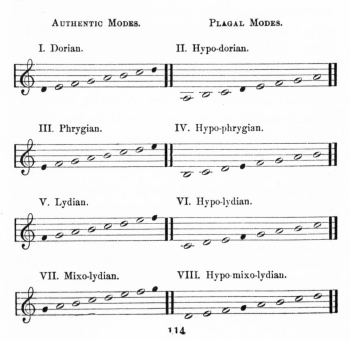

LATER ADDITIONS.

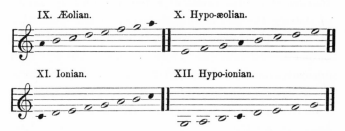

IX. Æolian.   X. Hypo-æolian.

XI. Ionian.   XII. Hypo-ionian.

To suppose that the chant in this period was sung
exactly as it appears in the office books of the present
day would be to ignore a very characteristic and universal usage in the Middle Age. No privilege was more
freely accorded to the mediæval chanter than that of
adding to the melody whatever embellishment he might
choose freely to invent on the impulse of the moment.
The right claimed by Italian opera singers down to
a very recent date to decorate the phrases with trills,
cadenzas, etc., even to the extent of altering the written
notes themselves, is only the perpetuation of a practice
generally prevalent in the mediæval Church, and which
may have come down, for anything we know to the
contrary, from remote antiquity. In fact, the require-
ment of singing the notes exactly as they are written
is a modern idea; no such rule was recognized as invariably binding until well into the nineteenth century.
It was no uncommon thing in Händel's time and after
to introduce free embellishments even into "I know
that my Redeemer liveth" in the "Messiah." In the
Middle Age the singers in church and convent took
great merit to themselves for the inventive ability and

115

vocal adroitness by which they were able to sprinkle the plain notes of the chant with improvised embellishments. " Moreover, there existed in the liturgic text a certain number of words upon which the singers had the liberty of dilating according to their fancy. According to an ancient Christian tradition, certain chants were followed by a number of notes sung upon meaningless vowels; these notes, called neumes or *jubili*, rendered, in accordance with a poetic thought, the faith and adoration of the worshipers who appeared to be unable to find words that could express their sentiments. These vocalizations or embroideries were sometimes longer than the chants themselves, and many authors complained of the importance given to these vocal fantasies." [1] Among the mnemonic signs which, before the invention of the staff and notation system, indicated the changes of pitch to be observed by the singer, there were many that unmistakably point to the traditional flourishes which had become an integral element in the Plain Song system. Many of these survived and were carried over into secular music after the method of chanting became more simple and severe. Similar license was also practised in the later period of part singing, and not only in the rude early counterpoint of the thirteenth and fourteenth centuries, but even in the highly developed and specialized chorus music of the sixteenth century. the embellishments which were reduced to a system and handed down by tradition, gave to this art a style and effect the nature of which has now fallen from the knowledge of men.

[1] Lemaire *Le · Chant, ses principes et son histoire.*

Such was the nature of the song which resounded about the altars of Roman basilicas and through convent cloisters in the seventh and eighth centuries, and which has remained the sanctioned official speech of the Catholic Church in her ritual functions to the present day. Nowhere did it suffer any material change or addition until it became the basis of a new harmonic art in Northern Europe in the twelfth and thirteenth centuries. The chant according to the Roman use began to extend itself over Europe in connection with the missionary efforts which emanated from Rome from the time of Gregory the Great. Augustine, the emissary of Gregory, who went to England in 597 to convert the Saxons, carried with him the Roman chant. "The band of monks," says Green, "entered Canterbury bearing before them a silver cross with a picture of Christ, and singing in concert the strains of the litany of their church."[1] And although the broad-minded Gregory instructed Augustine not to insist upon supplanting with the Roman use the liturgy already employed in the older British churches if such an attempt would create hostility, yet the Roman chant was adopted both at Canterbury and York.

The Roman chant was accepted eventually throughout the dominions of the Church as an essential element of the Roman liturgy. Both shared the same struggles and the same triumphs. Familiarity with the church song became an indispensable part of the equipment of every clergyman, monastic and secular. No missionary might go forth from Rome who was not adept in it. Monks made dangerous journeys to Rome from the remotest

[1] Green, *Short History of the English People.*

districts in order to learn it. Every monastery founded in the savage forests of Germany, Gaul, or Britain became at once a singing school, and day and night the holy strains went up in unison with the melodies of the far distant sacred city. The Anglo-Saxon monk Winfrid, afterward known as Boniface, the famous missionary to the Germans, planted the Roman liturgy in Thuringia and Hesse, and devoted untiring efforts to teaching the Gregorian song to his barbarous proselytes. In Spain, Ildefonso, about 600, is enrolled among the zealous promoters of sacred song according to the use of Rome. Most eminent and most successful of all who labored for the exclusive authority of the Roman chant as against the Milanese, Gallican, and other rival forms was Charlemagne, king of the Franks from 768 to 814, whose persistent efforts to implant the Gregorian song in every church and school in his wide dominions was an important detail of his labor in the interest of liturgic uniformity according to the Roman model.

Among the convent schools which performed such priceless service for civilization in the gloomy period of the early Middle Age, the monastery of St. Gall in Switzerland holds an especially distinguished place. This convent was established in the seventh century by the Irish monk from whom it took its name, rapidly increased in repute as a centre of piety and learning, and during the eighth, ninth, and tenth centuries numbered some of the foremost scholars of the time among its brotherhood. About 790 two monks, versed in all the lore of the liturgic chant, were sent from Rome into the empire of Charlemagne at the monarch's request.

One of them, Romanus, was received and entertained by
the monks of St. Gall, and was persuaded to remain with
them as teacher of church song according to the Antiphonary which he had brought with him from Rome.
St. Gall soon became famous as a place where the purest traditions of the Roman chant were taught and
practised.   Schubiger, in his extremely interesting work,
*Die Sängerschule St. Gallens vom VIII.–XII. Jahr-
hundert,* has given an extended account of the methods
of devotional song in use at St. Gall, which may serve
as an illustration of the general practice among the
pious monks of the Middle Age:

" In the reign of Charlemagne (803) the Council of Aachen
enjoined upon all monasteries the use of the Roman song,
and a later capitulary required that the monks should
perform this song completely and in proper order at the
divine office, in the daytime as well as at night.   According
to other rescripts during the reign of Louis the Pious (about
820) the monks of St. Gall were required daily to celebrate
Mass, and also to perform the service of all the canonical
hours.   The solemn melodies of the ancient psalmody resounded daily in manifold and precisely ordered responses ;
at the midnight hour the sound of the Invitatorium, Venite
exultamus Domino, opened the service of the nocturnal
vigils ; the prolonged, almost mournful tones of the responses alternated with the intoned recitation of the
lessons ; in the spaces of the temple on Sundays and festal
days, at the close of the nightly worship, there reëchoed
the exalted strains of the Ambrosian hymn of praise (Te
Deum laudamus) ; at the first dawn of day began the morning adoration, with psalms and antiphons, hymns and

prayers; to these succeeded in due order the remaining offices of the diurnal hours. The people were daily invited by the Introit to participate in the holy mysteries; they heard in solemn stillness the tones of the Kyrie imploring mercy; on festal days they were inspired by the song once sung by the host of angels; after the Gradual they heard the melodies of the Sequence which glorified the object of the festival in jubilant choral strains, and afterward the simple recitative tones of the Creed; at the Sanctus they were summoned to join in the praise of the Thrice Holy, and to implore the mercy of the Lamb who taketh away the sins of the world. These were the songs which, about the middle of the ninth century, arose on festal or ferial days in the cloister church of St. Gall. How much store the fathers of this convent set upon beauty and edification in song appears from the old regulations in which distinct pronunciation of words and uniformity of rendering are enjoined, and hastening or dragging the time sharply rebuked."

Schubiger goes on to say that three styles of performing the chant were employed; *viz.*, a very solemn one for the highest festivals, one less solemn for Sundays and saints' days, and an ordinary one for ferial days. An appropriate character was given to the different chants, — *e. g.*, a profound and mournful expression in the office for the dead; an expression of tenderness and sweetness to the hymns, the Kyrie, Sanctus, and Agnus Dei; and a dignified character (cantus gravis) to the antiphons, responses, and alleluia. Anything that could disturb the strict and euphonious rendering of the song was strictly forbidden. Harsh, unmusical voices were

not permitted to take part. Distinctness, precise conformity of all the singers in respect to time, and purity
of intonation were inflexibly demanded.

Special services, with processions and appropriate
hymns, were instituted on the occasion of the visit to
the monastery of the emperor or other high dignitary.
All public observances, the founding of a building, the
reception of holy relics, the consecration of a bell or
altar, — even many of the prescribed routine duties of
conventual life, such as drawing water, lighting lamps,
or kindling fires, — each had its special form of song. It
was not enthusiasm, but sober truth, that led Ekke-
hard V. to say that the rulers of this convent, " through
their songs and melodies, as also through their teachings,
filled the Church of God, not only in Germany, but in
all lands from one sea to the other, with splendor and
joy."

At the convent of St. Gall originated the class of liturgical hymns called Sequences, which includes some of
the finest examples of mediæval hymnody. At a very
early period it became the custom to sing the Alleluia
of the Gradual to a florid chant, the final vowel being
extended into an exceedingly elaborate flourish of notes.
Notker Balbulus, a notable member of the St. Gall
brotherhood in the ninth century, conceived the notion,
under the suggestion of a visiting monk, of making a
practical use of the long-winded final cadence of the
Alleluia. He extended and modified these melodious
passages and set words to them, thus constructing a
brief form of prose hymn. His next step was to invent
both notes and text, giving his chants a certain crude

121

form by the occasional repetition of a melodic strain. He preserved a loose connection with the Alleluia by retaining the mode and the first few tones. These experiments found great favor in the eyes of the brethren of St. Gall; others followed Notker's example, and the Sequence melodies were given honored places in the ritual on festal days and various solemn occasions. The custom spread; Pope Nicholas I. in 860 permitted the adoption of the new style of hymn into the liturgy. The early Sequences were in rhythmic prose, but in the hands of the ecclesiastical poets of the few centuries following they were written in rhymed verse. The Sequence was therefore distinguished from other Latin hymns only by its adoption into the office of the Mass as a regular member of the liturgy on certain festal days. The number increased to such large proportions that a sifting process was deemed necessary, and upon the occasion of the reform of the Missal through Pius V. after the Council of Trent only five were retained, *viz.*, Victimae paschali, sung on Easter Sunday; Veni Sancte Spiritus, appointed for Whit-Sunday; Lauda Sion, for Corpus Christi; Stabat Mater dolorosa, for Friday of Passion Week; and Dies Irae, which forms a portion of the Mass for the Dead.

Many beautiful and touching stories have come down to us, illustrating the passionate love of the monks for their songs, and the devout, even superstitious, reverence with which they regarded them. Among these are the tales of the Armorican monk Hervé, in the sixth century, who, blind from his birth, became the inspirer and teacher of his brethren by

122

means of his improvised songs, and the patron of mendicant singers, who still chant his legend in Breton verse. His mother, so one story goes, went one day to visit him in the cloister, and, as she was approaching, said: " I see a procession of monks advancing, and I hear the voice of my son. God be with you, my son! When, with the help of God, I get to heaven, you shall be warned of it, you shall hear the angels sing." The same evening she died, and her son, while at prayer in his cell, heard the singing of the angels as they welcomed her soul in heaven.[1] According to another legend, told by Gregory of Tours, a mother had taken her only son to a monastery near Lake Geneva, where he became a monk, and especially skilful in chanting the liturgic service. " He fell sick and died; his mother in despair came to bury him, and returned every night to weep and lament over his tomb. One night she saw St. Maurice in a dream attempting to console her, but she answered him, 'No, no; as long as I live I shall always weep for my son, my only child!' 'But,' answered the saint, 'he must not be wept for as if he were dead; he is with us, he rejoices in eternal life, and to-morrow, at Matins, in the monastery, thou shalt hear his voice among the choir of the monks; and not to-morrow only, but every day as long as thou livest.' The mother immediately arose, and waited with impatience the first sound of the bell for Matins, to hasten to the church of the monks. The precentor having intoned the response, when the monks in full choir took up the antiphon, the mother immediately recognized the voice of her child.

[1] Montalembert, *The Monks of the West*, vol. ii.

She gave thanks to God; and every day for the rest of her life, the moment she approached the choir she heard the voice of her well-beloved son mingle in the sweet and holy melody of the liturgic chant."[1]

As centuries went on, and these ancient melodies, gathering such stores of holy memory, were handed down in their integrity from generation to generation of praying monks, it is no wonder that the feeling grew that they too were inspired by the Holy Spirit. The legend long prevailed in the Middle Age that Gregory the Great one night had a vision in which the Church appeared to him in the form of an angel, magnificently attired, upon whose mantle was written the whole art of music, with all the forms of its melodies and notes. The pope prayed God to give him the power of recollecting all that he saw; and after he awoke a dove appeared, who dictated to him the chants which are ascribed to him.[2] Ambros quotes a mediæval Latin chronicler, Aurelian Reomensis, who relates that a blind man named Victor, sitting one day before an altar in the Pantheon at Rome, by direct divine inspiration composed the response Gaude Maria, and by a second miracle immediately received his sight. Another story from the same source tells how a monk of the convent of St. Victor, while upon a neighboring mountain, heard angels singing the response Cives Apostolorum, and after his return to Rome he taught the song to his brethren as he had heard it.[3]

[1] Montalembert, *The Monks of the West*, vol. ii.

[2] *Ibid.*

[3] Ambros, *Geschichte der Musik*, vol. ii.

In order to explain the feeling toward the liturgic chant which is indicated by these legends and the rapturous eulogies of mediæval and modern writers, we have only to remember that the melody was never separated in thought from the words, that these words were prayer and praise, made especially acceptable to God because wafted to him by means of his own gift of music. To the mediæval monks prayer was the highest exercise in which man can engage, the most efficacious of all actions, the chief human agency in the salvation of the world. Prayer was the divinely appointed business to which they were set apart. Hence arose the multiplicity of religious services in the convents, the observance of the seven daily hours of prayer, in some monasteries in France, as earlier in Syria and Egypt, extending to the so-called *laus perennis*, in which companies of brethren, relieving each other at stated watches, maintained, like the sacred fire of Vesta, an unbroken office of song by night and day.

Such was the liturgic chant in the ages of faith, before the invention of counterpoint and the first steps in modern musical science suggested new conceptions and methods in worship music. It constitutes to-day a unique and precious heritage from an era which, in its very ignorance, superstition, barbarism of manners, and ruthlessness of political ambition, furnishes strongest evidence of the divine origin of a faith which could triumph over such antagonisms. To the devout Catholic, the chant has a sanctity which transcends even its æsthetic and historic value, but non-Catholic as well as Catholic may reverence it as a direct creation and a token of a mode of thought which, as at no epoch since, conceived prayer and praise as a Christian's most urgent duty, and as an infallible means of gaining the favor of God.

The Catholic liturgic chant, like all other monumental forms of art, has often suffered through the vicissitudes of taste which have beguiled even those whose official responsibilities would seem to constitute them the special custodians of this sacred treasure. Even to-day there are many clergymen and church musicians who have but a faint conception of the affluence of lovely melody and profound religious expression contained in this vast body of mediæval music. Where purely æsthetic considerations have for a time prevailed, as they often will even in a Church in which tradition and symbolism exert so strong an influence as they do in the Catholic, this archaic form of melody has been neglected. Like all the older types (the sixteenth century *a capella* chorus and the German rhythmic choral, for example) its austere speech has not been able to prevail against the fascinations of the modern brilliant and emotional style of church music which has emanated from instrumental art and the Italian aria. Under this latter influence, and the survival of the seventeenth-century contempt for everything mediæval and "Gothic," the chant was long looked upon with disdain as the offspring of a barbarous age, and only maintained at all out of unwilling deference to ecclesiastical authority. In the last few decades, however, probably as a detail of the reawakening in all departments of a study of the great works of older art, there has appeared a reaction in favor of a renewed culture of the Gregorian chant. The tendency toward sensationalism in church music has now begun to subside. The true ideal is seen to be in the past. Together with the new appreciation of Palestrina, Bach, and the older Anglican Church composers, the Catholic chant is coming to its rights, and an enlightened modern taste is beginning to realize the melodious beauty, the liturgic appropriateness, and the edifying power that lie in the ancient unison song. This movement is even now only in its inception; in the majority of church centres there is still apathy, and in consequence corruption of the old forms, crudity and coldness in execution. Much has, however, been already achieved, and in the patient and acute scholarship applied in the field of textual criticism by the monks of Solesmes and the church musicians of Paris, Brussels, and Regensburg, in the enthusiastic zeal shown in many churches and seminaries of Europe and America for the attainment of a pure and expressive style of delivery, and in the restoration of the Plain Song to portions of the ritual from which it has long been banished, we see evidences of a movement which promises to be fruitful, not only in this special sphere, but also, as a direct consequence, in other domains of church music which have been too long neglected.

The historic status of the Gregorian chant as the basis of the magnificent structure of Catholic church music down to 1600, of the Anglican chant, and to a large extent of the German people's hymn-tune or choral, has always been known to scholars. The revived study of it has come from an awakened perception of its liturgic significance and its inherent beauty. The influence drawn from its peculiarly solemn and elevated quality has begun to penetrate the chorus work of the best Catholic composers of the recent time. Protestant church musicians are also beginning to find advantage in the study of the melody, the rhythm, the expression, and even the tonality of the Gregorian song. And every lover of church music will find a new pleasure and uplift in listening to its noble strains. He must, however, listen sympathetically, expelling from his mind all comparison with the modern styles to which he is accustomed, holding in clear view its historic relations and liturgic function. To one who so attunes his mind to its peculiar spirit and purport, the Gregorian Plain Song will seem worthy of the exalted place it holds in the veneration of the most august ecclesiastical institution in history.

CHAPTER V

THE DEVELOPMENT OF MEDIÆVAL CHORUS MUSIC

It has already been noted that the music of the Catholic Church has passed through three typical phases or styles, each complete in itself, bounded by clearly marked lines, corresponding quite closely in respect to time divisions with the three major epochs into which the history of the Western Church may be divided. These phases or schools of ecclesiastical song are so far from being mutually exclusive that both the first and second persisted after the introduction of the third, so that at the present day at least two of the three forms are in use in almost every Catholic congregation, the Gregorian chant being employed in the song of the priest and in the antiphonal psalms and responses, and either the second or third form being adopted in the remaining offices.[1]

Since harmony was unknown during the first one thousand years or more of the Christian era, and instrumental music had no independent existence, the whole vast system of chant melodies was purely unison and unaccompanied, its rhythm usually subordinated to that of the text. Melody, unsupported by harmony, soon

---

[1] The offices, chiefly conventual, in which the chant is employed throughout are exceptions to the general rule.

runs its course, and if no new principle had been added to this antique melodic method, European music would have become petrified or else have gone on copying itself indefinitely. But about the eleventh century a new conception made its appearance, in which lay the assurance of the whole magnificent art of modern music. This new principle was that of harmony, the combination of two or more simultaneous and mutually dependent parts. The importance of this discovery needs no emphasis. It not only introduced an artistic agency that is practically unlimited in scope and variety, but it made music for the first time a free art, with its laws of rhythm and structure no longer identical with those of language, but drawn from the powers that lie inherent in its own nature. Out of the impulse to combine two or more parts together in complete freedom from the constraints of verbal accent and prosody sprang the second great school of church music, which, likewise independent of instrumental accompaniment, developed along purely vocal lines, and issued in the contrapuntal chorus music which attained its maturity in the last half of the sixteenth century.

This mediæval school of *a capella* polyphonic music is in many respects more attractive to the student of ecclesiastical art than even the far more elaborate and brilliant style which prevails to-day. Modern church music, by virtue of its variety, splendor, and dramatic pathos, seems to be tinged with the hues of earthliness which belie the strictest conception of ecclesiastical art. It partakes of the doubt and turmoil of a skeptical and rebellious age, it is the music of impassioned longing

130

in which are mingled echoes of worldly allurements, it is not the chastened tone of pious assurance and self-abnegation. The choral song developed in the ages of faith is pervaded by the accents of that calm ecstasy of trust and celestial anticipation which give to mediæval art that exquisite charm of naïveté and sincerity never again to be realized through the same medium, because it is the unconscious expression of an unquestioning simplicity of conviction which seems to have passed away forever from the higher manifestations of the human creative intellect.

Such pathetic suggestion clings to the religious music of the Middle Age no less palpably than to the sculpture, painting, and hymnody of the same era, and combines with its singular artistic perfection and loftiness of tone to render it perhaps the most typical and lovely of all the forms of Catholic art. And yet to the generality of students of church and art history it is of all the products of the Middle Age the least familiar. Any intellectual man whom we might select would call himself but scantily educated if he had no acquaintance with me-diæval architecture and plastic art; yet he would probably not feel at all ashamed to confess total ignorance of that vast store of liturgic music which in the fifteenth and sixteenth centuries filled the incense-laden air of those very cathedrals and chapels in which his reverent feet so love to wander. The miracles of mediæval archi-tecture, the achievements of the Gothic sculptors and the religious painters of Florence, Cologne, and Flanders are familiar to him, but the musical craftsmen of the Low Countries, Paris, Rome, and Venice, who clothed every prayer, hymn, and Scripture lesson with strains of unique beauty and tenderness, are only names, if indeed their names are known to him at all. Yet in sheer bulk their works would doubtless be found to equal the whole amount of the music of every kind that has been written in the three centuries following their era; while in technical mastery and adaptation to its special end this school is not unworthy of comparison with the more brilliant and versatile art of the present day.

The period from the twelfth century to the close of the sixteenth was one of extraordinary musical activity. The thousands of cathedrals, chapels, parish churches, and convents were unceasing in their demands for new settings of the Mass and offices. Until the art of printing was applied to musical notes about the year 1500, followed by the foundation of musical publishing houses, there was but little duplication or exchange of musical compositions, and thus every important ecclesiastical establishment must be provided with its own corps of composers and copyists. The religious enthusiasm and the vigorous intellectual activity of the Middle Age found as free a channel of discharge in song as in any other means of embellishment of the church ceremonial. These conditions, together with the absence of an operatic stage, a concert system, or a musical public, turned the fertile musical impulses of the period to the benefit of the Church. The ecclesiastical musicians also set to music vast numbers of madrigals, chansons, villanellas, and the like, for the entertainment of aristocratic patrons, but this was only an incidental deflection from their more serious duties as ritual composers. In quality as well as quantity the mediæval chorus music was not unworthy of comparison with the architectural, sculptural, pictorial, and textile products which were created in the same epoch and under the same auspices. The world has never witnessed a more absorbed devotion to a single artistic idea, neither has there existed since the golden age of Greek sculpture another art form so lofty in expression and so perfect in workmanship as the polyphonic church chorus in the years of its maturity. That style of musical art which was brought to fruition by such men as Josquin des Prés, Orlandus Lassus, Willaert, Palestrina, Vittoria, the Anerios, the Gabrielis, and Lotti is not unworthy to be compared with the Gothic cathedrals in whose epoch it arose and with the later triumphs of Renaissance painting with which it culminated.

Of this remarkable achievement of genius the educated man above mentioned knows little or nothing. How is it possible, he might ask, that a school of art so opulent in results, capable of arousing so much admiration among the initiated, could have dominated all Europe for five such brilliant centuries, and yet have left so little impress upon the consciousness of the modern world, if it really possessed the high artistic merits that are claimed for it? The answer is not difficult. For the world at large music exists only as it is performed, and the difficulty and expense of musical performance insure, as a general rule, the neglect of compositions that do not arouse a public demand. Church music is less susceptible than secular to the tyranny of fashion, but even in this department changing tastes and the politic compromising spirit tend to pay court to

novelty and to neglect the antiquated. The revolution
in musical taste and practice which occurred early in the
seventeenth century — a revolution so complete that it
metamorphosed the whole conception of the nature and
purpose of music — swept all musical production off
into new directions, and the complex austere art of the
mediæval Church was forgotten under the fascination of
the new Italian melody and the vivid rhythm and tone-
color of the orchestra. Since then the tide of invention
has never paused long enough to enable the world at
large to turn its thought to the forsaken treasures of the
past. Moreover, only a comparatively minute part of
this multitude of old works has ever been printed, much
of it has been lost, the greater portion lies buried in the
dust of libraries ; whatever is accessible must be released
from an abstruse and obsolete system of notation, and
the methods of performance, which conditioned a large
measure of its effect, must be restored under the uncertain guidance of tradition. The usages of chorus singing
in the present era do not prepare singers to cope with
the peculiar difficulties of the *a capella* style ; a special
education and an unwonted mode of feeling are required
for an appreciation of its appropriateness and beauty.
Nevertheless, such is its inherent vitality, so magical is
its attraction to one who has come into complete harmony with its spirit, so true is it as an exponent of the
mystical submissive type of piety which always tends to
reassert itself in a rationalistic age like the present, that
the minds of churchmen are gradually returning to it,
and scholars and musical directors are tempting it forth
from its seclusion. Societies are founded for its study,

choirs in some of the most influential church centres are adding mediæval works to their repertories, journals and schools are laboring in its interest, and its influence is insinuating itself into the modern mass and anthem, lending to the modern forms a more elevated and spiritual quality. Little by little the world of culture is becoming enlightened in respect to the unique beauty and refinement of this form of art; and the more intelligent study of the Middle Age, which has now taken the place of the former prejudiced misinterpretation, is forming an attitude of mind that is capable of a sympathetic response to this most exquisite and characteristic of all the products of mediæval genius.

In order to seize the full significance of this school of Catholic music in its mature stage in the sixteenth century, it will be necessary to trace its origin and growth. The constructive criticism of the present day rests on the principle that we cannot comprehend works and schools of art unless we know their causes and environment. We shall find as we examine the history of mediæval choral song, that it arose in response to an instinctive demand for a more expansive form of music than the unison chant. Liturgic necessities can in no wise account for the invention of part singing, for even to-day the Gregorian Plain Song remains the one officially recognized form of ritual music in the Catholic Church. It was an unconscious impulse, prophesying a richer musical expression which could not at once be realized, — a blind revolt of the European mind against bondage to an antique and restrictive form of expression. For the Gregorian chant by its very nature as unaccompanied melody, rhythmically controlled by prose accent and measure, was incapable of further development, and it was impossible that music should remain at a standstill while all the other arts were undergoing the pains of growth. The movement which elicited the art of choral song from the latent powers of the liturgic chant was identical with the tendency which evolved Gothic and Renaissance architecture, sculpture, and painting out of Roman and Byzantine art. Melody unsupported soon runs its course ; harmony, music in parts, with contrast of consonance and dissonance, dynamics, and light and shade, must supplement melody, adding more opulent resources to the simple charm of tone and rhythm. The science of harmony, at least in the modern sense, was unknown in antiquity, and the Gregorian chant was but the projection of the antique usage into the modern world. The history of modern European music, therefore, begins with the first authentic instances of singing in two or more semi-independent parts, these parts being subjected to a definite proportional notation.

A century or so before the science of part writing had taken root in musical practice, a strange barbaric form of music meets our eyes. A manuscript of the tenth century, formerly ascribed to Hucbald of St. Armand, who lived, however, a century earlier, gives the first distinct account, with rules for performance, of a divergence from the custom of unison singing, by which the voices of the choir, instead of all singing the same notes, move along together separated by octaves and fourths or octaves and fifths ; or else a second voice accompanies the first by a movement sometimes direct, sometimes oblique, and sometimes contrary. The author of this manuscript makes no claim to the invention of this manner of singing, but alludes to it as something already well known. Much speculation has been expended upon the question of the origin and purpose of the first form of this barbarous organum or diaphony, as it was called. Some conjecture that it was suggested by the sound of the ancient Keltic stringed instrument crowth or crotta, which was tuned in fifths and had a flat finger-board; others find in it an imitation of the early organ with its several rows of pipes sounding fifths like a modern mixture stop; while others suppose, with some reason, that it was a survival of a fashion practised among the Greeks and Romans. The importance of the organum in music history has, however, been greatly overrated, for properly speaking it was not harmony or part singing at all, but only another kind of unison. Even the second form of organum was but little nearer the final goal, for the attendant note series was not free enough to be called an organic element in a harmonic structure. As soon, however, as the accompanying part was allowed ever so little unconstrained life of its own, the first steps in genuine part writing were taken, and a new epoch in musical history had begun.

EXAMPLE OF ORGANUM OR DIAPHONY, FIRST SPECIES.

Nos . .   qui vi - vi - mus be - ne - di - ci - mus Do - mi-

num ex hoc nunc et us - que En se - cu - lum. . .

EXAMPLE OF ORGANUM OR DIAPHONY, SECOND SPECIES.

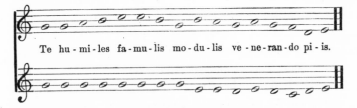

Te hu - mi - les fa - mu - lis mo - du - lis ve - ne - ran - do pi - is.

The freer and more promising style which issued from the treadmill of the organum was called in its initial stages discant (Lat. *discantus*), and was at first wholly confined to an irregular mixture of octaves, unisons, fifths and fourths, with an occasional third as a sort of concession to the criticism of the natural ear upon antique theory. At first two parts only were employed. Occasional successions of parallel fifths and fourths, the heritage of the organum, long survived, but they were gradually eliminated as hollow and unsatisfying, and the principle of contrary motion, which is the very soul of all modern harmony and counterpoint, was slowly established. It must be borne in mind, as the clue to all mediæval music, that the practice of tone combination involved no idea whatever of chords, as modern theory conceives them. The characteristic principle of the vastly preponderating portion of the music of the last three centuries is harmony, technically so called, *i. e.*, chords, solid or distributed, out of which melody is primarily evolved. Homophony, monody — one part sustaining the tune while all others serve as the support and, so to speak, the coloring material also — is now the ruling postulate. The chorus music of Europe down to the seventeenth century was, on the other hand, based on melody; the composer never thought of his combination as chords, but worked, we might say, horizontally, weaving together several semi-independent melodies into a flexible and accordant tissue.[1]

The transition from organum to discant was effected about the year 1100. There was for a time no thought of the invention of the component melodies. Not only the *cantus firmus* (the principal theme), but also the counterpoint (the melodic " running mate "), was borrowed, the second factor being frequently a folk-tune altered to fit the chant melody, according to the simple laws of euphony then admitted. In respect to the words the discant may be divided into two classes : the words might be the same in both parts ; or one voice would sing the text of the office of the Church, and the other the words of the secular song from which the accompanying tune was taken. In the twelfth century the monkish musicians, stirred to bolder flights by the satisfactory results of their two-part discant, essayed three parts, with

[1] This distinction between harmony and counterpoint is fundamental, but no space can be given here to its further elucidation. The point will easily be made clear by comparing an ordinary modern hymn tune with the first section of a fugue.

results at first childishly awkward, but with growing
ease and smoothness.   Free invention of the accompany-

EXAMPLE OF DISCANT IN THREE PARTS WITH DIFFERENT
WORDS (TWELFTH CENTURY).

From Coussemaker, *Histoire de l'harmonie au moyen age.*   Translated
into modern notation.

ing parts took the place of the custom of borrowing
the entire melodic framework, for while two borrowed
themes might fit each other, it was practically impossible
to find three that would do so without almost complete
alteration. As a scientific method of writing developed,
with the combination of parallel and contrary motion,
the term discant gave way to counterpoint (Lat. *punctus
contra punctum*). But there was never any thought of
inventing the *cantus firmus* ; this was invariably taken
from a ritual book or a popular tune, and the whole art
of composition consisted in fabricating melodic figures
that would unite with it in an agreeable synthesis.
These contrapuntal devices, at first simple and often
harsh, under the inevitable law of evolution became
more free and mellifluous at the same time that they
became more complex. The primitive discant was one
note against one note ; later the accompanying part was
allowed to sing several notes against one of the *cantus
firmus.* Another early form consisted of notes inter-
rupted by rests. In the twelfth century such progress
had been made that thirds and sixths were abundantly
admitted, dissonant intervals were made to resolve upon

consonances, consecutive fifths were avoided, passing notes and embellishments were used in the accompanying voices, and the beginnings of double counterpoint and imitation appeared. Little advance was made in the thirteenth century; music was still chiefly a matter of scholastic theory, a mechanical handicraft. Considerable dexterity had been attained in the handling of three simultaneous, independent parts. Contrary and parallel motion alternating for variety's sake, contrast of consonance and dissonance, a system of notation by which time values as well as differences of pitch could be indicated, together with a recognition of the importance of rhythm as an ingredient in musical effect, — all this foreshadowed the time when the material of tonal art would be plastic in the composer's hand, and he would be able to mould it into forms of fluent grace, pregnant with meaning. This final goal was still far away; the dull, plodding round of apprenticeship must go on through the fourteenth century also, and the whole conscious aim of effort must be directed to the invention of scientific combinations which might ultimately provide a vehicle for the freer action of the imagination.

The period from the eleventh to the fifteenth centuries was, therefore, not one of expressive art work, but rather of slow and arduous experiment. The problem was so to adjust the semi-independent melodious parts that an unimpeded life might be preserved in all the voices, and yet the combined effect be at any instant pure and beautiful. The larger the number of parts, the greater the skill required to weave them together into a varied, rich, and euphonious pattern. Any one of these parts might for the moment hold the place of the leading part which the others were constrained to follow through the mazes of the design. Hence the term polyphonic, *i. e.*, many-voiced. Although each voice part was as important as any other in this living musical texture, yet each section took its cue from a single melody — a fragment of a Gregorian chant or a folk-tune and called the *cantus firmus*, and also known as the tenor, from *teneo*, to hold — and the voice that gave out this melody came to be called the tenor voice. In the later phases of this art the first utterance of the theme was assigned indifferently to any one of the voice parts.

After confidence had been gained in devising two or more parts to be sung simultaneously, the next step was to bring in one part after another. Some method of securing unity amid variety was now necessary, and this was found in the contrivance known as " imitation," by which one voice follows another through the same or approximate intervals, the part first sounded acting as a model for a short distance, then perhaps another taking up the leadership with a new melodic figure, the intricate network of parts thus revealing itself as a coherent organism rather than a fortuitous conjunction of notes, the composer's invention and the hearers' impression controlled by a conscious plan to which each melodic part is tributary.

When a number of parts came to be used together, the need of fixing the pitch and length of notes with precision became imperative. So out of the antique mnemonic signs, which had done useful service during

143

the exclusive régime of the unison chant, there was gradually developed a system of square-headed notes, together with a staff of lines and spaces. But instead of simplicity a bewildering complexity reigned for centuries. Many clefs were used, shifting their place on the staff in order to keep the notes within the lines; subtleties, many and deep, were introduced, and the matter of rhythm, key relations, contrapuntal structure, and method of singing became a thing abstruse and recondite. Composition was more like algebraic calculation than free art; symbolisms of trinity and unity, of perfect and imperfect, were entangled in the notation, to the delight of the ingenious monkish intellect and the despair of the neophyte and the modern student of mediæval manuscripts. Progress was slowest at the beginning. It seemed an interminable task to learn to put a number of parts together with any degree of ease, and for many generations after it was first attempted the results were harsh and uncouth.

Even taking into account the obstacles to rapid development which exist in the very nature of music as the most abstract of the arts, it seems difficult to understand why it should have been so long in acquiring beauty and expression. There was a shorter way to both, but the church musicians would not take it. All around them bloomed a rich verdure of graceful expressive melody in the song and instrumental play of the common people. But the monkish musicians and choristers scorned to follow the lead of anything so artless and obvious. In a scholastic age they were musical scholastics; subtilty and fine pedantic distinctions were

144

their pride. They had become infatuated with the for·
mal and technical, and they seemed indifferent to the
claims of the natural and simple while carried away by
a passion for intricate structural problems.

The growth of such an art as this, without models,
must necessarily be painfully slow. Many of the cloistered experimenters passed their lives in nursing an infant
art without seeing enough progress to justify any very
strong faith in the bantling's future. Their floundering
helplessness is often pathetic, but not enough so to overcome a smile at the futility of their devices. Practice and
theory did not always work amiably together. In studying the chorus music of the Middle Age, we must observe
that, as in the case of the liturgic chant, the singers did
not deem it necessary to confine themselves to the
notes actually written. In this formative period of
which we are speaking it was the privilege of the
singers to vary and decorate the written phrases according to their good pleasure. These adornments were
sometimes carefully thought out, incorporated into the
stated method of delivery, and handed down as traditions.[1] But it is evident that in the earlier days of
counterpoint these variations were often extemporized
on the spur of the moment. The result of this habit on
the part of singers who were ignorant of the laws of
musical consonance and proportion, and whose ears were
as dull as their understandings, could easily be conceived
even if we did not have before us the indignant testi-

---

[1] Mendelssohn, in his letter to Zelter describing the music of the Six-
tine Chapel, is enthusiastic over the beautiful effect of the *abellimenti* in
Allegri's Miserere.

mony of many musicians and churchmen of the period. Jean Cotton, in the eleventh century, says that he could only compare the singers with drunken men, who indeed find their way home, but do not know how they get there. The learned theorist, Jean de Muris, of the fourteenth century, exclaims: "How can men have the face to sing discant who know nothing of the combination of sounds! Their voices roam around the *cantus firmus* without regard to any rule; they throw their tones out by luck, just as an unskilful thrower hurls a stone, hitting the mark once in a hundred casts." As he broods over the abuse his wrath increases. "O roughness, O bestiality! taking an ass for a man, a kid for a lion, a sheep for a fish. They cannot tell a consonance from a dissonance. They are like a blind man trying to strike a dog." Another censor apostrophizes the singers thus: "Does such oxen bellowing belong in the Church? Is it believed that God can be graciously inclined by such an uproar?" Oelred, the Scottish abbot of Riverby in the twelfth century, rails at the singers for jumbling the tones together in every kind of distortion, for imitating the whinnying of horses, or (worst of all in his eyes) sharpening their voices like those of women. He tells how the singers bring in the aid of absurd gestures to enhance the effect of their preposterous strains, swaying their bodies, twisting their lips, rolling their eyes, and bending their fingers, with each note. A number of popes, notably John XXII., tried to suppress these offences, but the extemporized discant was too fascinating a plaything to be dropped, and ridicule and pontifical rebuke were alike powerless.

Such abuses were, of course, not universal, perhaps not general, — as to that we cannot tell; but they illustrate the chaotic condition of church music in the three or four centuries following the first adoption of part singing. The struggle for light was persistent, and music, however crude and halting, received abundant measure of the reverence which, in the age that saw the building of the Gothic cathedrals, was accorded to everything that was identified with the Catholic religion. There were no forms of music that could rival the song of the Church, — secular music at the best was a plaything, not an art. The whole endeavor of the learned musicians was addressed to the enrichment of the church service, and the wealthy and powerful princes of France, Italy, Austria, Spain, and England turned the patronage of music at their courts in the same channel with the patronage of the Church. It was in the princely chapels of Northern France and the schools attached to them that the new art of counterpoint was first cultivated. So far as the line of progress can be traced, the art originated in Paris or its vicinity, and slowly spread over the adjacent country. The home of Gothic architecture was the home of mediæval chorus music, and the date of the appearance of these two products is the same. The princes of France and Flanders (the term France at that period meaning the dominions of the Capetian dynasty) faithfully guarded the interests of religious music, and the theorists and composers of this time were officers of the secular government as well as of the Church. We should naturally suppose that church music would be actively supported by a king so pious as Robert of France (eleventh century), who discarded his well-beloved wife at the command of Pope Gregory V. because she was his second cousin, who held himself pure and magnanimous in the midst of a fierce and corrupt age, and who composed many beautiful hymns, including (as is generally agreed) the exquisite Sequence, Veni Sancte Spiritus. He was accustomed to lead the choir in his chapel by voice and gesture. He carried on all his journeys a little prayer chamber in the form of a tent, in which he sang at the stated daily hours to the praise of God. Louis IX. also, worthily canonized for the holiness of his life, made the cultivation of church song one of the most urgent of his duties. Every day he heard two Masses, sometimes three or four. At the canonical hours hymns and prayers were chanted by his chapel choir, and even on his crusades his choristers went before him on the march, singing the office for the day, and the king, a priest by his side, sang in a low voice after them. Rulers of a precisely opposite character, the craftiest and most violent in a guileful and brutal age, were zealous patrons of church music. Even during that era of slaughter and misery when the French kingship was striding to supremacy over the bodies of the great vassals, and struggling with England for very existence in the One Hundred Years' War, the art of music steadily advanced, and the royal and ducal chapels flourished. Amid such conditions and under such patronage accomplished musicians were nurtured in France and the Low Countries, and thence they went forth to teach all Europe the noble art of counterpoint.

About the year 1350 church music had cast off its

swaddling bands and had entered upon the stage that was soon to lead up to maturity. With the opening of the fifteenth century compositions worthy to be called artistic were produced. These were hardly yet beautiful according to modern standards, certainly they had little or no characteristic expression, but they had begun to be pliable and smooth sounding, showing that the notes had come under the composer's control, and that he was no longer an awkward apprentice. From the early part of the fifteenth century we date the epoch of artistic polyphony, which advanced in purity and dignity until it culminated in the perfected art of the sixteenth century. So large a proportion of the fathers and high priests of mediæval counterpoint belonged to the districts now included in Northern France, Belgium, and Holland that the period bounded by the years 1400 and 1550 is known in music history as " the age of the Netherlanders." With limitless patience and cunning, the French and Netherland musical artificers applied themselves to the problems of counterpoint, producing works enormous in quantity and often of bewildering intricacy. Great numbers of pupils were trained in the convents and chapel schools, becoming masters in their turn, and exercising commanding influence in the churches and cloisters of all Europe. Complexity in part writing steadily increased, not only in combinations of notes, but also in the means of indicating their employment. It often happened that each voice must sing to a measure sign that was different from that provided for the other voices. Double and triple rhythm alternated, the value of notes of the same character varied in different circumstances ; a highly sophisticated symbolism was invented, known as " riddle canons," by which adepts were enabled to improvise accompanying parts to the *cantus firmus*; and counterpoint, single and double, augmented and diminished, direct, inverted, and retrograde, became at once the end and the means of musical endeavor. Rhythm was obscured and the words almost hopelessly lost in the web of crossing parts. The *cantus firmus*, often extended into notes of portentous length, lost all expressive quality, and was treated only as a thread upon which this closely woven fabric was strung. Composers occupied themselves by preference with the mechanical side of music; quite unimaginative, they were absorbed in solving technical problems; and so they went on piling up difficulties for their fellow-craftsmen to match, making music for the eye rather than for the ear, for the logical faculty rather than for the fancy or the emotion.

It would, however, be an error to suppose that such labored artifice was the sole characteristic of the scientific music of. the fifteenth century. The same composers who revelled in the exercise of this kind of scholastic subtlety also furnished their choirs with a vast amount of music in four, five, and six parts, complex and difficult indeed from the present point of view, but for the choristers as then trained perfectly available, in which there was a striving for solemn devotional effect, a melodious leading of the voices, and the adjustment of phrases into bolder and more symmetrical patterns. Even among the master fabricators of musical labyrinths we find glimpses of a recognition of the true final aim of music, a soul dwelling in the tangled skeins of their polyphony, a grace and inwardness of expression comparable to the poetic suggestiveness which shines through the naïve and often rude forms of Gothic sculpture. The growing fondness on the part of the austere church musicians for the setting of secular poems — madrigals, chansons, villanellas, and the like — in polyphonic style gradually brought in a simpler construction, more obvious melody, and a more characteristic and pertinent expression, which reacted upon the mass and motet in the promotion of a more direct and flexible manner of treatment. The *stile famigliare*, in which the song moves note against note, syllable against syllable, suggesting modern chord progression, is no invention of Palestrina, with whose name it is commonly associated, but appears in many episodes in the works of his Netherland masters.

The contrapuntal chorus music of the Middle Age reached its maturity in the middle of the sixteenth century. For five hundred years this art had been growing, constantly putting forth new tendrils, which interlaced in luxuriant and ever-extending forms until they overspread all Western Christendom. It was now given to one man, Giovanni Pierluigi, called Palestrina from the place of his birth, to put the finishing touches upon this wonder of mediæval genius, and to impart to it all of which its peculiar nature was capable in respect to technical completeness, tonal purity and majesty, and elevated devotional expression. Palestrina was more than a flawless artist, more than an Andrea del Sarto; he was so representative of that inner spirit which has uttered itself in the most sincere works of Catholic art that the very heart of the institution to which he devoted his life may be said to find a voice in his music.

Palestrina was born probably in 1526 (authority of Haberl) and died in 1594. He spent almost the whole of his art life as director of music at Rome in the service of the popes, being at one time also a singer in the papal chapel. He enriched every portion of the ritual with compositions, the catalogue of his works including ninety-five masses. Among his contemporaries at Rome were men such as Vittoria, Marenzio, the Anerios, and the Naninis, who worked in the same style as Palestrina. Together they compose the "Roman school" or the "Palestrina school," and all that may be said of Palestrina's style would apply in somewhat diminished degree to the writings of this whole group.

Palestrina has been enshrined in history as the "savior of church music" by virtue of a myth which has until recent years been universally regarded as a historic fact. The first form of the legend was to the effect that the reforming Council of Trent (1545–1563) had serious thoughts of abolishing the chorus music of the Church everywhere, and reducing all liturgic music to the plain unison chant; that judgment was suspended at the request of Pope Marcellus II. until Palestrina could produce a work that should be free from all objectionable features; that a mass of his composition — the Mass of Pope Marcellus — was performed before a commission of cardinals, and that its beauty and refinement so impressed the judges that polyphonic music was saved and Palestrina's style proclaimed as the most perfect model of artistic music. This tale has undergone gradual reduction until it has been found that the Council of Trent contented itself with simply recommending to the bishops that they exclude from the churches " all musical compositions in which anything impure or lascivious is mingled," yet not attempting to define what was meant by " impure " and " lascivious." The commission of cardinals had jurisdiction only over some minor questions of discipline in the papal choir, and if Palestrina had the mass in question sung before them (which is doubtful) it had certainly been composed a number of years earlier.

Certain abuses that called for correction there doubtless were in church music in this period. The prevalent practice of borrowing themes from secular songs for the *cantus firmus*, with sometimes the first few words of the original song at the beginning — as in the mass of " The Armed Man," the " Adieu, my Love " mass, etc. — was certainly objectionable from the standpoint of propriety, although the intention was never profane, and the impression received was not sacrilegious. Moreover, the song of the Church had at times become so artificial and sophisticated as to belie the true purpose of worship music. But among all the records of complaint we find only one at all frequent, and that was that the sacred words could not be understood in the elaborate contrapuntal interweaving of the voices. In the history of every church, in all periods, down even to the present time, there has always been a party that discountenances everything that looks like art for the sake of art, satisfied only with the simplest and rudest

form of music, setting the reception of the sacred text
so far above the pleasure of the sense that all artistic
embellishment seems to them profanation. This class
was represented at the Council of Trent, but it was
never in the majority, and never strenuous for the total
abolition of figured music. No reform was instituted
but such as would have come about inevitably from the
ever-increasing refinement of the art and the assertion
of the nobler traditions of the Church in the Counter-
Reformation. An elevation of the ideal of church music
there doubtless was at this time, and the genius of
Palestrina was one of the most potent factors in its promotion; but it was a natural growth, not a violent
turning of direction.

The dissipation of the halo of special beatification
which certain early worshipers of Palestrina have
attempted to throw about the Mass of Pope Marcellus has in no wise dimmed its glory. It is not
unworthy of the renown which it has so dubiously
acquired. Although many times equalled by its author,
he never surpassed it, and few will be inclined to dispute
the distinction it has always claimed as the most perfect
product of mediæval musical art. Its style was not
new; it does not mark the beginning of a new era,
as certain writers but slightly versed in music history
have supposed, but the culmination of an old one. It
is essentially in the manner of the Netherland school,
which the myth-makers would represent as condemned
by the Council of Trent. Josquin des Prés, Orlandus
Lassus, Goudimel, and many others had written music
in the same style, just as chaste and subdued, with the

154

same ideal in mind, and almost as perfectly beautiful. It is not a simple work, letting the text stand forth in clear and obvious relief, as the legend would require. It is a masterpiece of construction, abounding in technical subtleties, differing from the purest work of the Netherlanders only in being even more delicately tinted and sweet in melody than the best of them could attain. It was in the quality of melodious grace that Palestrina soared above his Netherland masters. Melody, as we know, is the peculiar endowment of the Italians, and Palestrina, a typical son of Italy, crowned the Netherland science with an ethereal grace of movement which completed once for all the four hundred years' striving of contrapuntal art, and made it stand forth among the artistic creations of the Middle Age perhaps the most divinely radiant of them all.

It may seem strange at first thought that a form which embodied the deepest and sincerest religious feeling that has ever been projected in tones should have been perfected in an age when all other art had become to a large degree sensuous and worldly, and when the Catholic Church was under condemnation, not only by its enemies, but also by many of its grieving friends, for its political ambition, avarice, and corruption. The papacy was at that moment reaping the inevitable harvest of spiritual indifference and moral decline, and had fallen upon days of struggle, confusion, and humiliation. The Lutheran, Calvinistic, and Anglican revolt had rent from the Holy See some of the fairest of its dominions, and those that remained were in a condition of political and intellectual turmoil. That a reform " in head and members " was indeed needed is established not by the accusations of hostile witnesses alone, but by the demands of many of the staunchest prelates of the time and the admissions of unimpeachable Catholic historians. But, as the sequel proved, it was the head far more than the members that required surgery. The lust for sensual enjoyments, personal and family aggrandizement, and the pomp and luxury of worldly power, which had made the papacy of the fifteenth and first half of the sixteenth centuries a byword in Europe, the decline of faith in the early ideals of the Church, the excesses of physical and emotional indulgence which came in with the Renaissance as a natural reaction against mediæval repression, — all this had produced a moral degeneracy in Rome and its dependencies which can hardly be exaggerated. But the assertion that the Catholic Church at large, or even in Rome, was wholly given over to corruption and formalism is sufficiently refuted by the sublime manifestation of moral force which issued in the Catholic Reaction and the Counter-Reformation, the decrees of the Council of Trent, and the deeds of such moral heroes as Carlo Borromeo, Phillip Neri, Ignatius Loyola, Francis Xavier, Theresa of Jesus, Francis de Sales, Vincent de Paul, and the founders and leaders of the Capuchins, Theatines, Ursulines, and other beneficent religious orders, whose lives and achievements are the glory not only of Catholicism, but of the human race.

The great church composers of the sixteenth century were kindred to such spirits as these, and the reviving piety of the time found its most adequate symbol in the realm of art in the masses and hymns of Palestrina and his compeers. These men were nurtured in the cloisters and choirs. The Church was their sole patron, and no higher privilege could be conceived by them than that of lending their powers to the service of that sublime institution into which their lives were absorbed. They were not agitated by the political and doctrinal ferment of the day. No sphere of activity could more completely remove a man from mundane influences than the employment of a church musician of that period. The abstract nature of music as an art, together with the engrossing routine of a liturgic office, kept these men, as it were, close to the inner sanctuary of their religion, where the ecclesiastical traditions were strongest and purest. The music of the Church in the fifteenth and sixteenth centuries was unaffected by the influences which had done so much to make other forms of Italian art ministers to pride and sensual gratification. Music, through its very limitations, possessed no means of flattering the appetites of an Alexander VI., the luxurious tastes of a Leo X., or the inordinate pride of a Julius II. It was perforce allowed to develop unconstrained along the line of austere tradition. Art forms seem often to be under the control of a law which requires that when once set in motion they must run their course independently of changes in their environment. These two factors, therefore, — the compulsion of an advancing art demanding completion, and the uncontaminated springs of piety whence the liturgy and its musical setting drew their life, — will explain the splendid achievements of religious music in the hands of the Catholic composers of the sixteenth century amid conditions which would at first thought seem unfavorable to the nurture of an art so pure and austere.

Under such influences, impelled by a zeal for the glory of God and the honor of his Church, the polyphony of the Netherland school put forth its consummate flower in the "Palestrina style." In the works of this later school we may distinguish two distinct modes of treatment: (1) the intricate texture and solidity of Netherland work; (2) the "familiar style," in which the voices move together in equal steps, without canonic imitations. In the larger compositions we have a blending and alternation of these two, and the scholastic Netherland polyphony appears clarified, and moulded into more plastic outlines for the attainment of a more refined vehicle of expression.

The marked dissimilarity between the music of the mediæval school and that of the present era is to a large extent explained by the differences between the key and harmonic systems upon which they are severally based. In the modern system the relationship of notes to the antithetic tone-centres of tonic and dominant, and the freedom of modulation from one key to another by means of the introduction of notes that do not exist in the first, give opportunities for effect which are not obtainable in music based upon the Gregorian modes, for the reason that these modes do not differ in the notes employed (since they include only the notes represented by the white keys of the pianoforte plus the B flat), but only in the relation of the intervals to the note which forms the keynote or "final." The conception of music based on the latter system is, strictly speaking, melodic, not harmonic in the modern technical sense, and the resulting combinations of sounds are not conceived as chords built upon a certain tone taken as a fundamental, but rather as consequences of the conjunction of horizontally moving series of single notes. The harmony, therefore, seems both vague and monotonous to the ear trained in accordance with the laws of modern music, because, in addition to being almost purely diatonic, it lacks the stable pivotal points which give symmetry, contrast, and cohesion to modern tone structure. The old system admits chromatic changes but sparingly, chiefly in order to provide a leading tone in a cadence, or to obviate an objectionable melodic interval. Consequently there is little of what we should call variety or positive color quality. There is no pronounced leading melody to which the other parts are subordinate. The theme consists of a few chant-like notes, speedily taken up by one voice after another under control of the principle of " imitation." For the same reasons the succession of phrases, periods, and sections which constitutes the architectonic principle of form in modern music does not appear. Even in the " familiar style," in which the parts move together like blocks of chords of equal length, the implied principle is melodic in all the voices, not tune above and accompaniment beneath ; and the progression is not guided by the necessity of revolving about mutually supporting tone-centres.

In this " familiar style " which we may trace backward to the age of the Netherlanders, we find a remote anticipation of the modern harmonic feeling. A vague sense of complementary colors of tonic and dominant, caught perhaps from the popular music with which the most scientific composers of the fifteenth and sixteenth centuries always kept closely in touch, is sometimes evident for brief moments, but never carried out systematically to the end. This plain style is employed in hymns and short sentences, in connection with texts of an especially mournful or pleading expression, as, for instance, the Improperia and the Miserere, or, for contrast's sake, in the more tranquil passages of masses or motets. It is a style that is peculiarly tender and gracious, and may be found reflected in the sweetest of modern Latin and English hymn-tunes. In the absence of chromatic changes it is the most serene form of music in existence, and is suggestive of the confidence and repose of spirit which is the most refined essence of the devotional mood.

EXAMPLE OF THE SIMPLE STYLE (*stile famigliare*). PALESTRINA.

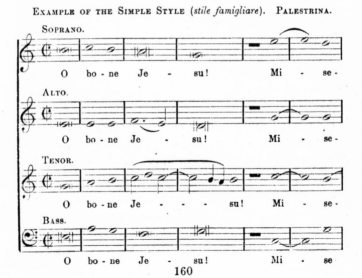

San - gui - ne tu - o prae - ti - o - sis - - - si - mo.

San - gui - ne tu - o prae - ti - o - sis - si - mo.

San - gui - ne tu - o prae - ti - o - sis - si - mo.

San - gui - ne tu - o prae - ti - o - sis - si - mo.

The intricate style commonly prevails in larger works — masses, motets, and the longer hymns. Only after careful analysis can we appreciate the wonderful art that has entered into its fabrication. Upon examining works of this class we find the score consisting of four or more parts, but not usually exceeding eight. The most obvious feature of the design is that each part appears quite independent of the others; the melody does not lie in one voice while the others act as accompaniment, but each part is as much a melody as any other; each voice pursues its easy, unfettered way, now one acting as leader, now another, the voices often crossing each other, each melody apparently quite regardless of its mates in respect to the time of beginning, culminating, and ending, the voices apparently not subject to any common law of accent or rhythm, but each busy with its own individual progress. The onward movement is like a series of waves; no sooner is the mind fixed upon one than it is lost in the ordered confusion of those that follow. The music seems also to have no definite rhythm. Each single voice part is indeed rhythmical, as a sentence of prose may be rhythmical, but since the melodic constituents come in upon different parts of the measure, one culminating at one moment, another at another, the parts often crossing each other, so that while the mind may be fixed upon one melody which seems to lead, another, which has been coming up from below, strikes in across the field, — the result of all this is that the attention is constantly being dislodged from one tonal centre and shifted to another, and the whole scheme of design seems without form, a fluctuating mass swayed hither and thither without coherent plan. The music does not lack dynamic change or alteration of speed, but these contrasts are often so subtly graded that it is not apparent where they begin or end. The whole effect is measured, subdued, solemn. We are never startled, there is nothing that sets the nerves throbbing. But as we hear this music again and again, analyzing its properties, shutting out all preconceptions, little by little there steal over us sensations of surprise, then of wonder, then of admiration. These delicately shaded harmonies develop unimagined beauties. Without sharp contrast of dissonance and consonance they are yet full of shifting lights and hues, like a meadow under breeze and sunshine, which to the careless eye seems only a mass of unvarying green, but which reveals to the keener sense infinite modulation of the scale of color. No melody lies conspicuous upon the surface, but the whole harmonic substance is full of undulating melody, each voice pursuing its confident, unfettered motion amid the ingenious complexity of which it is a constituent part.

FRAGMENT OF KYRIE, FROM THE MASS OF POPE MARCELLUS. NO-VELLO'S EDITION. PALESTRINA.

In considering further the technical methods and the final aims of this marvellous style, we find in its culminating period that the crown of the mediæval contrapuntal art upon its æsthetic side lies in the attainment of beauty of tone effect in and of itself — the gratification of the sensuous ear, rich and subtly modulated sound quality, not in the individual boys' and men's

voices, but in the distribution and combination of voices of different *timbre.* That mastery toward which orchestral composers have been striving during the past one hundred years — the union and contrast of stringed and wind instruments for the production of impressions upon the ear analogous to those produced upon the eye by the color of a Rembrandt or a Titian — this was also sought, and, so far as the slender means went, achieved in a wonderful degree by the tone-masters of the Roman

and Venetian schools. The chorus, we must remind ourselves, was not dependent upon an accompaniment, and sensuous beauty of tone must, therefore, result not merely from the individual quality of the voices, but still more from the manner in which the notes were grouped. The distribution of the components of a chord in order to produce the greatest sonority ; the alternation of the lower voices with the higher; the elimination of voices as a section approached its close, until the harmony was reduced at the last syllable to two higher voices in *pianissimo*, as though the strain were vanishing into the upper air; the resolution of tangled polyphony into a sun-burst of open golden chords; the subtle intrusion of veiled dissonances into the fluent gleaming concord ; the skilful blending of the vocal registers for the production of exquisite contrasts of light and shade, — these and many other devices were employed for the attainment of delicate and lustrous sound tints, with results to which modern chorus writing affords no parallel. The culmination of this tendency could not be reached until the art of interweaving voices according to regular but flexible patterns had been fully mastered, and composers had learned to lead their parts with the confidence with which the engraver traces his lines to shape them into designs of beauty.

The singular perfection of the work of Palestrina has served to direct the slight attention which the world now gives to the music of the sixteenth century almost exclusively to him; yet he was but one master among a goodly number whose productions are but slightly inferior to his, — *primus inter pares.* Orlandus Lassus in

Munich, Willaert, and the two Gabrielis, Andrea and Giovanni, and Croce in Venice, the Naninis, Vittoria, and the Anerios in Rome, Tallis in England, are names which do not pale when placed beside that of the "prince of music." Venice, particularly, was a worthy rival of Rome in the sphere of church song. The catalogue of her musicians who flourished in the sixteenth and early part of the seventeenth centuries contains the names of men who were truly sovereigns in their art, not inferior to Palestrina in science, compensating for a comparative lack of the super-refined delicacy and tremulous pathos which distinguished the Romans by a larger emphasis upon contrast, color variety, and characteristic expression. It was as though the splendors of Venetian painting had been emulated, although in reduced shades, by these masters of Venetian music. In admitting into their works contrivances for effect which anticipated a coming revolution in musical art, the Venetians, rather than the Romans, form the connecting link between mediæval and modern religious music. In the Venetian school we find triumphing over the ineffable calmness and remote impersonality of the Romans a more individual quality — a strain almost of passion and stress, and a far greater sonority and pomp. Chromatic changes, at first irregular and unsystematized, come gradually into use as a means of attaining greater intensity; dissonances become more pronounced, foreshadowing the change of key system with all its consequences. The contrapuntal leading of parts, in whose cunning labyrinths the expression of feeling through melody strove to lose itself, tended under the different ideal cherished by the Venetians to condense into more massive harmonies, with bolder outlines and melody rising into more obvious relief. As far back as the early decades of the sixteenth century Venice had begun to loosen the bands of mediæval choral law, and by a freer use of dissonances to prepare the ear for a new order of perceptions. The unprecedented importance given to the organ by the Venetian church composers, and the appearance of the beginnings of an independent organ style, also contributed strongly to the furtherance of the new tendencies. In this broader outlook, more individual stamp, and more self-conscious aim toward brilliancy the music of Venice simply shared those impulses that manifested themselves in the gorgeous canvases of her great painters and in the regal splendors of her public spectacles.

The national love of pomp and ceremonial display was shown in the church festivals hardly less than in the secular pageants, and all that could embellish the externals of the church solemnities was eagerly adopted. All the most distinguished members of the line of Venetian church composers were connected with the church of St. Mark as choir directors and organists, and they imparted to their compositions a breadth of tone and warmth of color fully in keeping with the historic and artistic glory of this superb temple. The founder of the sixteenth-century Venetian school was Adrian Willaert, a Netherlander, who was chapel-master at St. Mark's from 1527 to 1563. It was he who first employed the method which became a notable feature of the music of St. Mark's, of dividing the choir and thus obtaining novel effects of contrast and climax by means of antiphonal chorus singing. The hint was given to Willaert by the construction of the church, which contains two music galleries opposite each other, each with its organ. The freer use of dissonances, so characteristic of the adventurous spirit of the Venetian composers, first became a significant trait in the writings of Willaert.

The tendency to lay less stress upon interior intricacy and more upon harmonic strength, striking tone color, and cumulative grandeur is even more apparent in Willaert's successors at St. Mark's, — Cyprian de Rore, Claudio Merulo, and the two Gabrielis. Andrea and Giovanni Gabrieli carried the splendid tonal art of Venice to unprecedented heights, adding a third choir to the two of Willaert, and employing alternate choir singing, combinations of parts, and massing of voices in still more ingenious profusion. Winterfeld, the chief historian of this epoch, thus describes the performance of a twelve-part psalm by G. Gabrieli: "Three choruses, one of deep voices, one of higher, and the third consisting of the four usual parts, are separated from each other. Like a tender, fervent prayer begins the song in the deeper chorus, 'God be merciful unto us and bless us.' Then the middle choir continues with similar expression, 'And cause his face to shine upon us.' The higher chorus strikes in with the words, 'That thy way may be known upon earth.' In full voice the strain now resounds from all three choirs, 'Thy saving health among all nations.' The words, 'Thy saving health,' are given with especial earnestness, and it is to be noticed that this utterance comes not from all the choirs together, nor from a single one entire, but from selected voices from each choir in full-toned interwoven parts. We shall not attempt to describe how energetic and fiery the song, ' Let all the people praise thee, O God,' pours forth from the choirs in alternation; how tastefully the master proclaims the words, ' Let the nations be glad and sing for joy,' through change of measure and limitation to selected voices from all the choirs; how the words, ' And God shall bless us,' are uttered in solemn masses of choral song. Language could give but a feeble suggestion of the magnificence of this music." [1]

Great as Giovanni Gabrieli was as master of all the secrets of mediæval counterpoint and also of the special applications devised by the school of Venice, he holds an even more eminent station as the foremost of the founders of modern instrumental art, which properly took its starting point in St. Mark's church in the sixteenth century. These men conceived that the organ might claim a larger function than merely aiding the voices here and there, and they began to experiment with independent performances where the ritual permitted such innovation. So we see the first upspringing of a lusty growth of instrumental forms, if they may properly be called forms, — canzonas (the modern fugue in embryo), toccatas, ricercare (at first nothing more than vocal counterpoint transferred to the organ), fantasias, etc., — rambling, amorphous, incoherent pieces but vastly significant as holding the promise and potency of a new art. Of these far-sighted experimenters Giovanni Gabrieli was easily chief. Consummate

[1] Winterfeld, *Johannes Gabrieli und sein Zeitalter.*

master of the ancient forms, he laid the first pier of the arch which was to connect two epochs; honoring the old traditions by his achievements in chorus music, and leading his disciples to perceive possibilities of expression which were to respond to the needs of a new age.

Another composer of the foremost rank demands attention before we take leave of the mediæval contrapuntal school. Orlandus Lassus (original Flemish Roland de Lattre, Italianized Orlando di Lasso) was a musician whose genius entitles him to a place in the same inner circle with Palestrina and Gabrieli. He lived from 1520 to 1594. His most important field of labor was Munich. In force, variety, and range of subject and treatment he surpasses Palestrina, but is inferior to the great Roman in pathos, nobility, and spiritual fervor. His music is remarkable in view of its period for energy, sharp contrasts, and bold experiments in chromatic alteration. "Orlando," says Ambros, "is a Janus who looks back toward the great past of music in which he arose, but also forward toward the approaching epoch." An unsurpassed master of counterpoint, he yet depended much upon simpler and more condensed harmonic movements. The number of his works reaches 2337, of which 765 are secular. His motets hold a more important place than his masses, and in many of the former are to be found elements that are so direct and forceful in expression as almost to be called dramatic. His madrigals and choral songs are especially notable for their lavish use of chromatics, and also for a lusty sometimes rough humor, which shows his keen sympathy with the popular currents that were running strongly in the learned music of his time. Lassus has more significance in the development of music than Palestrina, for the latter's absorption in liturgic duties kept him within much narrower boundaries. Palestrina's music is permeated with the spirit of the liturgic chant; that of Lassus with the racier quality of the folk-song. Lassus, although his religious devotion cannot be questioned, had the temper of a citizen of the world; Palestrina that of a man of the cloister. Palestrina's music reaches a height of ecstasy which Lassus never approached; the latter is more instructive in respect to the tendencies of the time.

Turning again to the analysis of the sixteenth-century chorus and striving to penetrate still further the secret of its charm, we are obliged to admit that it is not its purely musical qualities or the learning and cleverness displayed in its fabrication that will account for its long supremacy or for the enthusiasm which it has often excited in an age so remote as our own. Its æsthetic effect can never be quite disentangled from the impressions drawn from its religious and historic associations. Only the devout Catholic can feel its full import, for to him it shares the sanctity of the liturgy, — it is not simply ear-pleasing harmony, but prayer; not merely a decoration of the holy ceremony, but an integral part of the sacrifice of praise and supplication. And among Protestants those who eulogize it most warmly are those whose opinions on church music are liturgical and austere. Given in a concert hall, in implied competition with modern chorus music, its effect is feeble. It is as religious music — ritualistic religious music — identified with what is most solemn and suggestive in the traditions and ordinances of an ancient faith, that this antiquated form of art makes its appeal to modern taste. No other phase of music is so dependent upon its setting.

There can be no question that the Catholic Church has always endeavored, albeit with a great deal of wavering and inconsistency, to maintain a certain ideal or standard in respect to those forms of art which she employs in her work of education. The frequent injunctions of popes, prelates, councils, and synods for century after century have always held the same tone upon this question. They have earnestly reminded their followers that the Church recognizes a positive norm or canon in ecclesiastical art, that there is a practical distinction between ecclesiastic art and secular art, and that it is a pious duty on the part of churchmen to preserve this distinction inviolate. The Church, however, has never had the courage of this conviction. As J. A. Symonds says, she has always compromised; and so has every church compromised. The inroads of secular styles and modes of expression have always been irresistible except here and there in very limited times and localities. The history of church art, particularly of church music, is the history of the conflict between the sacerdotal conception of art and the popular taste.

What, then, is the theory of ecclesiastical art which the heads of the Catholic Church have maintained in precept and so often permitted to be ignored in practice? What have been the causes and the results of the secularization of religious art, particularly music?

These questions are of the greatest practical interest to the student of church music, and the answers to them will form the centre around which all that I have to say from this point about Catholic music will mainly turn.

The strict idea of religious art, as it has always stood more or less distinctly in the thought of the Catholic Church, is that it exists not for the decoration of the offices of worship (although the gratification of the senses is not considered unworthy as an incidental end), but rather for edification, instruction, and inspiration. As stated by an authoritative Catholic writer: "No branch of art exists for its own sake alone. Art is a servant, and it serves either God or the world, the eternal or the temporal, the spirit or the flesh. Ecclesiastical art must derive its rule and form solely from the Church." "These rules and determinations [in respect to church art] are by no means arbitrary, no external accretion; they have grown up organically from within outward, from the spirit which guides the Church, out of her views and out of the needs of her worship. And herein lies the justification of her symbolism and emblematic expression in ecclesiastical art so long as this holds itself within the limits of tradition. The church of stone must be a speaking manifestation of the living Church and her mysteries. The pictures on the walls and on the altars are not mere adornment for the pleasure of the eye, but for the heart a book full of instruction, a sermon full of truth. And hereby art is raised to be an instrument of edification to the believer, it becomes a profound expositor for thousands, a transmitter and preserver of great ideas for all the centuries." [1] The Catholic Church in her art would subject the literal to the ideal, the particular to the general, the definitive to the symbolic. "The phrase 'emancipation of the individual,'" says Jakob again, "is not heard in the Church. Art history teaches that the Church does not oppose the individual conception, but simply restrains that false freedom which would make art the servant of personal caprice or of fashion."

The truth of this principle as a fundamental canon of ecclesiastical art is not essentially affected by the fact that it is only in certain periods and under favorable conditions that it has been strictly enforced. Whenever art reaches a certain point in development, individual determination invariably succeeds in breaking away from tradition. The attainment of technic, attended by the inevitable pride in technic, liberates its possessors. The spirit of the Italian religious painters of the fourteenth and early fifteenth centuries, content to submit their skill to further the educational purposes of the Church, could no longer persist in connection with the growing delight in new technical problems and the vision of the new fields open to art when face to face with reality. The conventional treatment of the Memmis and Fra Angelicos was followed by the naturalistic representation of the Raphaels, the Da Vincis, and the Titians. The same result has followed where pure art has decayed, or where no real appreciation of art ever existed. The stage of church

[1] Jakob, *Die Kunst im Dienste der Kirche.*

art in its purest and most edifying form is, therefore, only temporary. It exists in the adolescent period of an art, before the achievement of technical skill arouses desire for its unhampered exercise, and when religious ideas are at the same time dominant and pervasive. Neither is doubt to be cast upon the sincerity of the religious motive in this phase of art growth when we discover that its technical methods are identical with those of secular art at the same period. In fact, this general and conventional style which the Church finds suited to her ends is most truly characteristic when the artists have virtually no choice in their methods. The motive of the Gothic cathedral builders was no less religious because their modes of construction and decoration were also common to the civic and domestic architecture of the time. A distinctive ecclesiastical style has never developed in rivalry with contemporary tendencies in secular art, but only in unison with them. The historic church styles are also secular styles, carried to the highest practicable degree of refinement and splendor. These styles persist in the Church after they have disappeared in the mutations of secular art; they become sanctified by time and by the awe which the claim of supernatural commission inspires, and the world at last comes to think of them as inherently rather than conventionally religious.

All these principles must be applied to the sixteenth-century *a capella* music. In fact, there is no better illustration; its meaning and effect cannot be otherwise understood. Growing up under what seem perfectly natural conditions, patronized by the laity as well as by the clergy, this highly organized, severe, and impersonal style was seen, even before the period of its maturity, to conform to the ideal of liturgic art cherished by the Church; and now that it has become completely isolated in the march of musical progress, this conformity appears even more obvious under contrast. No other form of chorus music has existed so objective and impersonal, so free from the stress and stir of passion, so plainly reflecting an exalted spiritualized state of feeling. This music is singularly adapted to reinforce the impression of the Catholic mysteries by reason of its technical form and its peculiar emotional appeal. The devotional mood that is especially nurtured by the Catholic religious exercises is absorbed and mystical; the devotee strives to withdraw into a retreat within the inner shrine of religious contemplation, where no echoes of the world reverberate, and where the soul may be thrilled by the tremulous ecstasy of half-unveiled heavenly glory. It is the consciousness of the nearness and reality of the unseen world that lends such a delicate and reserved beauty to those creations of Catholic genius in which this ideal has been most directly symbolized. Of this cloistral mood the church music of the Palestrina age is the most subtle and suggestive embodiment ever realized in art. It is as far as possible removed from profane suggestion; in its ineffable calmness, and an indescribable tone of chastened exultation, pure from every trace of struggle, with which it vibrates, it is the most adequate emblem of that eternal repose toward which the believer yearns.

It is not true, however, as often alleged, that this form of music altogether lacks characterization, and that the style of Kyrie, Gloria, Crucifixus, Resurrexit, and of the motets and hymns whatever their subject, is always the same. The old masters were artists as well as churchmen, and knew how to adapt their somewhat unresponsive material to the more obvious contrasts of the text; and in actual performance a much wider latitude in respect to *nuance* and change of speed was permitted than could be indicated in the score. We know, also, that the choristers were allowed great license in the use of embellishments, more or less florid, upon the written notes, sometimes improvised, sometimes carefully invented, taught and handed down as a prescribed code, the tradition of which, in all but a few instances, has been lost. But the very laws of the Gregorian modes and the strict contrapuntal system kept such excursions after expression within narrow bounds, and the traditional view of ecclesiastical art forbade anything like a drastic descriptive literalism.

This mediæval polyphonic music, although the most complete example in art of the perfect adaptation of means to a particular end, could not long maintain its exclusive prestige. . It must be supplanted by a new style as soon as the transformed secular music was strong enough to react upon the Church. It was found that a devotional experience that was not far removed from spiritual trance, which was all that the old music could express, was not the only mental attitude admissible in worship. The new-born art strove to give more apt and detailed expression to the words, and why should not this permission be granted to church music? The musical revolution of the seventeenth century involved

the development of an art of solo singing and its supremacy over the chorus, the substitution of the modern
major and minor transposing scales for the Gregorian
modal system, a homophonic method of harmony for the
mediæval polyphony, accompanied music for the *a capella*, secular and dramatic for religious music, the rise
of instrumental music as an independent art, the transfer
of patronage from the Church to the aristocracy and ultimately to the common people. All the modern forms,
both vocal and instrumental, which have come to maturity in recent times suddenly appeared in embryo at the
close of the sixteenth or early in the seventeenth century.
The ancient style of ecclesiastical music did not indeed
come to a standstill. The grand old forms continued to
be cultivated by men who were proud to wear the mantle
of Palestrina; and in the eighteenth and nineteenth
centuries the traditions of the Roman and Venetian schools
of church music have had sufficient vitality to inspire
works not unworthy of comparison with their venerable
models. The strains of these later disciples, however,
are but scanty reverberations of the multitudinous
voices of the past. The instrumental mass and motet,
embellished with all the newly discovered appliances
of melody, harmony, rhythm, and tone color, led the
art of the Church with flying banners into wider
regions of conquest, and the *a capella* contrapuntal
chorus was left behind, a stately monument upon the
receding shores of the Middle Age.

[NOTE. A very important agent in stimulating a revival of interest in
the mediæval polyphonic school is the St. Cecilia Society, which was
founded at Regensburg in 1868 by Dr. Franz Xaver Witt, a devoted priest

and learned musician, for the purpose of restoring a more perfect relation between music and the liturgy and erecting a barrier against the intrusion of dramatic and virtuoso tendencies. Flourishing branches of this society exist in many of the chief church centres of Europe and America. It is the patron of schools of music, it has issued periodicals, books, and musical compositions, and has shown much vigor in making propaganda for its views.

Not less intelligent and earnest is the Schola Cantorum of Paris, which is exerting a strong influence upon church music in the French capital and thence throughout the world by means of musical performances, editions of musical works, lectures, and publications of books and essays.]

CHAPTER VI

THE MODERN MUSICAL MASS

To one who is accustomed to study the history of art in the light of the law of evolution, the contrast between the reigning modern style of Catholic church music and that of the Middle Age seems at first sight very difficult of explanation. The growth of the *a capella* chorus, which reached its perfection in the sixteenth century, may be traced through a steady process of development, every step of which was a logical consequence of some prior invention. But as we pass onward into the succeeding age and look for a form of Catholic music which may be taken as the natural offspring and successor of the venerable mediæval style, we find what appears to be a break in the line of continuity. The ancient form maintains its existence throughout the seventeenth century and a portion of the eighteenth, but it is slowly crowded to one side and at last driven from the field altogether by a style which, if we search in the field of church art alone, appears to have no antecedent. The new style is opposed to the old in every particular. Instead of forms that are polyphonic in structure, vague and indefinite in plan, based on an antique key system, the new compositions are homophonic, definite, and sectional in plan, revealing an

182

entirely novel principle of tonality, containing vocal solos as well as choruses, and supported by a free instrumental accompaniment. These two contrasted phases of religious music seem to have nothing in common so far as technical organization is concerned, and it is perfectly evident that the younger style could not have been evolved out of the elder. Hardly less divergent are they in respect to ideal of expression, the ancient style never departing from a moderate, unimpassioned uniformity, the modern abounding in variety and contrast, and continually striving after a sort of dramatic portrayal of moods. To a representative of the old school, this florid accompanied style would seem like an intruder from quite an alien sphere of experience, and the wonder grows when we discover that it sprung from the same national soil as that in which its predecessor ripened, and was likewise cherished by an institution that has made immutability in all essentials a cardinal principle. Whence came the impulse that effected so sweeping a change in a great historic form of art, where we might expect that liturgic necessities and ecclesiastical tradition would decree a tenacious conservatism? What new conception had seized upon the human mind so powerful that it could even revolutionize a large share of the musical system of the Catholic Church? Had there been a long preparation for a change that seems so sudden? Were there causes working under the surface, antecedent stages, such that the violation of the law of continuity is apparent only, and not real? These questions are easily answered if we abandon the useless attempt to find the parentage of the modern church style in the ritual music of the previous period; and by surveying all the musical conditions of the age we shall quickly discover that it was an intrusion into the Church of musical methods that were fostered under purely secular auspices. The Gregorian chant and the mediæval *a capella* chorus were born and nurtured within the fold of the Church, growing directly out of the necessity of adapting musical cadences to the rhythmical phrases of the liturgy. The modern sectional and florid style, on the contrary, was an addition from without, and was not introduced in response to any liturgic demands whatever. In origin and affiliations it was a secular style, adopted by the Church under a necessity which she eventually strove to turn into a virtue.

This violent reversal of the traditions of Catholic music was simply a detail of that universal revolution in musical practice and ideal which marked the passage from the sixteenth century to the seventeenth. The learned music of Europe had been for centuries almost exclusively in the care of ecclesiastical and princely chapels, and its practitioners held offices that were primarily clerical. The professional musicians, absorbed in churchly functions, had gone on adding masses to masses, motets to motets, and hymns to hymns, until the Church had accumulated a store of sacred song so vast that it remains the admiration and despair of modern scholars. These works, although exhibiting every stage of construction from the simplest to the most intricate, were all framed in accordance with principles derived from the mediæval conception of melodic combination. The secular songs which these same composers produced in great numbers, notwithstanding their greater flexibility and lightness of touch, were also written for chorus, usually unaccompanied, and were theoretically constructed according to the same system as the church pieces. Nothing like operas or symphonies existed; there were no orchestras worthy of the name; pianoforte, violin, and organ playing, in the modern sense, had not been dreamed of; solo singing was in its helpless infancy. When we consider, in the light of our present experience, how large a range of emotion that naturally utters itself in tone was left unrepresented through this lack of a proper secular art of music, we can understand the urgency of the demand which, at the close of the sixteenth century, broke down the barriers that hemmed in the currents of musical production and swept music out into the vast area of universal human interests. The spirit of the Renaissance had led forth all other art forms to share in the multifarious activities and joys of modern life at a time when music was still the satisfied inmate of the cloister. But it was impossible that music also should not sooner or later feel the transfiguring touch of the new human impulse. The placid, austere expression of the clerical style, the indefinite forms, the Gregorian modes precluding free dissonance and regulated chromatic change, were incapable of rendering more than one order of ideas. A completely novel system must be forthcoming, or music must confess its impotence to enter into the fuller emotional life which had lately been revealed to mankind.

The genius of Italy was equal to the demand. Usually when any form of art becomes complete a period of degeneracy follows; artists become mere imitators, inspiration and creative power die out, the art becomes a handicraft; new growth appears only in another period or another nation, and under altogether different auspices. Such would perhaps have been the case with church music in Italy if a method diametrically opposed to that which had so long prevailed in the Church had not inaugurated a new school and finally extended its conquest into the venerable precincts of the Church itself. The opera and instrumental music — the two currents into which secular music divided — sprang up, as from hidden fountains, right beside the old forms which were even then just attaining their full glory, as if to show that the Italian musical genius so abounded in energy that it could never undergo decay, but when it had gone to its utmost limits in one direction could instantly strike out in another still more brilliant and productive.

The invention of the opera about the year 1600 is usually looked upon as the event of paramount importance in the transition period of modern music history, yet it was only the most striking symptom of a radical, sweeping tendency. Throughout the greater part of the sixteenth century a search had been in progress after a style of music suited to the solo voice, which could lend itself to the portrayal of the change and development of emotion involved in dramatic representation. The folk-song, which is only suited to the expression of a single simple frame of mind, was of course inadequate. The old church music was admirably adapted to the expression of the consciousness of man in his relations to the divine — what was wanted was a means of expressing the emotions of man in his relations to his fellow-men. Lyric and dramatic poetry flourished, but no proper lyric or dramatic music. The Renaissance had done its mighty work in all other fields of art, but so far as music was concerned in the fourteenth and fifteenth centuries a Renaissance did not exist. Many reasons might be given why the spirit of the Renaissance had no appreciable effect in the musical world until late in the sixteenth century. Musical forms are purely subjective in their conception; they find no models or even suggestions in the natural world, and the difficulty of choosing the most satisfactory arrangements of tones out of an almost endless number of possible combinations, together with the necessity of constantly new adjustments of the mind in order to appreciate the value of the very forms which itself creates, makes musical development a matter of peculiar slowness and difficulty. The enthusiasm for the antique, which gave a definite direction to the revival of learning and the new ambitions in painting and sculpture, could have little practical value in musical invention, since the ancient music, which would otherwise have been chosen as a guide, had been completely lost. The craving for a style of solo singing suited to dramatic purposes tried to find satisfaction by means that were childishly insufficient. Imitations of folk-songs, the device of singing one part in a madrigal, while the other parts were played by instruments, were some of the futile efforts to solve the problem. The sense of disappointment broke forth in bitter wrath

187

against the church counterpoint, and a violent conflict raged between the bewildered experimenters and the adherents of the scholastic methods.

The discovery that was to satisfy the longings of a century and create a new art was made in Florence. About the year 1580 a circle of scholars, musicians, and amateurs began to hold meetings at the house of a certain Count Bardi, where they discussed, among other learned questions, the nature of the music of the Greeks, and the possibility of its restoration. Theorizing was supplemented by experiment, and at last Vincenzo Galilei, followed by Giulio Caccini, hit upon a mode of musical declamation, half speech and half song, which was enthusiastically hailed as the long-lost style employed in the Athenian drama. A somewhat freer and more melodious manner was also admitted in alternation with the dry, formless recitation, and these two related methods were employed in the performance of short lyric, half-dramatic monologues. Such were the Monodies of Galilei and the Nuove Musiche of Caccini. More ambitious schemes followed. Mythological masquerades and pastoral comedies, which had held a prominent place in the gorgeous spectacles and pageants of the Italian court festivals ever since the thirteenth century, were provided with settings of the new declamatory music, or *stile recitativo*, and behold, the opera was born.

The Florentine inventors of dramatic music builded better than they knew. They had no thought of setting music free upon a new and higher flight; they never dreamed of the consequences of releasing melody from the fetters of counterpoint. Their sole intention was to make poetry more expressive and emphatic by the employment of tones that would heighten the natural inflections of speech, and in which there should be no repetition or extension of words (as in the contrapuntal style) involving a subordination of text to musical form. The ideal of recitative was the expression of feeling by a method that permits the text to follow the natural accent of declamatory speech, unrestrained by a particular musical form or tonality, and dependent only upon the support of the simplest kind of instrumental accompaniment. In this style of music, said Caccini, speech is of the first importance, rhythm second, and tone last of all. These pioneers of dramatic music, as they declared over and over again, simply desired a form of music that should allow the words to be distinctly understood. They condemned counterpoint, not on musical grounds, but because it allowed the text to be obscured and the natural rhythm broken. There was no promise of a new musical era in such an anti-musical pronunciamento as this. But a relation between music and poetry in which melody renounces all its inherent rights could not long be maintained. The genius of Italy in the seventeenth century was musical, not poetic. Just so soon as the infinite possibilities of charm that lie in free melody were once perceived, no theories of Platonizing pedants could check its progress. The demands of the new age, reinforced by the special Italian gift of melody, created an art form in which absolute music triumphed over the feebler claims of poetry and rhetoric. The cold, calculated Florentine music-drama gave way to the vivacious, impassioned opera of Venice and Naples. Although the primitive dry recitative survived, the far more expressive accompanied recitative was evolved from it, and the grand aria burst into radiant life out of the brief lyrical sections which the Florentines had allowed to creep into their tedious declamatory scenes. Vocal colorature, which had already appeared in the dramatic pieces of Caccini, became the most beloved means of effect. The little group of simple instruments employed in the first Florentine music-dramas was gradually merged in the modern full orchestra. The original notion of making the poetic and scenic intention paramount was forgotten, and the opera became cultivated solely as a means for the display of all the fascinations of vocalism.

Thus a new motive took complete possession of the art of music. By virtue of the new powers revealed to them, composers would now strive to enter all the secret precincts of the soul and give a voice to every emotion, simple or complex, called forth by solitary meditation or by situations of dramatic stress and conflict. Music, like painting and poetry, should now occupy the whole world of human experience. The stupendous achievements of the tonal art of the past two centuries are the outcome of this revolutionary impulse. But not at once could music administer the whole of her new possession. She must pass through a course of training in technic, to a certain extent as she had done in the fourteenth and fifteenth centuries, but under far more favorable conditions and quite different circumstances. The shallowness of the greater part

of the music of the seventeenth and eighteenth centuries is partly due to the difficulty that composers found in mastering the new forms. A facility in handling the material must be acquired before there could be any clear consciousness of the possibilities of expression which the new forms contained. The first problem in vocal music was the development of a method of technic; and musical taste, fascinated by the new sensation, ran into an extravagant worship of the human voice. There appeared in the seventeenth and eighteenth centuries the most brilliant group of singers, of both sexes, that the world has ever seen. The full extent of the morbid, we might almost say the insane, passion for sensuous, nerve-exciting tone is sufficiently indicated by the encouragement in theatre and church of those outrages upon nature, the male soprano and alto. A school of composers of brilliant melodic genius appeared in Italy, France, and Germany, who supplied these singers with showy and pathetic music precisely suited to their peculiar powers. Italian melody and Italian vocalism became the reigning sensation in European society, and the opera easily took the primacy among fashionable amusements. The Italian grand opera, with its solemn travesty of antique characters and scenes, its mock heroics, its stilted conventionalities, its dramatic feebleness and vocal glitter, was a lively reflection of the taste of this age of "gallant" poetry, rococo decoration, and social artificiality. The musical element consisted of a succession of arias and duets stitched together by a loose thread of *secco* recitative. The costumes were those of contemporary fashion, although the characters were named after worthies of ancient Greece and Rome. The plots were in no sense historic, but consisted of love tales and conspiracies concocted by the playwright. Truth to human nature and to locality was left to the despised comic opera. Yet we must not suppose that the devotees of this music were conscious of its real superficiality. They adored it not wholly because it was sensational, but because they believed it true in expression; and indeed it was true to those light and transient sentiments which the voluptuaries of the theatre mistook for the throbs of nature. Tender and pathetic these airs often were, but it was the affected tenderness and pathos of fashionable eighteenth-century literature which they represented. To the profounder insight of the present they seem to express nothing deeper than the make-believe emotions of children at their play.

Under such sanctions the Italian grand aria became the dominant form of melody. Not the appeal to the intellect and the genuine experiences of the heart was required of the musical performer, but rather brilliancy of technic and seductiveness of tone. Ephemeral nerve excitement, incessant novelty within certain conventional bounds, were the demands laid by the public upon composer and singer. The office of the poet became hardly less mechanical than that of the costumer or the decorator. Composers, with a few exceptions, yielded to the prevailing fashion, and musical dramatic art lent itself chiefly to the portrayal of stereotyped sentiments and the gratification of the sense. I would not be understood as denying the germ of truth that lay in this art element contributed by Italy to the modern world. Its later results were sublime and beneficent, for Italian melody has given direction to well-nigh all the magnificent achievements of secular music in the past two centuries. I am speaking here of the first outcome of the infatuation it produced, in the breaking down of the taste for the severe and elevated, and the production of a transient, often demoralizing intoxication.

It was not long before the charming Italian melody undertook the conquest of the Church. The popular demand for melody and solo singing overcame the austere traditions of ecclesiastical song. The dramatic and concert style invaded the choir gallery. The personnel of the choirs was altered, and women, sometimes male sopranos and altos, took the place of boys. The prima donna, with her trills and runs, made the choir gallery the parade ground for her arts of fascination. The chorus declined in favor of the solo, and the church aria vied with the opera aria in bravura and languishing pathos. Where the chorus was retained in mass, motet, or hymn, it abandoned the close-knit contrapuntal texture in favor of a simple homophonic structure, with strongly marked rhythmical movement. The orchestral accompaniment also lent to the composition a vivid dramatic coloring, and brilliant solos for violins and flutes seemed often to convert the sanctuary into a concert hall. All this was inevitable, for the Catholic musicians of the seventeenth and eighteenth centuries were artists as well as churchmen; they shared the æsthetic convictions of their time, and could not be expected to forego the opportunities for effect which the new methods put into their hands. They were

13

no longer dependent upon the Church for commissions; the opera house and the salon gave them sure means of subsistence and fame. The functions of church and theatre composers were often united in a single man. The convents and cathedral chapels were made training-schools for the choir and the opera stage on equal terms. It was in a monk's cell that Bernacchi and other world-famous opera singers of the eighteenth century were educated. Ecclesiastics united with aristocratic laymen in the patronage of the opera; cardinals and archbishops owned theatre boxes, and it was not considered in the least out of character for monks and priests to write operas and superintend their performance. Under such conditions it is not strange that church and theatre reacted upon each other, and that the sentimental style, beloved in opera house and salon, should at last be accepted as the proper vehicle of devotional feeling.

In this adornment of the liturgy in theatrical costume we find a singular parallel between the history of church music in the transition period and that of religious painting in the period of the Renaissance. Pictorial art had first to give concrete expression to the conceptions evolved under the influence of Christianity, and since the whole intent of the pious discipline was to turn the thought away from actual mundane experience, art avoided the representation of ideal physical loveliness on the one hand and a scientific historical correctness on the other. Hence arose the naïve, emblematic pictures of the fourteenth century, whose main endeavor was to attract and indoctrinate with delineations that were

194

symbolic and intended mainly for edification. Painting was one of the chief means employed by the Church to impart instruction to a constituency to whom writing was almost inaccessible. Art, therefore, even when emancipated from Byzantine formalism, was still essentially hieratic, and the painter willingly assumed a semi-sacerdotal office as the efficient coadjutor of the preacher and the confessor. With the fifteenth century came the inrush of the antique culture, uniting with native Italian tendencies to sweep art away into a passionate quest of beauty wherever it might be found. The conventional religious subjects and the traditional modes of treatment could no longer satisfy those whose eyes had been opened to the magnificent materials for artistic treatment that lay in the human form, draped and undraped, in landscape, atmosphere, color, and light and shade, and who had been taught by the individualistic trend of the age that the painter is true to his genius only as he frees himself from formulas and follows the leadings of his own instincts. But art could not wholly renounce its original pious mission. The age was at least nominally Christian, sincerely so in many of its elements, and the patronage of the arts was still to a very large extent in the hands of the clergy. And here the Church prudently consented to a modification of the established ideals of treatment of sacred themes. The native Italian love of elegance of outline, harmony of form, and splendor of color, directed by the study of the antique, overcame the earlier austerity and effected a combination of Christian tradition and pagan sensuousness which, in such work as that of Correggio and the

195

great Venetians, and even at times in the pure Raphael and the stern Michael Angelo, quite belied the purpose of ecclesiastical art, aiming not to fortify dogma and elevate the spirit, but to gratify the desire of the eye and the delight in the display of technical skill. Painting no longer conformed to a traditional religious type; it followed its genius, and that genius was really inspired by the splendors of earth, however much it might persuade itself that it ministered to holiness.

A noted example of this self-deception, although an extreme one, is the picture entitled " The Marriage at Cana," by Paolo Veronese. Christ is the central figure, but his presence has no vital significance. He is simply an imposing Venetian grandee, and the enormous canvas, with its crowd of figures elegantly attired in fashionable sixteenth-century costume, its profusion of sumptuous dishes and gorgeous tapestries, is nothing more or less than a representation of a Venetian state banquet. Signorelli and Michael Angelo introduced naked young men into pictures of the Madonna and infant Christ. Others, such as Titian, lavished all the resources of their art with apparently equal enthusiasm upon Madonnas and nude Venuses. The other direction which was followed by painting, aiming at historical verity and rigid accuracy in anatomy and expression, may be illustrated by comparing Rubens's " Crucifixion " in the Antwerp Museum with a crucifixion, for example, by Fra Angelico. Each motive was sincere, but the harsh realism of the Fleming shows how far art, even in reverent treatment of religious themes, had departed from the unhistoric symbolism formerly imposed by the

Church. In all this there was no disloyal intention; art had simply issued its declaration of independence; its sole aim was henceforth beauty and reality; the body as well as the soul seemed worthy of study and adoration; and the Church adopted the new skill into its service, not seeing that the world was destined to be the gainer, and not religion.

The same impulse produced analogous results in the music of the Catholic Church. The liturgic texts that were appropriated to choral setting remained as they had been, the place and theoretic function of the musical offices in the ceremonial were not altered, but the music, in imitating the characteristics of the opera and exerting a somewhat similar effect upon the mind, became animated by an ideal of devotion quite apart from that of the liturgy, and belied that unimpassioned, absorbed and universalized mood of worship of which the older forms of liturgic art are the most complete and consistent embodiment. Herein is to be found the effect of the spirit of the Renaissance upon church music. It is not simply that it created new musical forms, new styles of performance, and a more definite expression; the significance of the change lies rather in the fact that it transformed the whole spirit of devotional music by endowing religious themes with sensuous charm, and with a treatment inspired by the arbitrary will of the composer and not by the traditions of the Church.

At this point we reach the real underlying motive, however unconscious of it individual composers may have been, which compelled the revolution in liturgic music. A new ideal of devotional expression made inevitable the abandonment of the formal, academic style of the Palestrina school. The spirit of the age which required a more subjective expression in music, involved a demand for a more definite characterization in the setting of the sacred texts. The composer could no longer be satisfied with a humble imitation of the forms which the Church had sealed as the proper expression of her attitude toward the divine mysteries, but claimed the privilege of coloring the text according to the dictates of his own feeling as a man and his peculiar method as an artist. The mediæval music was that of the cloister and the chapel. It was elevated, vague, abstract; it was as though it took up into itself all the particular and temporary emotions that might be called forth by the sacred history and articles of belief, and sifted and refined them into a generalized type, special individual experience being dissolved in the more diffused sense of awe and rapture which fills the hearts of an assembly in the attitude of worship. It was the mood of prayer which this music uttered, and that not the prayer of an individual agitated by his own personal hopes and fears, but the prayer of the Church, which embraces all the needs which the believers share in common, and offers them at the Mercy Seat with the calmness that comes of reverent confidence. Thus in the old masses the Kyrie eleison and the Miserere nobis are never agonizing; the Crucifixus does not attempt to portray the grief of an imaginary spectator of the scene on Calvary; the Gloria in excelsis and the Sanctus never force the jubilant tone into a frenzied excitement; the setting of the Dies

198

Iræ in the Requiem mass makes no attempt to paint a realistic picture of the terrors of the day of judgment.

Now compare a typical mass of the modern dramatic school and see how different is the conception. The music of Gloria and Credo revels in all the opportunities for change and contrast which the varied text supplies; the Dona nobis pacem dies away in strains of tender longing. Consider the mournful undertone that throbs through the Crucifixus of Schubert's Mass in A flat, the terrifying crash that breaks into the Miserere nobis in the Gloria of Beethoven's Mass in D, the tide of ecstasy that surges through the Sanctus of Gounod's St. Cecilia Mass and the almost cloying sweetness of the Agnus Dei, the uproar of brass instruments in the Tuba mirum of Berlioz's Requiem. Observe the strong similarity of style at many points between Verdi's Requiem and his opera "Aïda." In such works as these, which are fairly typical of the modern school, the composer writes under an independent impulse, with no thought of subordinating himself to ecclesiastical canons or liturgic usage. He attempts not only to depict his own state of mind as affected by the ideas of the text, but he also often aims to make his music picturesque according to dramatic methods. He does not seem to be aware that there is a distinction between religious concert music and church music. The classic example of this confusion is in the Dona nobis pacem of Beethoven's Missa Solemnis, where the composer introduces a strain of military music in order to suggest the contrasted horrors of war. This device, as Beethoven employs it, is exceedingly striking and beautiful, but it is precisely antagonistic to the

199

meaning of the text and the whole spirit of the liturgy. The conception of a large amount of modern mass music seems to be, not that the ritual to which it belongs is prayer, but rather a splendid spectacle intended to excite the imagination and fascinate the sense. It is this altered conception, lying at the very basis of the larger part of modern church music, that leads such writers as Jakob to refuse even to notice the modern school in his sketch of the history of Catholic church music, just as Rio condemns Titian as the painter who mainly contributed to the decay of religious painting.

In the Middle Age artists were grouped in schools or in guilds, each renouncing his right of initiative and shaping his productions in accordance with the legalized formulas of his craft. The modern artist is a separatist, his glory lies in the degree to which he rises above hereditary technic, and throws into his work a personal quality which becomes his own creative gift to the world. The church music of the sixteenth century was that of a school; the composers, although not actually members of a guild, worked on exactly the same technical foundations, and produced masses and motets of a uniformity that often becomes academic and monotonous. The modern composer carries into church pieces his distinct personal style. The grandeur and violent contrasts of Beethoven's symphonies, the elegiac tone of Schubert's songs, the enchantments of melody and the luxuries of color in the operas of Verdi and Gounod, are also characteristic marks of the masses of these composers. The older music could follow the text submissively, for there was no prescribed musical form to be worked out, and cadences could occur whenever a sentence came to an end. The modern forms, on the other hand, consisting of consecutive and proportional sections, imply the necessity of contrast, development, and climax — an arrangement that is not necessitated by any corresponding system in the text. This alone would often result in a lack of congruence between text and music, and the composer would easily fall into the way of paying more heed to the sheer musical working out than to the meaning of the words. Moreover, in the fifteenth and sixteenth centuries there was no radical conflict between the church musical style and the secular; so far as secular music was cultivated by the professional composers it was no more than a slight variation from the ecclesiastical model. Profane music may be said to have been a branch of religious music. In the modern period this relationship is reversed; secular music in opera and instrumental forms has remoulded church music, and the latter is in a sense a branch of the former.

Besides the development of the sectional form, another technical change acted to break down the old obstacles to characteristic expression. An essential feature of the mediæval music, consequent upon the very nature of the Gregorian modes, was the very slight employment of chromatic alteration of notes, and the absence of free dissonances. Modulation in the modern sense cannot exist in a purely diatonic scheme. The breaking up of the modal system was foreshadowed when composers became impatient with the placidity and colorlessness of the modal harmonies and began to introduce unexpected dissonances for the sake of variety The chromatic changes that occasionally appear in the old music are scattered about in a hap-hazard fashion; they give an impression of helplessness to the modern ear when the composer seems about to make a modulation and at once falls back again into the former tonality. It was a necessity, therefore, as well as a virtue, that the church music of the old régime should maintain the calm, equable flow that seems to us so pertinent to its liturgic intention. For these reasons it may perhaps be replied to what has been said concerning the devotional ideal embodied in the calm, severe strains of the old masters, that they had no choice in the matter. Does it follow, it may be asked, that these men would not have written in the modern style if they had had the means? Some of them probably would have done so, others almost certainly would not. Many writers who carried the old form into the seventeenth century did have the choice and resisted it; they stanchly defended the traditional principles and condemned the new methods as destructive of pure church music. The laws that work in the development of ecclesiastical art also seem to require that music should pass through the same stages as those that sculpture and painting traversed, — first, the stage of symbolism, restraint within certain conventions in accordance with ecclesiastical prescription; afterwards, the deliverance from the trammels of school formulas, emancipation from all laws but those of the free determination of individual genius. At this point authority ceases, dictation gives way to persuasion, and art still ministers to the higher ends of the Church, not through fear, but through reverence for the teachings and appeals which the Church sends forth as her contribution to the nobler influences of the age.

The writer who would trace the history of the modern musical mass has a task very different from that which meets the historian of the mediæval period. In the latter case, as has already been shown, generalization is comparatively easy, for we deal with music in which differences of nationality and individual style hardly appear. The modern Catholic music, on the other hand, follows the currents that shape the course of secular music. Where secular music becomes formalized, as in the early Italian opera, religious music tends to sink into a similar routine. When, on the other hand, men of commanding genius, such as Beethoven, Berlioz, Liszt, Verdi, contribute works of a purely individual stamp to the general development of musical art, their church compositions form no exception, but are likewise sharply differentiated from others of the same class. The influence of nationality makes itself felt — there is a style characteristic of Italy, another of South Germany and Austria, another of Paris, although these distinctions tend to disappear under the solvent of modern cosmopolitanism. The Church does not positively dictate any particular norm or method, and hence local tendencies have run their course almost unchecked.

Catholic music has shared all the fluctuations of European taste. The levity of the eighteenth and early part of the nineteenth centuries was as apparent in the mass as in the opera. The uplift in musical culture during the last one hundred years has carried church composition along with it, so that almost all the works produced since Palestrina, of which the Church has most reason to be proud, belong to the nineteenth century. One of the ultimate results of the modern license in style and the tendency toward individual expression is the custom of writing masses as free compositions rather than for liturgic uses, and of performing them in public halls or theatres in the same manner as oratorios. Mozart wrote his Requiem to the order of a private patron. Beethoven's Missa Solemnis, not being ready when wanted for a consecration ceremony, outgrew the dimensions of a service mass altogether, and was finished without any liturgic purpose in view. Cherubini's mass in D minor and Liszt's Gran Mass were each composed for a single occasion, and both of them, like the Requiems of Berlioz and Dvořák, although often heard in concerts, have but very rarely been performed in church worship. Masses have even been written by Protestants, such as Bach, Schumann, Hauptmann, Richter, and Becker. Masses that are written under the same impulse as ordinary concert and dramatic works easily violate the ecclesiastical spirit, and pass into the category of religious works that are non-churchly, and it may often seem necessary to class them with cantatas on account of their semi-dramatic tone. In such productions as Bach's B minor Mass, Beethoven's Missa Solemnis, and Berlioz's Requiem we have works that constitute a separate phase of art, not masses in the proper sense, for they do not properly blend with the Church ceremonial nor contribute to the special devotional mood which the Church aims to promote, while yet in their general conception they are held by a loose band to the altar. So apart do these mighty creations stand that they may almost be said to glorify religion in the abstract rather than the confession of the Catholic Church.

The changed conditions in respect to patronage have had the same effect upon the mass as upon other departments of musical composition. In former periods down to the close of the eighteenth century, the professional composer was almost invariably a salaried officer, attached as a personal retainer to a court, lay or clerical, and bound to conform his style of composition in a greater or less degree to the tastes of his employer. A Sixtus V. could reprove Palestrina for failing to please with a certain mass and admonish him to do better work in the future. Haydn could hardly venture to introduce any innovation into the style of religious music sanctioned by his august masters, the Esterhazys. Mozart wrote all his masses, with the exception of the Requiem, for the chapel of the prince archbishop of Salzburg. In this establishment the length of the mass was prescribed, the mode of writing and performance, which had become traditional, hindered freedom of development, and therefore Mozart's works of this class everywhere give evidence of constraint. On the other hand, the leading composers of the present century that have occupied themselves with the mass have been free from such arbitrary compulsions. They have written masses, not as a part of routine duty, but as they were inspired by the holy words and by the desire to offer the free gift of their genius at the altar of the Church. They have been, as a rule, devoted churchmen, but they have felt that they had the sympathy of the Church in asserting the rights of the artist as against prelatical conservatism and local usage. The outcome is seen in a group of works which, whatever the strict censors may deem their defects in edifying quality, at least indicate that in the field of musical art there is no necessary conflict between Catholicism and the free spirit of the age.

Under these conditions the mass in the modern musical era has taken a variety of directions and assumed distinct national and individual complexions. The Neapolitan school, which gave the law to Italian opera in the eighteenth century, endowed the mass with the same soft sensuousness of melody and sentimental pathos of expression, together with a dry, calculated kind of harmony in the chorus portions, the work never touching deep chords of feeling, and yet preserving a tone of sobriety and dignity. As cultivated in Italy and France the mass afterward degenerated into rivalry on equal terms with the shallow, captivating, cloying melody of the later Neapolitans and their successors, Rossini and Bellini. In this school of so-called religious music all sense of appropriateness was often lost, and a florid, profane treatment was not only permitted but encouraged. Perversions which can hardly be called less than blasphemous had free rein in the ritual music. Franz Liszt, in a letter to a Paris journal, written in 1835, bitterly attacks the music that flaunted itself in the Catholic churches of the city. He complains of the sacrilegious virtuoso displays of the prima donna, the wretched choruses, the vulgar antics of the organist.playing galops and variations from comic operas in the most solemn

206

moments of the holy ceremony. Similar testimony has from time to time come from Italy, and it would appear that the most lamentable lapses from the pure church tradition have occurred in some of the very places where one would expect that the strictest principles would be loyally maintained. The most celebrated surviving example of the consequences to which the virtuoso tendencies in church music must inevitably lead when unchecked by a truly pious criticism is Rossini's Stabat Mater. This frivolous work is frequently performed with great *éclat* in Catholic places of worship, as though the clergy were indifferent to the almost incredible levity which could clothe the heart-breaking pathos of Jacopone's immortal hymn — a hymn properly honored by the Church with a place among the five great Sequences — with strains better suited to the sprightly abandon of opera buffa.

Another branch of the mass was sent by the Neapolitan school into Austria, and here the results, although unsatisfactory to the better taste of the present time, were far nobler and more fruitful than in Italy and France. The group of Austrian church composers, represented by the two Haydns, Mozart, Eybler, Neukomm, Sechter and others of the period, created a form of church music which partook of much of the dry, formal, pedantic spirit of the day, in which regularity of form, scientific correctness, and a conscious propriety of manner were often more considered than emotional fervor. Certain conventions, such as a florid contrapuntal treatment of the Kyrie with its slow introduction followed by an Allegro, the fugues at the Cum Sanctu Spiritu and the Et Vitam, the regular alternation of solo and chorus numbers, give the typical Austrian mass a somewhat rigid, perfunctory air, and in practice produce the effect which always results when expression becomes stereotyped and form is exalted over substance. Mozart's masses, with the exception of the beautiful Requiem (which was his last work and belongs in a different category), were the production of his boyhood, written before his genius became self-assertive and under conditions distinctly unfavorable to the free exercise of the imagination.

The masses of Joseph Haydn stand somewhat apart from the strict Austrian school, for although as a rule they conform externally to the local conventions, they are far more individual and possess a freedom and buoyancy that are decidedly personal. It has become the fashion among the sterner critics of church music to condemn Haydn's masses without qualification, as conspicuous examples of the degradation of taste in religious art which is one of the depressing legacies of the eighteenth century. Much of this censure is deserved, for Haydn too often loses sight of the law which demands that music should reinforce, and not contradict, the meaning and purpose of the text. Haydn's mass style is often indistinguishable from his oratorio style. His colorature arias are flippant, often introduced at such solemn moments as to be offensive. Even where the voice part is subdued to an appropriate solemnity, the desired impression is frequently destroyed by some tawdry flourish in the orchestra. The brilliancy of the choruses is often pompous and hollow. Haydn's genius was primarily instrumental; he was the virtual creator of the modern symphony and string quartet; his musical forms and modes of expression were drawn from two diverse sources which it was his great mission to conciliate and idealize, *viz.*, the Italian aristocratic opera, and the dance and song of the common people. An extraordinary sense of form and an instinctive sympathy with whatever is spontaneous, genial, and racy made him what he was. The joviality of his nature was irrepressible. To write music of a sombre cast was out of his power. There is not a melancholy strain in all his works; pensiveness was as deep a note as he could strike. He tried to defend the gay tone of his church music by saying that he had such a sense of the goodness of God that he could not be otherwise than joyful in thinking of him. This explanation was perfectly sincere, but Haydn was not enough of a philosopher to see the weak spot in this sort of æsthetics. Yet in spite of the obvious faults of Haydn's mass style, looking at it from a historic point of view, it was a promise of advance, and not a sign of degeneracy. For it marked the introduction of genuine, even if misdirected feeling into worship music, in the place of dull conformity to routine. Haydn was far indeed from solving the problem of church music, but he helped to give new life to a form that showed danger of becoming atrophied.

Two masses of world importance rise above the mediocrity of the Austrian school, like the towers of some Gothic cathedral above the monotonous tiled roofs of a mediæval city, — the Requiem of Mozart and the Missa Solemnis of Beethoven. The unfinished masterpiece of Mozart outsoars all comparison with the religious works of his youth, and as his farewell to the world he could impart to it a tone of pathos and exaltation which had hardly been known in the cold, objective treatment of the usual eighteenth-century mass. The hand of death was upon Mozart as he penned the immortal pages of the Requiem, and in this crisis he could feel that he was free from the dictation of fashion and precedent. This work is perhaps not all that we might look for in these solemn circumstances. Mozart's exquisite genius was suited rather to the task, in which lies his true glory, of raising the old Italian opera to its highest possibilities of grace and truth to nature. He had not that depth of feeling and sweep of imagination which make the works of Bach, Händel, and Beethoven the sublimest expression of awe in view of the mysteries of life and death. Yet it is wholly free from the fripperies which disfigure the masses of Haydn, as well as from the dry scholasticism of much of Mozart's own early religious work. Such movements as the Confutatis, the Recordare, and the Lacrimosa — movements inexpressibly earnest, consoling, and pathetic — gave evidence that a new and loftier spirit had entered the music of the Church.

The Missa Solemnis of Beethoven, composed 1818–1822, can hardly be considered from the liturgic point of view. In the vastness of its dimensions it is quite disproportioned to the ceremony to which it theoretically belongs, and its almost unparalleled difficulty of execution and the grandeur of its choral climaxes remove it beyond the reach of all but the most exceptional choirs. It is, therefore, performed only as a concert work by choral societies with a full orchestral equipment. For these reasons it is not to be classed with the service masses of the Catholic Church, but may be placed beside the B minor Mass of Sebastian Bach, both holding a position outside all ordinary comparisons. Each of these colossal creations stands on its own solitary eminence, the projection in tones of the religious conceptions of two gigantic, all-comprehending intellects. For neither of these two works is the Catholic Church strictly responsible. They do not proceed from within the Church. Bach was a strict Protestant; Beethoven, although nominally a disciple of the Catholic Church, had almost no share in her communion, and his religious belief, so far as the testimony goes, was a sort of pantheistic mysticism. Both these supreme artists in the later periods of their careers gave free rein to their imaginations and not only well-nigh exceeded all available means of performance, but also seemed to strive to force musical forms and the powers of instruments and voices beyond their limits in the efforts to realize that which is unrealizable through any human medium. In this endeavor they went to the very verge of the sublime, and produced achievements which excite wonder and awe. These two masses defy all imitation, and represent no school. The spirit of individualism in religious music can go no further.

The last masses of international importance produced on Austrian soil are those of Franz Schubert. Of his six Latin masses four are youthful works, pure and graceful, but not especially significant. In his E flat and A flat masses, however, he takes a place in the upper rank of mass composers of this century. The E flat Mass is weakened by the diffuseness which was Schubert's besetting sin; the A flat is more terse and sustained in excellence, and thoroughly available for practical use. Both of them contain movements of purest ideal beauty and sincere worshipful spirit, and often rise to a grandeur that is unmarred by sensationalism and wholly in keeping with the tone of awe which pervades even the most exultant moments of the liturgy.

The lofty idealism exemplified in such works as Mozart's Requiem, Beethoven's Mass in D, Schubert's last two masses, and in a less degree in Weber's Mass in E flat has never since been lost from the German mass, in spite of local and temporary reactions. Such composers as Kiel, Havert, Grell, and Rheinberger have done noble service in holding German Catholic music fast to the tradition of seriousness and truth which has been taking form all through this century in German secular music. It must be said, however, that the German Catholic Church at large, especially in the country districts, has been too often dull to the righteous claims of the profounder expression of devotional feeling, and has maintained the vogue of the Italian mass and the shallower products of the Austrian school. Against this indifference the St. Cecilia Society has directed its noble missionary labors, with as yet but partial success.

If we turn our observation to Italy and France we find that the music of the Church is at every period sympathetically responsive to the fluctuations in secular music. Elevated and dignified, if somewhat cold and constrained, in the writings of the nobler spirits of the Neapolitan school such as Durante and Jomelli, sweet and graceful even to effeminacy in Pergolesi, sensuous and saccharine in Rossini, imposing and massive, rising at times to epic grandeur, in Cherubini, by turns ecstatic and voluptuous in Gounod, ardent and impassioned in Verdi — the ecclesiastical music of the Latin nations offers works of adorable beauty, sometimes true to the pure devotional ideal, sometimes perverse, and by their isolation serving to illustrate the dependence of the church composer's inspiration upon the general conditions of musical taste and progress. Not only were those musicians of France and Italy who were prominent as church composers also among the leaders in opera, but their ideals and methods in opera were closely paralleled by those displayed in their religious productions. It is impossible to separate the powerful masses of Cherubini, with their pomp and majesty of movement, their reserved and pathetic melody, their grandiose dimensions and their sumptuous orchestration, from those contemporary tendencies in dramatic art which issued in the "historic school" of grand opera as exemplified in the pretentious works of Spontini and Meyerbeer. They may be said to be the reflection in church art of the hollow splendor of French imperialism. Such an expression, however, may be accused of failing in justice to the undeniable merits of Cherubini's masses. As a man and as a musician Cherubini commands unbounded respect for his unswerving sincerity in an age of sham, his uncompromising assertion of his dignity as an artist in an age of sycophancy, and the solid worth of his achievement in the midst of shallow aims and mediocre results. As a church composer he towers so high above his predecessors of the eighteenth century in respect to learning and imagination that his masses are not unworthy to stand beside Beethoven's Missa Solemnis as auguries of the loftier aims that were soon to prevail in the realm of religious music. His Requiem in C minor, particularly, by reason of its exquisite tenderness, breadth of thought, nobility of expression, and avoidance of all excess either of agitation or of gloom, must be ranked among the most admirable modern examples of pure Catholic art.

The effort of Lesueur (1763–1837) to introduce into church music a picturesque and imitative style — which, in spite of much that was striking and attractive in result, must be pronounced a false direction in church music — was characteristically French and was continued in such works as Berlioz's Requiem and to a certain extent in the masses and psalms of Liszt. The genius of Liszt, notwithstanding his Hungarian birth, was closely akin to the French in his tendency to connect every musical impulse with a picture or with some mental conception which could be grasped in distinct concrete outline. In his youth Liszt, in his despair over the degeneracy of liturgic music in France and its complete separation from the real life of the people, proclaimed the necessity of a *rapprochement* between church music and popular music. In an article written for a Paris journal in 1834, which remains a fragment, he imagined a new style of religious music which should " unite in colossal relations theatre and church, which should be at the same time dramatic and solemn, imposing and simple, festive and earnest, fiery and unconstrained, stormy and reposeful, clear and fervent." These expressions are too vague to serve as a program for a new art movement. They imply, however, a protest against the one-sided operatic tendency of the day, at the same time indicating the conviction that the problem is not to be solved in a pedantic reaction toward the ancient austere ideal, and yet that the old and new endeavors, liturgic appropriateness and characteristic expression, reverence of mood and recognition of the claims of contemporary taste, should in some way be made to harmonize. The man who all his life conceived the theatre as a means of popular education, and who strove to realize that conception as court music director at Weimar, would also lament any alienation between the church ceremony and the intellectual and emotional habitudes and inclinations of the people. A devoted churchman reverencing the ancient ecclesiastical tradition, and at the same time a musical artist of the advanced modern type, Liszt's instincts yearned more or less blindly towards an alliance between the sacerdotal conception of religious art and the general artistic spirit of the age. Some such vision evidently floated before his mind in the masses, psalms, and oratorios of his later years, as shown in their frequent striving after the picturesque, together with an inclination toward the older ecclesiastical forms. These two ideals are probably incompatible; at any rate Liszt did not possess the genius to unite them in a convincing manner.

Among the later ecclesiastical composers of France, Gounod shines out conspicuously by virtue of those fascinating melodic gifts which have made the fame of the St. Cecilia mass almost conterminous with that of the opera "Faust." Indeed, there is hardly a better example of the modern propensity of the dramatic and religious styles to reflect each other's lineaments than is found in the close parallelism which appears in Gounod's secular and church productions. So pliable, or perhaps we might say, so neutral is his art, that a similar quality of melting cadence is made to portray the mutual avowals of love-lorn souls and the raptures of heavenly aspiration. Those who condemn Gounod's religious music on this account as sensuous have some reason on their side, yet no one has ever ventured to accuse Gounod of insincerity, and it may well be that his wide human sympathy saw enough correspondence between the worship of an earthly ideal and that of a heavenly — each implying the abandonment of self-consciousness in the yearning for a happiness which is at the moment the highest conceivable — as to make the musical expression of both essentially similar. This is to say that the composer forgets liturgic claims in behalf of the purely human. This principle no doubt involves the destruction of church music as a distinctive form of art, but it is certain that the world at large, as evinced by the immense popularity of Gounod's religious works, sees no incongruity and does not feel that such

216

usage is profane. Criticism on the part of all but the most austere is disarmed by the pure, seraphic beauty which this complacent art of Gounod often reveals. The intoxicating sweetness of his melody and harmony never sinks to a Rossinian flippancy. Of Gounod's reverence for the Church and for its art ideals, there can be no question. A man's views of the proper tone of church music will be controlled largely by his temperament, and Gounod's temperament was as warm as an Oriental's. He offered to the Church his best, and as the Magi brought gold, frankincense, and myrrh to a babe born among cattle in a stable, so Gounod, with a consecration equally sincere, clothed his prayers in strains so ecstatic that compared with them the most impassioned accents of "Faust" and "Romeo and Juliet" are tame. He was a profound student of Palestrina, Mozart, and Cherubini, and strong traces of the styles of these masters are apparent in his works.

Somewhat similar qualities, although far less sensational, are found in the productions of that admirable band of organists and church composers that now lends such lustre to the art life of the French capital. The culture of such representatives of this school as Guilmant, Widor, Saint-Saëns, Dubois, Gigout is so solidly based, and their views of religious music so judicious, that the methods and traditions which they are conscientiously engaged in establishing need only the reinforcement of still higher genius to bring forth works which will confer even greater honor upon Catholicism than she has yet received from the devotion of her musical sons in France. No purer or nobler type of religious music has appeared in these latter days than is to be found in the compositions of César Franck (1822–1890). For the greater part of his life overlooked or disdained by all save a devoted band of disciples, in spirit and in learning he was allied to the Palestrinas and the Bachs, and there are many who place him in respect to genius among the foremost of the French musicians of the nineteenth century.

The religious works of Verdi might be characterized in much the same terms as those of Gounod. In Verdi also we have a truly filial devotion to the Catholic Church, united with a temperament easily excited to a white heat when submitted to his musical inspiration, and a genius for melody and seductive harmonic combinations in which he is hardly equalled among modern composers. In his Manzoni Requiem, Stabat Mater, and Te Deum these qualities are no less in evidence than in " Aïda " and " Otello," and it would be idle to deny their devotional sincerity on account of their lavish profusion of nerve-exciting effects. The controversy between the contemners and the defenders of the Manzoni Requiem is now somewhat stale and need not be revived here. Any who may wish to resuscitate it, however, on account of the perennial importance of the question of what constitutes purity and appropriateness in church art, must in justice put themselves into imaginative sympathy with the racial religious feeling of an Italian, and make allowance also for the undeniable suggestion of the dramatic in the Catholic ritual, and for the natural effect of the Catholic ceremonial and its peculiar atmosphere upon the more ardent, enthusiastic order of minds.

The most imposing contributions that have been made to Catholic liturgic music since Verdi's Requiem are undoubtedly the Requiem Mass and the Stabat Mater of Dvořák. All the wealth of tone color which is contained upon the palette of this master of harmony and instrumentation has been laid upon these two magnificent scores. Inferior to Verdi in variety and gorgeousness of melody, the Bohemian composer surpasses the great Italian in massiveness, dignity, and in unfailing good taste. There can be no question that Dvořák's Stabat Mater is supreme over all other settings — the only one, except Verdi's much shorter work, that is worthy of the pathos and tenderness of this immortal Sequence. The Requiem of Dvořák in spite of a tendency to monotony, is a work of exceeding beauty, rising often to grandeur, and is notable, apart from its sheer musical qualities, as the most precious gift to Catholic art that has come from the often rebellious land of Bohemia.

It would be profitless to attempt to predict the future of Catholic church music. In the hasty survey which we have made of the Catholic mass in the past three centuries we have been able to discover no law of development except the almost unanimous agreement of the chief composers to reject law and employ the sacred text of Scripture and liturgy as the basis of works in which not the common consciousness of the Church shall be expressed, but the emotions aroused by the action of sacred ideas upon different temperaments and divergent artistic methods. There is no sign that this principle of individual liberty will be renounced. Nevertheless, the increasing deference that is paid to authority, the growing study of the works and ideals of the past which is so apparent in the culture of the present day, will here and there issue in partial reactions. The mind of the present, having seen the successful working out of certain modern problems and the barrenness of others, is turning eclectic. Nowhere is this more evident than in the field of musical culture, both religious and secular. We see that in many influential circles the question becomes more and more insistent, what is truth and appropriateness? — whereas formerly the demand was for novelty and "effect." Under this better inspiration many beautiful works are produced which are marked by dignity, moderation, and an almost austere reserve, drawing a sharp distinction between the proper ecclesiastical tone and that suited to concert and dramatic music, restoring once more the idea of impersonality, expressing in song the conception of the fathers that the Church is a refuge, a retreat from the tempests of the world, a place of penitence and restoration to confidence in the near presence of heaven.

Such masses as the Missa Solemnis of Beethoven, the D minor of Cherubini, the Messe Solennelle of Rossini, the St. Cecilia of Gounod, the Requiems of Berlioz and Verdi, sublime and unspeakably beautiful as they are from the broadly human standpoint, are yet in a certain sense sceptical. They reveal a mood of agitation which is not that intended by the ministrations of the Church in her organized acts of worship. And yet such works will continue to be produced, and the Church will accept them, in grateful recognition of the sincere homage which their creation implies. It is of the nature of the highest artistic genius that it cannot restrain its own fierce impulses out of conformity to a type or external tradition. It will express its own individual emotion or it will become paralyzed and mute. The religious compositions that will humbly yield to a strict liturgic standard in form and expression will be those of writers of the third or fourth grade, just as the church hymns have been, with few exceptions, the production, not of the great poets, but of men of lesser artistic endowment, and who were primarily churchmen, and poets only by second intention. This will doubtless be the law for all time. The Michael Angelos, the Dantes, the Beethovens will forever break over rules, even though they be the rules of a beloved mother Church.

The time is past, however, when we may fear any degeneracy like to that which overtook church music one hundred or more years ago. The principles of such consecrated church musicians as Witt, Tinel, and the leaders of the St. Cecilia Society and the Paris Schola Cantorum, the influence of the will of the Church implied in all her admonitions on the subject of liturgic song, the growing interest in the study of the masters of the past, and, more than all, the growth of sound views of art as a detail of the higher and the popular education, must inevitably promote an increasing conviction among clergy, choir leaders, and people of the importance of purity and appropriateness in the music of the Church. The need of reform in many of the Catholic churches of this and other

countries is known to every one. Doubtless one cause
of the frequent indifference of priests to the condition of
the choir music in their churches is the knowledge that the
chorus and organ are after all but accessories ; that the
Church possesses in the Gregorian chant a form of song
that is the legal, universal, and unchangeable foundation
of the musical ceremony, and that any corruption in the
gallery music can never by any possibility extend to the
heart of the system. The Church is indeed fortunate in
the possession of this altar song, the unifying chain
which can never be loosened. All the more reason,
therefore, why this consciousness of unity should pervade all portions of the ceremony, and the spirit of the
liturgic chant should blend even with the large freedom
of modern musical experiment.

CHAPTER VII

THE music of the Protestant Church of Germany, while adopting many features from its great antagonist, presents certain points of contrast which are of the highest importance not only in the subsequent history of ecclesiastical song, but also as significant of certain national traits which were conspicuous among the causes of the schism of the sixteenth century. The musical system of the Catholic Church proceeded from the Gregorian chant, which is strictly a detail of the sacerdotal office. The Lutheran music, on the contrary, is primarily based on the congregational hymn. The one is clerical, the other laic; the one official, prescribed, liturgic, unalterable, the other free, spontaneous, and democratic. In these two forms and ideals we find reflected the same conceptions which especially characterize the doctrine, worship, and government of these oppugnant confessions.

The Catholic Church, as we have seen, was consistent in withdrawing the office of song from the laity and assigning it to a separate company who were at first taken from the minor clergy, and who even in later periods were conceived as exercising a semi-clerical function. Congregational singing, although not officially and without exception discountenanced by the Catholic Church, has never been encouraged, and song, like prayer, is looked upon as essentially a liturgic office.

In the Protestant Church the barrier of an intermediary priesthood between the believer and his God is broken down. The entire membership of the Christian body is recognized as a universal priesthood, with access to the Father through one mediator, Jesus Christ. This conception restores the offices of worship to the body of believers, and they in turn delegate their administration to certain officials, who, together with certain independent privileges attached to the office, share with the laity in the determination of matters of faith and polity.

It was a perfectly natural result of this principle that congregational song should hold a place in the Protestant cultus which the Catholic Church has never sanctioned. The one has promoted and tenaciously maintained it; the other as consistently repressed it, — not on æsthetic grounds, nor primarily on grounds of devotional effect, but really through a more or less distinct perception of its significance in respect to the theoretical relationship of the individual to the Church. The struggles over popular song in public worship which appear throughout the early history of Protestantism are thus to be explained. The emancipated layman found in the general hymn a symbol as well as an agent of the assertion of his new rights and privileges in the Gospel. The people's song of early Protestantism has therefore a militant ring. It marks its epoch no less significantly than Luther's ninety-five theses and the Augsburg Confession. It was a sort of spiritual *Triumphlied*, proclaiming to the universe that the day of spiritual emancipation had dawned.

The second radical distinction between the music of the Protestant Church and that of the Catholic is that the vernacular language takes the place of the Latin. The natural desire of a people is that they may worship in their native idiom; and since the secession from the ancient Church inevitably resulted in the formation of national or independent churches, the necessities which maintained in the Catholic Church a common liturgic language no longer obtained, and the people fell back upon their national speech.

Among the historic groups of hymns that have appeared since Clement of Alexandria and Ephraëm the Syrian set in motion the tide of Christian song, the Lutheran hymnody has the greatest interest to the student of church history. In sheer literary excellence it is undoubtedly surpassed by the Latin hymns of the mediæval Church and the English-American group; in musical merit it no more than equals these; but in historic importance the Lutheran song takes the foremost place. The Latin and the English hymns belong only to the history of poetry and of inward spiritual experience; the Lutheran have a place in the annals of politics and doctrinal strifes as well. German Protestant hymnody dates from Martin Luther; his lyrics were the models of the hymns of the reformed Church in Germany for a century or more. The principle that lay at the basis of his movement gave them their character.

15   225

istic tone; they were among the most efficient agencies in carrying this principle to the mind of the common people, and they also contributed powerfully to the enthusiasm which enabled the new faith to maintain itself in the conflicts by which it was tested. The melodies to which the hymns of Luther and his followers were set became the foundation of a musical style which is the one school worthy to be placed beside the Italian Catholic music of the sixteenth century. This hymnody and its music afforded the first adequate outlet for the poetic and musical genius of the German people, and established the pregnant democratic traditions of German art as against the aristocratic traditions of Italy and France. As we cannot overestimate the spiritual and intellectual force which entered the European arena with Luther and his disciples, so we must also recognize the analogous elements which asserted themselves at the same moment and under the same inspiration in the field of art expression, and gave to this movement a language which helps us in a peculiar way to understand its real import.

The first questions which present themselves in tracing the historic connections of the early Lutheran hymnody are: What was its origin? Had it models, and if so, what and where were they? In giving a store of congregational songs to the German people was Luther original, or only an imitator? In this department of his work does he deserve the honor which Protestants have awarded him?

Protestant writers have, as a rule, bestowed unstinted praise upon Luther as the man who first gave the people a voice with which to utter their religious emotions in song. Most of these writers are undoubtedly aware that a national poesy is never the creation of a single man, and that a brilliant epoch of national literature or art must always be preceded by a period of experiment and fermentation; yet they are disposed to make little account of the existence of a popular religious song in Germany before the Reformation, and represent Luther almost as performing the miracle of making the dumb to speak. Even those who recognize the fact of a pre-existing school of hymnody usually seek to give the impression that pure evangelical religion was almost, if not quite, unknown in the popular religious poetry of the centuries before the Reformation, and that the Lutheran hymnody was composed of altogether novel elements. They also ascribe to Luther creative work in music as well as in poetry. Catholic writers, on the other hand, will allow Luther no originality whatever; they find, or pretend to find, every essential feature of his work in the Catholic hymns and tunes of the previous centuries, or in those of the Bohemian sectaries. They admit the great influence of Luther's hymns in disseminating the new doctrines, but give him credit only for cleverness in dressing up his borrowed ideas and forms in a taking popular guise. As is usually the case in controversy, the truth lies between the two extremes. Luther's originality has been overrated by Protestants, and the true nature of the germinal force which he imparted to German congregational song has been misconceived by Catholics. It was not new forms, but a new spirit, which Luther gave to his Church. He did not break with the past, but found in the past a new standing-ground. He sought truth in the Scriptures, in the writings of the fathers and the mediæval theologians; he rejected what he deemed false or barren in the mother Church, adopted and developed what was true and fruitful, and moulded it into forms whose style was already familiar to the people. In poetry, music, and the several details of church worship Luther recast the old models, and gave them to his followers with contents purified and adapted to those needs which he himself had made them to realize. He understood the character of his people; he knew where to find the nourishment suited to their wants; he knew how to turn their enthusiasms into practical and progressive directions. This was Luther's achievement in the sphere of church art, and if, in recognizing the precise nature of his work, we seem to question his reputation for creative genius, we do him better justice by honoring his practical wisdom.

The singing of religious songs by the common people in their own language in connection with public worship did not begin in Germany with the Reformation. The German popular song is of ancient date, and the religious lyric always had a prominent place in it. The Teutonic tribes before their conversion to Christianity had a large store of hymns to their deities, and afterward their musical fervor turned itself no less ardently to the service of their new allegiance. Wackernagel, in the second volume of his monumental collection of German hymns from the earliest time to the beginning of the seventeenth century, includes fourteen hundred and forty-eight religious lyrics in the German tongue composed between the year 868 and 1518.[1] This collection, he says, is as complete as possible, but we must suppose that a very large number written before the invention of printing have been lost. About half the hymns in this volume are of unknown authorship. Among the writers whose names are given we find such notable poets as Walther von der Vogelweide, Gottfried von Strassburg, Hartmann von Aue, Frauenlob, Reinmar der Zweter, Kunrad der Marner, Heinrich von Loufenberg, Michel Behem, and Hans Sachs, besides famous churchmen like Eckart and Tauler, who are not otherwise known as poets. A great number of these poems are hymns only in a qualified sense, having been written, not for public use, but for private satisfaction; but many others are true hymns, and have often resounded from the mouths of the people in social religious functions.

Down to the tenth century the only practice among the Germans that could be called a popular church song was the ejaculation of the words *Kyrie eleison, Christe eleison*. These phrases, which are among the most ancient in the Mass and the litanies, and which came originally from the Eastern Church, were sung or shouted by the German Christians on all possible occasions. In processions, on pilgrimages, at burials, greeting of distinguished visitors, consecration of a church or prelate, in many subordinate liturgic offices, invocations of supernatural aid in times of dis-

[1] Wackernagel, *Das deutsche Kirchenlied von der ältesten Zeit bis zu Anfang des XVII. Jahrhunderts.*

tress, on the march, going into battle, — in almost every social action in which religious sanctions were involved the people were in duty bound to utter this phrase, often several hundred times in succession. The words were often abbreviated into *Kyrieles*, *Kyrie eleis*, *Kyrielle*, *Kerleis*, and *Kles*, and sometimes became mere inarticulate cries.

When the phrase was formally sung, the Gregorian tones proper to it in the church service were employed. Some of these were florid successions of notes, many to a syllable, as in the Alleluia from which the Sequences sprung, — a free, impassioned form of emotional utterance which had extensive use in the service of the earlier Church, both East and West, and which is still employed, sometimes to extravagant lengths, in the Orient. The custom at last arose of setting words to these exuberant strains. This usage took two forms, giving rise in the ritual service to the "farced Kyries" or Tropes, and in the freer song of the people producing a more regular kind of hymn, in which the *Kyrie eleison* became at last a mere refrain at the end of each stanza. These songs came to be called *Kirleisen*, or *Leisen*, and sometimes *Leiche*, and they exhibit the German congregational hymn in its first estate.

Religious songs multiplied in the centuries following the tenth almost by geometrical progression. The tide reached a high mark in the twelfth and thirteenth centuries under that extraordinary intellectual awakening which distinguished the epoch of the Crusades, the Stauffen emperors, the Minnesingers, and the court epic poets. Under the stimulus of the ideals of chivalric honor and knightly devotion to woman, the adoration of the Virgin Mother, long cherished in the bosom of the Church, burst forth in a multitude of ecstatic lyrics in her praise. Poetic and musical inspiration was communicated by the courtly poets to the clergy and common people, and the love of singing at religious observances grew apace. Certain heretics, who made much stir in this period, also wrote hymns and put them into the mouths of the populace, thus following the early example of the Arians and the disciples of Bardasanes. To resist this perversion of the divine art, orthodox songs were composed, and, as in the Reformation days, schismatics and Romanists vied with each other in wielding this powerful proselyting agent.

Mystics of the fourteenth century — Eckart, Tauler, and others — wrote hymns of a new tone, an inward spiritual quality, less objective, more individual, voicing a yearning for an immediate union of the soul with God, and the joy of personal love to the Redeemer. Poetry of this nature especially appealed to the religious sisters, and from many a convent came echoes of these chastened raptures, in which are heard accents of longing for the comforting presence of the Heavenly Bridegroom.

Those half-insane fanatics, the Flagellants, and other enthusiasts of the thirteenth and fourteenth centuries, also contributed to the store of pre-Reformation hymnody. Hoffmann von Fallersleben has given a vivid account of the barbaric doings of these bands of self-tormentors, and it is evident that their singing was not the least uncanny feature of their performances.[1]

In the fourteenth century appeared the device which played so large a part in the production of the Reformation hymns — that of adapting secular tunes to religious poems, and also making religious paraphrases of secular ditties. Praises of love, of out-door sport, even of wine, by a few simple alterations were made to express devotional sentiments. A good illustration of this practice is the recasting of the favorite folk-song, "Den liepsten Bulen den ich han," into "Den liepsten Herren den ich han." Much more common, however, was the transfer of melodies from profane poems to religious, a method which afterward became an important reliance for supplying the reformed congregations with hymn-tunes.

Mixed songs, part Latin and part German, were at one time much in vogue. A celebrated example is the

> " In dulce jubilo
> Nu singet und seyt fro "

of the fourteenth century, which has often been heard in the reformed churches down to a recent period.

In the fifteenth century the popular religious song flourished with an affluence hardly surpassed even in the first two centuries of Protestantism. Still under the control of the Catholic doctrine and discipline, it nevertheless betokens a certain restlessness of mind; the native individualism of the German spirit is pre-

[1] Hoffmann von Fallersleben, *Geschichte des deutschen Kirchenliedes bis auf Luther's Zeit.*

paring to assert itself. The fifteenth was a century of stir and inquiry, full of premonitions of the upheaval soon to follow. The Revival of Learning began to shake Germany, as well as Southern and Western Europe, out of its superstition and intellectual subjection. The religious and political movements in Bohemia and Moravia, set in motion by the preaching and martyrdom of Hus, produced strong effect in Germany. Hus struck at some of the same abuses that aroused the wrath of Luther, notably the traffic in indulgences. The demand for the use of the vernacular in church worship was even more fundamental than the similar desire in Germany, and preceded rather than followed the movement toward reform. Hus was also a prototype of Luther in that he was virtually the founder of the Bohemian hymnody. He wrote hymns both in Latin and in Czech, and earnestly encouraged the use of vernacular songs by the people. The Utraquists published a song-book in the Czech language in 1501, and the Unitas Fratrum one, containing four hundred hymns, in 1505. These two antedated the first Lutheran hymn-book by about twenty years. The Bohemian reformers, like Luther after them, based their poetry upon the psalms, the ancient Latin hymns, and the old vernacular religious songs; they improved existing texts, and set new hymns in place of those that contained objectionable doctrinal features. Their tunes also were derived, like those of the German reformers, from older religious and secular melodies.

These achievements of the Bohemians, answering

popular needs that exist at all times, could not remain without influence upon the Germans. Encouragement to religious expression in the vernacular was also exerted by certain religious communities known as Brethren of the Common Life, which originated in Holland in the latter part of the fourteenth century, and extended into North and Middle Germany in the fifteenth. Thomas à Kempis was a member of this order. The purpose of these Brethren was to inculcate a purer religious life among the people, especially the young; and they made it a ground principle that the national language should be used so far as possible in prayer and song. Particularly effective in the culture of sacred poetry and music among the artisan class were the schools of the Mastersingers, which flourished all over Germany in the fourteenth, fifteenth, and sixteenth centuries.

Standing upon the threshold of the Reformation, and looking back over the period that elapsed since the pagan myths and heroic lays of the North began to yield to the metrical gospel narrative of the "Heliand" and the poems of Otfried, we can trace the same union of pious desire and poetic instinct which, in a more enlightened age, produced the one hundred thousand evangelical hymns of Germany. The pre-Reformation hymns are of the highest importance as casting light upon the condition of religious belief among the German laity. We find in them a great variety of elements, — much that is pure, noble, and strictly evangelical, mixed with crudity, superstition, and crass realism. In the nature of the case they do not, on the whole, rise to the poetic and spiritual level of the contemporary Latin hymns of the Church. There is nothing in them comparable with the Dies Iræ, the Stabat Mater, the Hora Novissima, the Veni Sancte Spiritus, the Ad Perennis Vitæ Fontem, the Passion Hymns of St. Bernard, or scores that might be named which make up the golden chaplet of Latin religious verse from Hilary to Xavier. The latter is the poetry of the cloister, the work of men separated from the world, upon whom asceticism and scholastic philosophizing had worked to refine and subtilize their conceptions. It is the poetry, not of laymen, but of priests and monks, the special and peculiar utterance of a sacerdotal class, wrapt in intercessory functions, straining ever for glimpses of the Beatific Vision, whose one absorbing effort was to emancipate the soul from time and discipline it for eternity. It is poetry of and for the temple, the sacramental mysteries, the hours of prayer, for seasons of solitary meditation; it blends with the dim light sifted through stained cathedral windows, with incense, with majestic music. The simple layman was not at home in such an atmosphere as this, and the Latin hymn was not a familiar expression of his thought. His mental training was of a coarser, more commonplace order. He must particularize, his religious feeling must lay hold of something more tangible, something that could serve his childish views of things, and enter into some practical relation with the needs of his ordinary mechanical existence.

The religious folk-song, therefore, shows many traits similar to those found in the secular folk-song, and we can easily perceive the influence of one upon the other. In both we can see how receptive the common people were to anything that savored of the marvellous, and how their minds dwelt more upon the external wonder than upon the lesson that it brings. The connection of these poems with the ecclesiastical dramas, which form such a remarkable chapter in the history of religious instruction in the Middle Age, is also apparent, and scores of them are simply narratives of the Nativity, the Crucifixion, the Resurrection, and the Ascension, told over and over in almost identical language. These German hymns show in what manner the dogmas and usages of the Church took root in the popular heart, and affected the spirit of the time. In all other mediæval literature we have the testimony of the higher class of minds, the men of education, who were saved by their reflective intelligence from falling into the grosser superstitions, or at least from dwelling in them. But in the folk poetry the great middle class throws back the ideas imposed by its religious teachers, tinged by its own crude mental operations. The result is that we have in these poems the doctrinal perversions and the mythology of the Middle Age set forth in their baldest form. Beliefs that are the farthest removed from the teaching of the Scriptures, are carried to lengths which the Catholic Church has never authoritatively sanctioned, but which are natural consequences of the action of her dogmas upon untrained, superstitious minds. There are hymns which teach the preëxistence of Mary with God before the creation; that in and through her all things were created. Others, not

236

content with the church doctrine of her intercessory office in heaven, represent her as commanding and controlling her Son, and even as forgiving sins in her own right. Hagiolatry, also, is carried to its most dubious extremity. Power is ascribed to the saints to save from the pains of hell. In one hymn they are implored to intercede with God for the sinner, because, the writer says, God will not deny their prayer. It is curious to see in some of these poems that the attributes of love and compassion, which have been removed from the Father to the Son, and from the Son to the Virgin Mother, are again transferred to St. Ann, who is implored to intercede with her daughter in behalf of the suppliant.

All this, and much more of a similar sort, the product of vulgar error and distorted thinking, cannot be gainsaid. But let us, with equal candor, acknowledge that there is a bright side to this subject. Corruption and falsehood are not altogether typical of the German religious poetry of the Middle Age. Many Protestant writers represent the mediæval German hymns as chiefly given over to mariolatry and much debasing superstition, and as therefore indicative of the religious state of the nation. This, however, is very far from being the case, as a candid examination of such a collection as Wackernagel's will show. Take out everything that a severe Protestant would reject, and there remains a large body of poetry which flows from the pure, undefiled springs of Christian faith, which from the evangelical standpoint is true and edifying, gems of expression not to be matched by the poetry of

Luther and his friends in simplicity and refinement of language. Ideas common to the hymnody of all ages are to be found there. One comes to mind in which there is carried out in the most touching way the thought of John Newton in his most famous hymn, where in vision the look of the crucified Christ seems to charge the arrested sinner with his death. Another lovely poem expresses the shrinking of the disciple in consciousness of mortal frailty when summoned by Christ to take up the cross, and the comfort that he receives from the Saviour's assurance of his own sufficient grace. A celebrated hymn by Tauler describes a ship sent from heaven by the Father, containing Jesus, who comes as our Redeemer, and who asks personal devotion to himself and a willingness to live and die with and for him. Others set forth the atoning work of Christ's death, without mention of any other condition of salvation. Others implore the direct guidance and protection of Christ, as in the exquisite cradle hymn of Heinrich von Loufenberg, which is not surpassed in tenderness and beauty by anything in Keble's *Lyra Innocentium*, or the child verses of Blake.

This mass of hymns covers a wide range of topics: God in his various attributes, including mercy and a desire to pardon, — a conception which many suppose to have been absent from the thought of the Middle Age; the Trinity; Christ in the various scenes of his life, and as head of the Church; admonitions, confessions, translations of psalms, poems to be sung on pilgrimages, funeral songs, political songs, and many more which touch upon true relations between man and the divine. There is a wonderful pathos in this great body of national poetry, for it makes us see the dim but honest striving of the heart of the noble German people after that which is sure and eternal, and which could offer assurance of compensation amid the doubt and turmoil of that age of strife and tyranny. The true and the false in this poetry were alike the outcome of the conditions of the time and the authoritative religious teaching. The fourteenth and fifteenth centuries, in spite of the abuses which made the Reformation necessary, contained many saintly lives, beneficent institutions, much philanthropy, and inspired love of God. All these have their witness in many products of that era, and we need look no further than the mediæval religious poetry to find elements which show that on the spiritual side the Reformation was not strictly a moral revolution, restoring a lost religious feeling, but rather an intellectual process, establishing a hereditary piety upon reasonable and Scriptural foundations.

We see, therefore, how far Luther was from being the founder of German hymnody. In trying to discover what his great service to religious song really was, we must go on to the next question that is involved, and ask, What was the status and employment of the folk-hymn before the Reformation? Was it in a true sense a *church* song? Had it a recognized place in the public service? Was it at all liturgic, as the Lutheran hymn certainly was? This brings us to a definitive distinction between the two schools of hymnody.

The attitude of the Catholic Church to congregational singing has often been discussed, and is at present the object of a great deal of misconception. The fact of the matter is, that she ostensibly encourages the people to share in some of the subordinate Latin offices, but the very spirit of the liturgy and the development of musical practice have in course of time, with now and then an exception, reduced the congregation to silence. Before the invention of harmony all church music had more of the quality of popular music, and the priesthood encouraged the worshipers to join their voices in those parts of the service which were not confined by the rubrics to the ministers. But the Gregorian chant was never really adopted by the people, — its practical difficulties, and especially the inflexible insistence upon the use of Latin in all the offices of worship, virtually confined it to the priests and a small body of trained singers. The very conception and spirit of the liturgy, also, has by a law of historic development gradually excluded the people from active participation. Whatever may have been the thought of the fathers of the liturgy, the eucharistic service has come to be simply the vehicle of a sacrifice offered by and through the priesthood for the people, not a tribute of praise and supplication emanating from the congregation itself. The attitude of the worshiper is one of obedient faith, both in the supernatural efficacy of the sacrifice and the mediating authority of the celebrant. The liturgy is inseparably bound up with the central act of consecration and oblation, and is conceived as itself possessing a divine sanction. The liturgy is not in any sense the creation of the people, but comes down to them from a higher source, the gradual production of men believed to have been inspired by the Holy Spirit, and is accepted by the laity as a divinely authorized means in the accomplishment of the supreme sacerdotal function. The sacrifice of the Mass is performed for the people, but not through the people, nor even necessarily in their presence. And so it has come to pass that, although the Catholic Church has never officially recognized the existence of the modern mixed choir, and does not in its rubrics authorize any manner of singing except the unison Gregorian chant, nevertheless, by reason of the expansion and specialization of musical art, and the increasing veneration of the liturgy as the very channel of descending sacramental grace, the people are reduced to a position of passive receptivity.

As regards the singing of hymns in the national languages, the conditions are somewhat different. The laws of the Catholic Church forbid the vernacular in any part of the eucharistic service, but permit vernacular hymns in certain subordinate offices, as, for instance, Vespers. But even in these services the restrictions are more emphasized than the permissions. Here also the tacit recognition of a separation of function between the clergy and the laity still persists; there can never be a really sympathetic coöperation between the church language and the vernacular; there is a constant attitude of suspicion on the part of the authorities, lest the people's hymn should afford a rift for the subtle intrusion of heretical or unchurchly ideas.

The whole spirit and implied theory of the Catholic Church is therefore unfavorable to popular hymnody.

16

This was especially the case in the latter Middle Age. The people could put no heart into the singing of Latin. The priests and monks, especially in such convent schools as St. Gall, Fulda, Metz, and Reichenau, made heroic efforts to drill their rough disciples in the Gregorian chant, but their attempts were ludicrously futile. Vernacular hymns were simply tolerated on certain prescribed occasions. In the century or more following the Reformation, the Catholic musicians and clergy, taught by the astonishing popular success of the Lutheran songs, tried to inaugurate a similar movement in their own ranks, and the publication and use of Catholic German hymn-books attained large dimensions; but this enthusiasm finally died out. Both in mediæval and in modern times there has practically remained a chasm between the musical practice of the common people and that of the Church, and in spite of isolated attempts to encourage popular hymnody, the restrictions have always had a depressing effect, and the free, hearty union of clergy and congregation in choral praise and prayer is virtually unknown.

The new conceptions of the relationship of man to God, which so altered the fundamental principle and the external forms of worship under the Lutheran movement, manifested themselves most strikingly in the mighty impetus given to congregational song. Luther set the national impulse free, and taught the people that in singing praise they were performing a service that was well pleasing to God and a necessary part of public communion with him. It was not simply that Luther charged the popular hymnody with the energy of his world-transforming doctrine, — he also gave it a dignity which it had never possessed before, certainly not since the apostolic age, as a part of the official liturgic song of the Church. Both these facts gave the folk-hymn its wonderful proselyting power in the sixteenth century, — the latter gives it its importance in the history of church music.

Luther's work for the people's song was in substance a detail of his liturgic reform. His knowledge of human nature taught him the value of set forms and ceremonies, and his appreciation of what was universally true and edifying in the liturgy of the mother Church led him to retain many of her prayers, hymns, responses, etc., along with new provisions of his own. But in his view the service is constituted through the activity of the believing subject; the forms and expressions of worship are not in themselves indispensable — the one thing necessary is faith, and the forms of worship have their value simply in defining, inculcating, stimulating and directing this faith, and enforcing the proper attitude of the soul toward God in the public social act of devotion. The congregational song both symbolized and realized the principle of direct access of the believer to the Father, and thus exemplified in itself alone the whole spirit of the worship of the new Church. That this act of worship should be in the native language of the nation was a matter of course, and hence the popular hymn, set to familiar and appropriate melody, became at once the characteristic, official, and liturgic expression of the emotion of the people in direct communion with God.

The immense consequence of this principle was seen in the outburst of song that followed the founding of the new Church by Luther at Wittenberg. It was not that the nation was electrified by a poetic genius, or by any new form of musical excitement; it was simply that the old restraints upon self-expression were removed, and that the people could celebrate their new-found freedom in Christ Jesus by means of the most intense agency known to man, which they had been prepared by inherited musical temperament and ancient habit to use to the full. No wonder that they received this privilege with thanksgiving, and that the land resounded with the lyrics of faith and hope.

Luther felt his mission to be that of a purifier, not a destroyer. He would repudiate, not the good and evil alike in the ancient Church, but only that which he considered false and pernicious. This judicious conservatism was strikingly shown in his attitude toward the liturgy and form of worship, which he would alter only so far as was necessary in view of changes in doctrine and in the whole relation of the Church as a body toward the individual. The altered conception of the nature of the eucharist, the abolition of homage to the Virgin and saints, the prominence given to the sermon as the central feature of the service, the substitution of the vernacular for Latin, the intimate participation of the congregation in the service by means of hymn-singing, — all these changes required a recasting of the order of worship; but everything in the old ritual that was consistent with these changes was retained. Luther, like the founders of the reformed Church of England, was profoundly conscious of the truth and beauty of many of the prayers and hymns of the mother Church. Especially was he attached to her music, and would preserve the compositions of the learned masters alongside of the revived congregational hymn.

As regards the form and manner of service, Luther's improvements were directed (1) to the revision of the liturgy, (2) the introduction of new hymns, and (3) the arrangement of suitable melodies for congregational use.

Luther's program of liturgic reform is chiefly embodied in two orders of worship drawn up for the churches of Wittenberg, *viz.*, the Formula Missæ of 1523 and the Deutsche Messe of 1526.

Luther rejected absolutely the Catholic conception of the act of worship as in itself possessed of objective efficacy. The terms of salvation are found only in the Gospel; the worship acceptable to God exists only in the contrite attitude of the heart, and the acceptance through faith of the plan of redemption as provided in the vicarious atonement of Christ. The external act of worship in prayer, praise, Scripture recitation, etc., is designed as a testimony of faith, an evidence of thankfulness to God for his infinite grace, and as a means of edification and of kindling the devotional spirit through the reactive influence of its audible expression. The correct performance of a ceremony was to Luther of little account; the essential was the prayerful disposition of the heart and the devout acceptance of the word of Scripture. The substance of worship, said Luther, is "that our dear Lord speaks with us through his Holy Word, and we in return speak with him through prayer and song of praise." The sermon is of the greatest importance as an ally of the reading of the Word. The office of worship must be viewed as a means of instruction as well as a rite contrived as the promoter and expression of religious emotion; the believer is in no wise to be considered as having attained to complete ripeness and maturity, since if it were so religious worship would be unnecessary. Such a goal is not to be attained on earth. The Christian, said Luther, "needs baptism, the Word, and the sacrament, not as a perfected Christian, but as a sinner."

The Formula Missæ of 1523 was only a provisional office, and may be called an expurgated edition of the Catholic Mass. It is in Latin, and follows the order of the Roman liturgy with certain omissions, *viz.*, all the preliminary action at the altar as far as the Introit, the Offertory, the Oblation and accompanying prayers as far as the Preface, the Consecration, the Commemoration of the Dead, and everything following the Agnus Dei except the prayer of thanksgiving and benediction. That is to say, everything is removed which characterizes the Mass as a priestly, sacrificial act, or which recognizes the intercessory office of the saints. The musical factors correspond to the usage in the Catholic Mass; Luther's hymns with accompanying melodies were not yet prepared, and no trace of the Protestant choral appears in the Formula Missæ.

Although this order of 1523 was conceived only as a partial or temporary expedient, it was by no means set entirely aside by its author, even after the composition of a form more adapted to the needs of the people. In the preface to the Deutsche Messe of 1526, Luther cites the Latin Formula Missæ as possessing a special value. " This I will not abandon or have altered ; but as we have kept it with us heretofore, so must we still be free to use the same where and when it pleases us or occasion requires. I will by no means permit the Latin speech to be dropped out of divine worship, since it is important for the youth. And if I were able, and the Greek and Hebrew languages were as common with us as the Latin, and had as much music and song as the Latin has, we should hold Masses, sing and read every Sunday in all four languages, German, Latin, Greek, and Hebrew." It is important, he goes on to say, that the youth should be familiar with more languages than their own, in order that they may be able to give instruction in the true doctrine to those not of their own nation, Latin especially approving itself for this purpose as the common dialect of cultivated men.

The Deutsche Messe of 1526, Luther explains, was drawn up for the use of the mass of the people, who needed a medium of worship and instruction which was already familiar and native to them. This form is a still further simplification, as compared with the Formula Missæ, and consists almost entirely of offices in the German tongue. Congregational chorals also have a prominent place, since the publication of collections of vernacular religious songs had begun two years before. This liturgy consists of (1) a people's hymn or a German psalm, (2) Kyrie eleison, (3) Collect, (4) the Epistle, (5) congregational hymn, (6) the Gospel, (7) the German paraphrase of the Creed, " Wie glauben all'

247

an einen Gott," sung by the people; next follows the sermon; (8) the Lord's Prayer and exhortation preliminary to the Sacrament, (9) the words of institution and elevation, (10) distribution of the bread, (11) singing of the German Sanctus or the hymn " Jesus Christus unser Heiland," (12) distribution of the wine, (13) Agnus Dei, a German hymn, or the German Sanctus, (14) Collect of thanksgiving, (15) Benediction.

It was far from Luther's purpose to impose these or any particular forms of worship upon his followers through a personal assumption of authority. He reiterates, in his preface to the Deutsche Messe, that he has no thought of assuming any right of dictation in the matter, emphasizing his desire that the churches should enjoy entire freedom in their forms and manner of worship. At the same time he realizes the benefits of uniformity as creating a sense of unity and solidarity in faith, practice, and interests among the various districts, cities, and congregations, and offers these two forms as in his opinion conservative and efficient. He warns his people against the injury that may result from the multiplication of liturgies at the instigation of indiscreet or vain leaders, who have in view the perpetuation of certain notions of their own, rather than the honor of God and the spiritual welfare of their neighbors.

In connection with this work of reconstructing the ancient liturgy for use in the Wittenberg churches, Luther turned his attention to the need of suitable hymns and tunes. He took up this work not only out of his love of song, but also from necessity. He wrote to Nicholas Haussmann, pastor at Zwickau: "I would that we had many German songs which the people could sing during the Mass. But we lack German poets and musicians, or they are unknown to us, who are able to make Christian and spiritual songs, as Paul calls them, which are of such value that they can be used daily in the house of God. One can find but few that have the appropriate spirit." The reason for this complaint was short-lived; a crowd of hymnists sprang up as if by magic, and among them Luther was, as in all things, chief. His work as a hymn writer began soon after the completion of his translation of the New Testament, while he was engaged in translating the psalms. Then, as Koch says, "the spirit of the psalmists and prophets came over him." Several allusions in his letters show that he took the psalms as his model; that is to say, he did not think of a hymn as designed for the teaching of dogma, but as the sincere, spontaneous outburst of love and reverence to God for his goodness.

The first hymn-book of evangelical Germany was published in 1524 by Luther's friend and coadjutor, Johann Walther. It contained four hymns by Luther, three by Paul Speratus, and one by an unknown author. Another book appeared in the same year containing fourteen more hymns by Luther, in addition to the eight of the first book. Six more from Luther's pen appeared in a song-book edited by Walther in 1525. The remaining hymns of Luther (twelve in number) were printed in five song-books of different dates, ending with Klug's in 1543. Four hymn-books contain prefaces by Luther, the first written for Walther's book of 1525, and the last for one published by Papst in 1545. Luther's example was contagious. Other hymn writers at once sprang up, who were filled with Luther's spirit, and who took his songs as models. Printing presses were kept busy, song-books were multiplied, until at the time of Luther's death no less than sixty collections, counting the various editions, had been issued. There was reason for the sneering remark of a Catholic that the people were singing themselves into the Lutheran doctrine. The principles of worship promulgated by Luther and implied in his liturgic arrangements were adopted by all the Protestant communities; whatever variations there might be in the external forms of worship, in all of them the congregational hymn held a prominent place, and it is to be noticed that almost without exception the chief hymn writers of the Lutheran time were theologians and preachers.

Luther certainly wrote thirty-six hymns. A few others have been ascribed to him without conclusive evidence. By far the greater part of these thirty-six are not entirely original. Many of them are translations or adaptations of psalms, some of which are nearly literal transfers. Other selections from Scripture were used in a similar way, among which are the Ten Commandments, the Ter Sanctus, the song of Simeon, and the Lord's Prayer. Similar use, *viz.*, close translation or free paraphrase, was made of certain Latin hymns by Ambrose, Gregory, Hus, and others, and also of certain religious folk-songs of the pre-Reformation period. Five hymns only are completely original, not drawn in any way from

older compositions. Besides these five many of the tran-
scriptions of psalms and older hymns owe but little to
their models. The chief of these, and the most celebrated
of all Luther's hymns, "Ein' feste Burg," was suggested
by the forty-sixth Psalm, but nothing could be more original in spirit and phraseology, more completely characteristic of the great reformer. The beautiful poems, "Aus
tiefer Noth" (Ps. cxxx.), and "Ach Gott, vom Himmel
sieh' darein" (Ps. xii.), are less bold paraphrases, but
still Luther's own in the sense that their expression is a
natural outgrowth of the more tender and humble side of
his nature.

No other poems of their class by any single man have
ever exerted so great an influence, or have received so
great admiration, as these few short lyrics of Martin
Luther. And yet at the first reading it is not easy to
understand the reason for their celebrity. As poetry they
disappoint us; there is no artfully modulated diction, no
subtle and far-reaching imagination. Neither do they
seem to chime with our devotional needs ; there is a jar-
ring note of fanaticism in them. We even find expressions that give positive offence, as when he speaks of the
"Lamb roasted in hot love upon the cross." We say
that they are not universal, that they seem the outcome
of a temper that belongs to an exceptional condition.
This is really the fact; here is the clue to their proper
study. They do belong to a time, and not to all time.
We must consider that they are the utterance of a mind
engaged in conflict, and often tormented with doubt of
the outcome. They reveal the motive of the great pivotal
figure in modern religious history. More than that —

they have behind them the great impelling force of the Reformation. Perhaps the world has shown a correct instinct in fixing upon " Ein' feste Burg " as the typical hymn of Luther and of the Reformation. Heine, who called it " the Marseillaise of the Reformation;" Frederick the Great, who called its melody (not without reverence) "God Almighty's grenadier march;" Mendelssohn and Meyerbeer, who chose the same tune to symbolize aggressive Protestantism; and Wagner, who wove its strains into the grand march which celebrates the military triumphs of united Germany, — all these men had an accurate feeling for the patriotic and moral fire which burns in this mighty song. The same spirit is found in other of Luther's hymns, but often combined with a tenderer music, in which emphasis is laid more upon the inward peace that comes from trust in God, than upon the fact of outward conflict. A still more exalted mood is disclosed in such hymns as " Nun freut euch, lieben Christen g'mein," and " Von Himmel hoch da komm ich her " — the latter a Christmas song said to have been written for his little son Hans. The first of these is notable for the directness with which it sets forth the Lutheran doctrine of justification by faith alone. It is in this same directness and homely vigor and adaptation to the pressing needs of the time that we must find the cause of the popular success of Luther's hymns. He knew what the dumb, blindly yearning German people had been groping for during so many years, and the power of his sermons and poems lay in the fact that they offered a welcome spiritual gift in phrases that went straight to the popular heart. His speech was that of the people — idiomatic, nervous, and penetrating. He had learned how to talk to them in his early peasant home, and in his study of the folk-songs. Coarse, almost brutal at times, we may call him, as in his controversies with Henry VIII., Erasmus, and others; but it was the coarseness of a rugged nature, of a son of the soil, a man tremendously in earnest, blending religious zeal with patriotism, never doubting that the enemies of his faith were confederates of the devil, who was as real to him as Duke George or Dr. Eck. No English translation can quite do justice to the homely vigor of his verse. Carlyle has succeeded as well as possible in his translation of "Ein' feste Burg," but even this masterly achievement does not quite reproduce the jolting abruptness of the metre, the swing and fire of the movement. The greater number of Luther's hymns are set to a less strident pitch, but all alike speak a language which reveals in every line the ominous spiritual tension of this historic moment.

In philological history these hymns have a significance equal to that of Luther's translation of the Bible, in which scholars agree in finding the virtual creation of the modern German language. And the elements that should give new life to the national speech were to be found among the commonalty. "No one before Luther," says Bayard Taylor, "saw that the German tongue must be sought for in the mouths of the people — that the exhausted expression of the earlier ages could not be revived, but that the newer, fuller, and richer speech, then in its childhood, must at once be acknowledged and adopted. With all his scholarship Luther dropped the theological style, and sought among the people for phrases as artless and simple as those of the Hebrew writers." "The influence of Luther on German literature cannot be explained until we have seen how sound and vigorous and many-sided was the new spirit which he infused into the language." [1] All this will apply to the hymns as well as to the Bible translation. Here was one great element in the popular effect which these hymns produced. Their simple, home-bred, domestic form of expression caught the public ear in an instant. Those who have at all studied the history of popular eloquence in prose and verse are aware of the electrical effect that may be produced when ideas of pith and moment are sent home to the masses in forms of speech that are their own. Luther's hymns may not be poetry in the high sense; but they are certainly eloquence, they are popular oratory in verse, put into the mouths of the people by one of their own number.

In spite of the fact that these songs were the natural outcome of a period of spiritual and political conflict, and give evidence of this fact in almost every instance, yet they are less dogmatic and controversial than might be expected, for Luther, bitter and intolerant as he often was, understood the requirements of church song well enough to know that theological and political polemic should be kept out of it. Nevertheless these hymns are a powerful witness to the great truths which were the corner-stone of the doctrines of the reformed church. They constantly emphasize the principle that

1 Taylor, *Studies in German Literature.*

salvation comes not through works or sacraments or any human mediation, but only through the merits, of Christ and faith in his atoning blood. The whole machinery of mariolatry, hagiolatry, priestly absolution, and personal merit, which had so long stood between the individual soul and Christ, was broken down. Christ is no longer a stern, hardly appeasable Judge, but a loving Saviour, yearning over mankind, stretching out hands of invitation, asking, not a slavish submission to formal observances, but a free, spontaneous offering of the heart. This was the message that thrilled Germany. And it was through the hymns of Luther and those modelled upon them that the new evangel was most widely and quickly disseminated. The friends as well as the enemies of the Reformation asserted that the spread of the new doctrines was due more to Luther's hymns than to his sermons. The editor of a German hymn-book published in 1565 says: "I do not doubt that through that one song of Luther, 'Nun freut euch, lieben Christen g'mein,' many hundred Christians have been brought to the faith who otherwise would not have heard of Luther." An indignant Jesuit declared that "Luther's songs have damned more souls than all his books and speeches." We read marvellous stories of the effect of these hymns; of Lutheran missionaries entering Catholic churches during service and drawing away the whole congregation by their singing; of wandering evangelists standing at street corners and in the market places, singing to excited crowds, then distributing the hymns upon leaflets so that the populace might join in the pæan, and so winning entire cities to the new faith almost in a day. This is easily to be believed when we consider that the progress of events and the drift of ideas for a century and more had been preparing the German mind for Luther's message; that as a people the Germans are extremely susceptible to the enthusiasms that utter themselves in song; and that these hymns carried the truths for which their souls had been thirsting, in language of extraordinary force, clothed in melodies which they had long known and loved.

We lay especial stress upon the hymns of Luther, not simply on account of their inherent power and historic importance, but also because they are representative of a school. Luther was one of a group of lyrists which included bards hardly less trenchant than he. Koch gives the names of fifty-one writers who endowed the new German hymnody between 1517 and 1560.[1] He finds in them all one common feature, — the ground character of objectivity. "They are genuine church hymns, in which the common faith is expressed in its universality, without the subjective feeling of personality." "It is always we, not I, which is the prevailing word in these songs. The poets of this period did not, like those of later times, paint their own individual emotions with all kinds of figurative expressions, but, powerfully moved by the truth, they sang the work of redemption and extolled the faith in the free, undeserved grace of God in Jesus

[1] Koch, *Geschichte des Kirchenliedes und Kirchegesanges der christlichen insbesondere der deutschen evangelischen Kirche.*

Christ, or gave thanks for the newly given pure word of God in strains of joyful victory, and defied their foes in firm, godly trust in the divinity of the doctrine which was so new and yet so old. Therefore they speak the truths of salvation, not in dry doctrinal tone and sober reflection, but in the form of testimony or confession, and although in some of these songs are contained plain statements of belief, the reason therefor is simply in the hunger and thirst after the pure doctrine. Hence the speech of these poets is the Bible speech, and the expression forcible and simple. It is not art, but faith, which gives these songs their imperishable value."

The hymns of Luther and the other early Reformation hymnists of Germany are not to be classed with sacred lyrics like those of Vaughan and Keble and Newman which, however beautiful, are not of that universality which alone adapts a hymn for use in the public assembly. In writing their songs Luther and his compeers identified themselves with the congregation of believers; they produced them solely for common praise in the sanctuary, and they are therefore in the strict sense impersonal, surcharged not with special isolated experiences, but with the vital spirit of the Reformation. No other body of hymns was ever produced under similar conditions; for the Reformation was born and cradled in conflict, and in these songs, amid their protestations of confidence and joy, there may often be heard cries of alarm before powerful adversaries, appeals for help in material as well as spiritual exigencies, and sometimes also tones of wrath and defiance. Strains

17   257

such as the latter are most frequent perhaps in the paraphrases of the psalms, which the authors apply to the situation of an infant church encompassed with enemies. Yet there is no sign of doubt of the justice of the cause, or of the safety of the flock in the divine hands.

Along with the production of hymns must go the composition or arrangement of tunes, and this was a less direct and simple process. The conditions and methods of musical art forbade the ready invention of melodies. We have seen in our previous examination of the music of the mediæval Church that the invention of themes for musical works was no part of the composer's business. Down to about the year 1600 the scientific musician always borrowed his themes from older sources — the liturgic chant or popular songs — and worked them up into choral movements according to the laws of counterpoint. He was, therefore, a tune-setter, not a tune-maker. The same custom prevailed among the German musicians of Luther's day, and it would have been too much to expect that they should go outside their strict habits, and violate all the traditions of their craft, so far as to evolve from their own heads a great number of singable melodies for the people's use. The task of Luther and his musical assistants, therefore, was to take melodies from music of all sorts with which they were familiar, alter them to fit the metre of the new hymns, and add the harmonies. In course of time the enormous multiplication of hymns, each demanding a musical setting, and the requirements of simplicity in popular song, brought about a union of the functions of the tune-

maker and the tune-setter, and in the latter part of the
sixteenth century the modern method of inventing
melodies took the place of the mediæval custom of
borrowing and adapting, both in the people's song and
in larger works.

Down to a very recent period it has been universally
believed that Luther was a musician of the latter order
i. e., a tune-maker, and that the melodies of many of his
hymns were of his own production. Among writers on
this period no statement is more frequently made than
that Luther wrote tunes as well as hymns. This belief
is as tenacious as the myth of the rescue of church
music by Palestrina. Dr. L. W. Bacon, in the preface
to his edition of the hymns of Luther with their original
melodies, assumes, as an undisputed fact, that many of
these tunes are Luther's own invention.[1] Even Julian's
Dictionary of Hymnology, which is supposed to be the
embodiment of the most advanced scholarship in this
department of learning, makes similar statements. But
this is altogether an error. Luther composed no tunes.
Under the patient investigation of a half-century, the
melodies originally associated with Luther's hymns have
all been traced to their sources. The tune of " Ein' feste
Burg " was the last to yield; Bäumker finds the germ of
it in a Gregorian melody. Such proof as this is, of course,
decisive and final. The hymn-tunes, called chorals,
which Luther, Walther, and others provided for the
reformed churches, were drawn from three sources, *viz.*,
the Latin song of the Catholic Church, the tunes of

---

[1] Bacon and Allen, editors : *The Hymns of Martin Luther set to their Original Melodies, with an English Version.*

German hymns before the Reformation, and the secular folk-song.

1. If Luther was willing to take many of the prayers of the Catholic liturgy for use in his German Mass, still more ready was he to adopt the melodies of the ancient Church. In his preface to the Funeral Hymns (1542), after speaking of the forms of the Catholic Church which in themselves he did not disapprove, he says: " In the same way have they much noble music, especially in the abbeys and parish churches, used to adorn most vile, idolatrous words. Therefore have we undressed these lifeless, idolatrous, crazy words, stripping off the noble music, and putting it upon the living and holy word of God, wherewith to sing, praise, and honor the same, that so the beautiful ornament of music, brought back to its right use, may serve its blessed Maker, and his Christian people." A few of Luther's hymns were translations of old Latin hymns and Sequences, and these were set to the original melodies. Luther's labor in this field was not confined to the choral, but, like the founders of the musical service of the Anglican Church, he established a system of chanting, taking the Roman use as a model, and transferring many of the Gregorian tunes. Johann Walther, Luther's co-laborer, relates the extreme pains which Luther took in setting notes to the Epistle, Gospel, and other offices of the service. He intended to institute a threefold division of church song, — the choir anthem, the unison chant, and the congregational hymn. Only the first and third forms have been retained. The use of chants derived from the Catholic service was continued in some churches as late as the end of the

seventeenth century. But, as Helmore says, " the rage for turning creeds, commandments, psalms, and everything to be sung, into metre, gradually banished the chant from Protestant communities on the Continent."

2. In cases in which pre-Reformation vernacular hymns were adopted into the song-books of the new Church the original melodies were often retained, and thus some very ancient German tunes, although in modern guise, are still preserved in the hymn-books of modern Germany. Melodies of the Bohemian Brethren were in this manner transferred to the German song-books.

3. The secular folk-song of the sixteenth century and earlier was a very prolific source of the German choral. This was after Luther's day, however, for it does not appear that any of his tunes were of this class. Centuries before the age of artistic German music began, the common people possessed a large store of simple songs which they delighted to use on festal occasions, at the fireside, at their labor, in love-making, at weddings, christenings, and in every circumstance of social and domestic life. Here was a rich mine of simple and expressive melodies from which choral tunes might be fashioned. In some cases this transfer involved considerable modification, in others but little, for at that time there was far less difference between the religious and the secular musical styles than there is now. The associations of these tunes were not always of the most edifying kind, and some of them were so identified with unsanctified ideas that the strictest theologians protested against them, and some

were weeded out. In course of time the old secular associations were forgotten, and few devout Germans are now reminded that some of the grand melodies in which faith and hope find such appropriate utterance are variations of old love songs and drinking songs. There is nothing exceptional in this borrowing of the world's tunes for ecclesiastical uses. We find the same practice among the French, Dutch, English, and Scotch Calvinists, the English Wesleyans, and the hymn-book makers of America. This method is often necessary when a young and vigorously expanding Church must be quickly provided with a store of songs, but in its nature it is only a temporary recourse.

The choral tunes sung by the congregation were at first not harmonized. Then, as they began to be set in the strict contrapuntal style of the day, it became the custom for the people to sing the melody while the choir sustained the other parts. The melody was at first in the tenor, according to time-honored usage in artistic music, but as composers found that they must consider the vocal limitations of a mass of untrained singers a simpler form of harmony was introduced, and the custom arose of putting the melody in the upper voice, and the harmony below. This method prepared the development of a harmony that was more in the nature of modern chord progressions, and when the choir and congregation severed their incompatible union, the complex counterpoint in which the age delighted was allowed free range in the motet, while the harmonized choral became more simple and compact. The partnership of choir and congregation was dissolved about 1600, and the organ took the place of the trained singers in accompanying the unison song of the people.

One who studies the German chorals as they appear in the hymn-books of the present day (many of which hold honored places in English and American hymnals) must not suppose that he is acquainted with the religious tunes of the Reformation in their pristine form. As they are now sung in the German churches they have been greatly modified in harmony and rhythm, and even in many instances in melody also. The only scale and harmonic system then in vogue was the Gregorian. In respect to rhythm also, the alterations have been equally striking. The present choral is usually written in notes of equal length, one note to a syllable. The metre is in most cases double, rarely triple. This manner of writing gives the choral a singularly grave, solid and stately character, encouraging likewise a performance that is often dull and monotonous. There was far more variety and life in the primitive choral, the movement was more flexible, and the frequent groups of notes to a single syllable imparted a buoyancy and warmth that are unknown to the rigid modern form. The transformation of the choral into its present shape was completed in the eighteenth century, a result, some say, of the relaxation of spiritual energy in the period of rationalism. A party has been formed among German churchmen and musicians which labors for the restoration of the primitive rhythmic choral. Certain congregations have adopted the reform, but there is as yet no sign that it will ultimately prevail.

In spite of the mischievous influence ascribed to

Luther's hymns by his opponents, they could appreciate their value as aids to devotion, and in return for Luther's compliment to their hymns they occasionally borrowed some of his. Strange as it may seem, even "Ein' feste Burg" was one of these. Neither were the Catholics slow to imitate the Protestants in providing songs for the people, and as in the old strifes of Arians and orthodox in the East, so Catholics and Lutherans strove to sing each other down. The Catholics also translated Latin hymns into German, and transformed secular folk-songs into edifying religious rhymes. The first German Catholic song-book was published in 1537 by Michael Vehe, a preaching monk of Halle. This book contained fifty-two hymns, four of which were alterations of hymns by Luther. It is a rather notable fact that throughout the sixteenth century eminent musicians of both confessions contributed to the musical services of their opponents. Protestants composed masses and motets for the Catholic churches, and Catholics arranged choral melodies for the Protestants. This friendly interchange of good offices was heartily encouraged by Luther. Next to Johann Walther, his most cherished musical friend and helper was Ludwig Senfl, a devout Catholic. This era of relative peace and good-will, of which this musical sympathy was a beautiful token, did not long endure. The Catholic Counter-Reformation cut sharply whatever there might have been of mutual understanding and tolerance, and the frightful Thirty Years' War overwhelmed art and the spirit of humanity together.

The multiplication of hymns and chorals went on

264

throughout the sixteenth century and into the seventeenth with unabated vigor. A large number of writers of widely differing degrees of poetic ability contributed to the hymn-books, which multiplied to prodigious numbers in the generations next succeeding that of Luther. These songs harmonized in general with the tone struck by Luther and his friends, setting forth the doctrine of justification by faith alone, and the joy that springs from the consciousness of a freer approach to God, mingled, however, with more sombre accents called forth by the apprehension of the dark clouds in the political firmament which seemed to bode disaster to the Protestant cause. The tempest broke in 1618. Again and again during the thirty years' struggle the reformed cause seemed on the verge of annihilation. When the exhaustion of both parties brought the savage conflict to an end, the enthusiasm of the Reformation was gone. Religious poetry and music indeed survived, and here and there burned with a pure flame amid the darkness of an almost primitive barbarism. In times of deepest distress these two arts often afford the only outlet for grief, and the only testimony of hope amid national calamities. There were unconquerable spirits in Germany, notably among the hymnists, cantors, and organists, who maintained the sacred fire of religious art amid the moral devastations of the Thirty Years' War, whose miseries they felt only as a deepening of their faith in a power that overrules the wrath of man. Their trust fastened itself unfalteringly upon those assurances of divine sympathy which had been the inspiration of their cause from the beginning. This pious confidence, this unabated poetic glow, found in Paul Gerhardt (1607-1676) the most fervent and refined expression that has been reached in German hymnody.

The production of melodies kept pace with the hymns throughout the sixteenth century, and in the first half of the seventeenth a large number of the most beautiful songs of the German Church were contributed by such men as Andreas Hammerschmidt, Johann Crüger, J. R. Ahle, Johann Schop, Melchior Frank, Michael Altenburg, and scores of others not less notable. After the middle of the seventeenth century, however, the fountain began to show signs of exhaustion. The powerful movement in the direction of secular music which emanated from Italy began to turn the minds of composers toward experiments which promised greater artistic satisfaction than could be found in the plain congregational choral. The rationalism of the eighteenth century, accompanying a period of doctrinal strife and lifeless formalism in the Church, repressed those unquestioning enthusiasms which are the only source of a genuinely expressive popular hymnody. Pietism, while a more or less effective protest against cold ceremonialism and theological intolerance, and a potent influence in substituting a warmer heart service in place of dogmatic pedantry, failed to contribute any new stimulus to the church song; for the Pietists either endeavored to discourage church music altogether, or else imparted to hymn and melody a quality of effeminacy and sentimentality. False tastes crept into the Church. The homely vigor and forthrightness of the Lutheran hymn seemed to the shallow critical spirits of the day rough, prosaic, and repellant, and they began to smooth out and polish the old rhymes, and supplant the choral melodies and harmonies with the prettinesses and languishing graces of the Italian cantilena. As the sturdy inventive power of conservative church musicians was no longer available or desired, recourse was had, as in old times, to secular material, but not as formerly to the song of the people, — honest, sincere, redolent of the soil, — but rather to the light, artificial strains of the fashionable world, the modish Italian opera, and the affected pastoral poesy. It is the old story of the people's song declining as the art-song flourishes. As the stern temper of the Lutheran era grew soft in an age of security and indifference, so the grand old choral was neglected, and its performance grew perfunctory and cold. An effort has been made here and there in recent years to restore the old ideals and practice, but until a revival of spirituality strong enough to stir the popular heart breaks out in Germany, we may not look for any worthy successor to the sonorous proselyting song of the Reformation age.

CHAPTER VIII

THE history of German Protestant church music in the seventeenth century and onward is the record of a transformation not less striking and significant than that which the music of the Catholic Church experienced in the same period. In both instances forms of musical art which were sanctioned by tradition and associated with ancient and rigorous conceptions of devotional expression were overcome by the superior powers of a style which was in its origin purely secular. The revolution in the Protestant church music was, however, less sudden and far less complete. It is somewhat remarkable that the influences that prevailed in the music of the Protestant Church — the Church of discontent and change — were on the whole more cautious and conservative than those that were active in the music of the Catholic Church. The latter readily gave up the old music for the sake of the new, and so swiftly readjusted its boundaries that the ancient landmarks were almost everywhere obliterated. The Protestant music advanced by careful evolutionary methods, and in the final product nothing that was valuable in the successive stages through which it passed was lost. In both cases — Lutheran and Catholic — the motive was the same. Church music,

268

like secular, demanded a more comprehensive and a more individual style of expression. The Catholic musicians of the seventeenth and eighteenth centuries were very clear in their minds as to what they wanted and how to get it. The brilliant Italian aria was right at hand in all its glory, and its languishing strains seemed admirably suited to the appeals which the aggressive Church was about to make to the heart and the senses. The powers that ruled in German Protestant worship conceived their aims, consciously or unconsciously, in a somewhat different spirit. The new musical movement in German church music was less self-confident, it was uncertain of its final direction, at times restrained by reverence for the ancient forms and ideals, again wantonly breaking with tradition and throwing itself into the arms of the alluring Italian culture.

The German school entered the seventeenth century with three strong and pregnant forms to its credit, *viz.,* the choral, the motet (essentially a counterpart of the Latin sixteenth-century motet), and organ music. Over against these stood the Italian recitative and aria, associated with new principles of tonality, harmony, and structure. The former were the stern embodiment of the abstract, objective, liturgic conception of worship music; the latter, of the subjective, impassioned, and individualistic. Should these ideals be kept apart, or should they be in some way united? One group of German musicians would make the Italian dramatic forms the sole basis of a new religious art, recognizing the claims of the personal, the varied, and the brilliant, in ecclesiastical music as in secular. Another group

269

clung tenaciously to the choral and motet, resisting every influence that might soften that austere rigor which to their minds was demanded by historic association and liturgic fitness. A third group was the party of compromise. Basing their culture upon the old German choir chorus, organ music, and people's hymn-tune, they grafted upon this sturdy stock the Italian melody. It was in the hands of this school that the future of German church music lay. They saw that the opportunities for a more varied and characteristic expression could not be kept out of the Church, for they were based on the reasonable cravings of human nature. Neither could they throw away those grand hereditary types of devotional utterance which had become sanctified to German memory in the period of the Reformation's storm and stress. They adopted what was soundest and most suitable for these ends in the art of both countries, and built up a form of music which strove to preserve the high traditions of national liturgic song, while at the same time it was competent to gratify the tastes which had been stimulated by the recent rapid advance in musical invention. Out of this movement grew the Passion music and the cantata of the eighteenth century, embellished with all the expressive resources of the Italian vocal solo and the orchestral accompaniment, solidified by a contrapuntal treatment derived from organ music, and held unswervingly to the very heart of the liturgy by means of those choral tunes which had become identified with special days and occasions in the church year.

The nature of the change of motive in modern church

music, which broke the exclusive domination of the chorus by the introduction of solo singing, has been set forth in the chapter on the later mass. The most obvious fact in the history of this modification of church music in Germany is that the neglect in many quarters of the strong old music of choral and motet in favor of a showy concert style seemed to coincide with that melancholy lapse into formalism and dogmatic intolerance which, in the German Church of the seventeenth and eighteenth centuries, succeeded to the enthusiasms of the Reformation era. But it does not follow, as often assumed, that we have here a case of cause and effect. It is worth frequent reiteration that no style of music is in itself religious. There is no sacredness, says Ruskin, in round arches or in pointed, in pinnacles or buttresses; and we may say with equal pertinence that there is nothing sacred *per se* in sixteenth-century counterpoint, Lutheran choral, or Calvinist psalm-tune. The adoption of the new style by so many German congregations was certainly not due to a spirit of levity, but to the belief that the novel sensation which their æsthetic instincts craved was also an element in moral edification. From the point of view of our more mature experience, however, there was doubtless a deprivation of something very precious when the German people began to lose their love for the solemn patriotic hymns of their faith, and when choirs neglected those celestial harmonies with which men like Eccard and Hasler lent these melodies the added charm of artistic decoration. There would seem to be no real compensation in those buoyant songs, with their thin accompaniment, which

Italy offered as a substitute for a style grown cold and obsolete. But out of this decadence, if we call it such, came the cantatas and Passions of J. S. Bach, in which a reflective age like ours, trained to settle points of fitness in matters of art, finds the most heart-searching and heart-revealing strains that devotional feeling has ever inspired. These glorious works could never have existed if the Church had not sanctioned the new methods in music which Germany was so gladly receiving from Italy. Constructed to a large extent out of secular material, these works grew to full stature under liturgic auspices, and at last, transcending the boundaries of ritual, they became a connecting bond between the organized life of the Church and the larger religious intuitions which no ecclesiastical system has ever been able to monopolize.

Such was the gift to the world of German Protestantism, stimulated by those later impulses of the Renaissance movement which went forth in music after their mission had been accomplished in plastic art. In the Middle Age, we are told, religion and art lived together in brotherly union; Protestantism threw away art and kept religion, Renaissance rationalism threw away religion and retained art. In painting and sculpture this is very nearly the truth; in music it is very far from being true. It is the glory of the art of music that she has almost always been able to resist the drift toward sensuousness and levity, and where she has apparently yielded, her recovery has been speedy and sure. So susceptible is her very nature to the finest touches of religious feeling, that every revival of the pure spirit of devotion has always found her prepared to adapt herself to new spiritual demands, and out of apparent decline to develop forms of religious expression more beautiful and sublime even than the old.

Conspicuous among the forms with which the new movement endowed the German Church was the cantata. This form of music may be traced back to Italy, where the monodic style first employed in the opera about 1600 was soon adopted into the music of the salon. The cantata was at first a musical recitation by a single person, without action, accompanied by a few plain chords struck upon a single instrument. This simple design was expanded in the first half of the seventeenth century into a work in several movements and in many parts or voices. Religious texts were soon employed and the church cantata was born. The cantata was eagerly taken up by the musicians of the German Protestant Church and became a prominent feature in the regular order of worship. In the seventeenth century the German Church cantata consisted usually of an instrumental introduction, a chorus singing a Bible text, a " spiritual aria " (a strophe song, sometimes for one, sometimes for a number of voices), one or two vocal solos, and a choral. This immature form (known as " spiritual concerto," " spiritual dialogue " or " spiritual act of devotion "), consisting of an alternation of Biblical passages and church or devotional hymns, flourished greatly in the seventeenth and early part of the eighteenth centuries. In its complete development in the eighteenth century it also incorporated the recitative and the Italian aria form, and carried to

18   273

their full power the chorus, especially the chorus based on the choral melody, and the organ accompaniment. By means of the prominent employment of themes taken from choral tunes appointed for particular days in the church calendar, especially those days consecrated to the contemplation of events in the life of our Lord, the cantata became the most effective medium for the expression of those emotions called forth in the congregation by their imagined participation in the scenes which the ritual commemorated. The stanzas of the hymns which appear in the cantata illustrate the Biblical texts, applying and commenting upon them in the light of Protestant conceptions. The words refer to some single phase of religious feeling made conspicuous in the order for the day. A cantata is, therefore, quite analogous to the anthem of the Church of England, although on a larger scale. Unlike an oratorio, it is neither epic nor dramatic, but renders some mood, more or less general, of prayer or praise.

We have seen that the Lutheran Church borrowed many features from the musical practice of the Catholic Church, such as portions of the Mass, the habit of chanting, and ancient hymns and tunes. Another inheritance was the custom of singing the story of Christ's Passion, with musical additions, in Holy Week. This usage, which may be traced back to a remote period in the Middle Age, must be distinguished from the method, prevalent as early as the thirteenth century, of actually representing the events of Christ's last days in visible action upon the stage. The Passion play, which still survives in Oberammergau in Bavaria, and in other more obscure parts of Europe, was one of a great number of ecclesiastical dramas, classed as Miracle Plays, Mysteries, and Moralities, which were performed under the auspices of the Church for the purpose of impressing the people in the most vivid way with the reality of the Old and New Testament stories, and the binding force of doctrines and moral principles.

The observance out of which the German Passion music of the eighteenth century grew was an altogether different affair. It consisted of the mere recitation, without histrionic accessories, of the story of the trial and death of Christ, as narrated by one of the four evangelists, beginning in the synoptic Gospels with the plot of the priests and scribes, and in St. John's Gospel with the betrayal. This narration formed a part of the liturgic office proper to Palm Sunday, Holy Tuesday, Wednesday of Holy Week, and Good Friday. According to the primitive use, which originated in the period of the supremacy of the Gregorian chant, several officers took part in the delivery. One cleric intoned the evangelist's narrative, another the words of Christ, and a third those of Pilate, Peter, and other single personages. The ejaculations of the Jewish priests, disciples, and mob were chanted by a small group of ministers. The text was rendered in the simpler syllabic form of the Plain Song. Only in one passage did this monotonous recitation give way to a more varied, song-like utterance, *viz.*, in the cry of Christ upon the cross, " Eli, Eli, lama sabachthani," this phrase being delivered in an extended, solemn, but unrhythmical melody, to which was imparted all the pathos that the singer could command. The chorus parts were at first sung in unison, then, as the art of part-writing developed, they were set in simple four-part counterpoint.

Under the influence of the perfected contrapuntal art of the sixteenth century there appeared a form now known as the motet Passion, and for a short time it flourished vigorously. In this style everything was sung in chorus without accompaniment — evangelist's narrative, words of Christ, Pilate, and all. The large opportunities for musical effect permitted by this manner of treatment gained for it great esteem among musicians, for since this purely musical method of repeating the story of Christ's death was never conceived as in any sense dramatic, there was nothing inconsistent in setting the words of a single personage in several parts. The life enjoyed by this phase of Passion music was brief, for it arose only a short time before the musical revolution, heralded by the Florentine monody and confirmed by the opera, drove the mediæval polyphony into seclusion.

With the quickly won supremacy of the dramatic and concert solo, together with the radical changes of taste and practice which it signified, the chanted Passion and the motet Passion were faced by a rival which was destined to attain such dimensions in Germany that it occupied the whole field devoted to this form of art. In the oratorio Passion, as it may be called, the Italian recitative and aria and the sectional rhythmic chorus took the place of the unison chant and the ancient polyphony; hymns and poetic monologues supplemented and sometimes supplanted the Bible text; and the impassioned

276

vocal style, introducing the new principle of definite expression of the words, was reinforced by the lately emancipated art of instrumental music. For a time, these three forms of Passion music existed side by side, the latest in an immature state; but the stars in the firmament of modern music were fighting in their courses for the mixed oratorio style, and in the early part of the eighteenth century this latter form attained completion and stood forth as the most imposing gift bestowed by Germany upon the world of ecclesiastical art.

The path which German religious music was destined to follow in the seventeenth and eighteenth centuries, under the guidance of the new ideas of expression, was plainly indicated when Heinrich Schütz, the greatest German composer of the seventeenth century, and the worthy forerunner of Bach and Händel, wrote his "histories" and "sacred symphonies." Born in 1585, he came under the inspiring instruction of G. Gabrieli in Venice in 1609, and on a second visit to Italy in 1628 he became still more imbued with the dominant tendencies of the age. He was appointed chapel-master at the court of the Elector of Saxony at Dresden in 1615, and held this position, with a few brief interruptions, until his death in 1672. He was a musician of the most solid attainments, and although living in a transition period in the history of music, he was cautious and respectful in his attitude toward both the methods which were at that time in conflict, accepting the new discoveries in dramatic expression as supplementary, not antagonistic, to the old ideal of devotional music. In his psalms he employed contrasting and combining choral

277

masses, reinforced by a band of instruments. In the Symphoniæ sacræ are songs for one or more solo voices, with instrumental obligato, in which the declamatory recitative style is employed with varied and appropriate effect. In his dramatic religious works, the " Resurrection," the " Seven Words of the Redeemer upon the Cross," the " Conversion of Saul," and the Passions after the four evangelists, Schütz uses the vocal solo, the instrumental accompaniment, and the dramatic chorus in a tentative manner, attaining at times striking effects of definite expression quite in accordance with modern ideas, while anon he falls back upon the strict impersonal method identified with the ancient Plain Song and sixteenth-century motet. Most advanced in style and rich in expression is the " Seven Words." A feature characteristic of the rising school of German Passion music is the imagined presence of Christian believers, giving utterance in chorus to the emotions aroused by the contemplation of the atoning act. In the " Seven Words " the utterances of Jesus and the other separate personages are given in arioso recitative, rising at times to pronounced melody. The tone of the whole work is fervent, elevated, and churchly. The evangelist and all the persons except Christ sing to an organ bass, — the words of the Saviour are accompanied by the ethereal tones of stringed instruments, perhaps intended as an emblematic equivalent to the aureole in religious paintings. In Schütz's settings of the Passion, although they belong to the later years of his life, he returns to the primitive form, in which the parts of the evangelist and the single characters are rendered in the severe " collect tone " of the ancient Plain Song, making no attempt at exact expression of changing sentiments. Even in these restrained and lofty works, however, his genius as a composer and his progressive sympathies as a modern artist occasionally break forth in vivid expression given to the ejaculations of priests, disciples, and Jewish mob, attaining a quite remarkable warmth and reality of portrayal. Nevertheless, these isolated attempts at naturalism hardly bring the Passions of Schütz into the category of modern works. There is no instrumental accompaniment, and, most decisive of all, they are restrained within the limits of the mediæval conception by the ancient Gregorian tonality, which is maintained throughout almost to the entire exclusion of chromatic alteration.

The works of Schütz, therefore, in spite of their sweetness and dignity and an occasional glimpse of picturesque detail, are not to be considered as steps in the direct line of progress which led from the early Italian cantata and oratorio to the final achievements of Bach and Händel. These two giants of the culminating period apparently owed nothing to Schütz. It is not probable that they had any acquaintance with his works at all. The methods and the ideals of these three were altogether different. Considering how common and apparently necessary in art is the reciprocal influence of great men, it is remarkable that in the instance of the greatest German musician of the seventeenth century and the two greatest of the eighteenth, all working in the field of religious dramatic music, not one was affected in the slightest degree by the labors of either of the others. Here we have the individualism of modern art exhibited in the most positive degree upon its very threshold.

In the Passions of Schütz we find only the characters of the Bible story, together with the evangelist's narrative taken literally from the Gospel, — that is to say, the original frame-work of the Passion music with the chorus element elaborated. In the latter part of the seventeenth century the dramatic scheme of the Passion was enlarged by the addition of the Christian congregation, singing appropriate chorals, and the ideal company of believers, expressing suitable sentiments in recitatives, arias, and choruses. The insertion of church hymns was of the highest importance in view of the relation of the Passion music to the liturgy, for the more stress was laid upon this feature, the more the Passion, in spite of its semi-dramatic character, became fitted as a constituent into the order of service. The choral played here the same part as in the cantata, assimilating to the prescribed order of worship what would otherwise be an extraneous if not a disturbing feature. This was especially the case when, as in the beginning of the adoption of the choral in the Passion, the hymn verses were sung by the congregation itself. In Bach's time this custom had fallen into abeyance, and the choral stanzas were sung by the choir; but this change involved no alteration in the form or the conception of the Passion performance as a liturgic act.

The growth of the Passion music from Schütz to its final beauty and pathos under Sebastian Bach was by no means constant. In certain quarters, particularly at Hamburg, the aria in the shallow Italian form took an utterly disproportionate importance. The opera, which was flourishing brilliantly at Hamburg about 1700, exercised a perverting influence upon the Passion to such an extent that the ancient liturgic traditions were completely abandoned. In many of the Hamburg Passions the Bible text was thrown away and poems substituted, all of which were of inferior literary merit, and some quite contemptible. Incredible as it may seem, the comic element was sometimes introduced, the "humorous" characters being the servant Malthus whose ear was cut off by Peter, and a clownish peddler of ointment. It must be said that these productions were not given in the churches; they are not to be included in the same category with the strictly liturgic Passions of Sebastian Bach. The comparative neglect of the choral and also of the organ removes them altogether from the proper history of German church music.

Thus we see how the new musical forms, almost creating the emotions which they were so well adapted to express, penetrated to the very inner shrine of German church music. In some sections, as at Hamburg, the Italian culture supplanted the older school altogether. In others it encountered sterner resistance, and could do no more than form an alliance, in which old German rigor and reserve became somewhat ameliorated and relaxed without becoming perverted. To produce an art work of the highest order out of this union of contrasting principles, a genius was needed who should possess so true an insight into the special capabilities of each that he should be able by their amalgamation to create a form of religious music that should be conformed to the purest conception of the mission of church song, and at the same time endowed with those faculties for moving the affections which were demanded by the tastes of the new age. In fulness of time this genius appeared. His name was Johann Sebastian Bach.

CHAPTER IX

THE CULMINATION OF GERMAN PROTESTANT MUSIC: JOHANN SEBASTIAN BACH

THE name of Bach is the greatest in Protestant church music, — there are many who do not hesitate to say that it is the greatest in all the history of music, religious and secular. The activity of this man was many-sided, and his invention seems truly inexhaustible. He touched every style of music known to his day except the opera, and most of the forms that he handled he raised to the highest power that they have ever attained. Many of his most admirable qualities appear in his secular works, but these we must pass over. In viewing him exclusively as a composer for the Church, however, we shall see by far the most considerable part of him, for his secular compositions, remarkable as they are, always appear rather as digressions from the main business of his life. His conscious life-long purpose was to enrich the musical treasury of the Church he loved, to strengthen and signalize every feature of her worship which his genius could reach: and to this lofty aim he devoted an intellectual force and an energy of loyal enthusiasm unsurpassed in the annals of art.

Johann Sebastian Bach is one of the monumental figures in the religious history of Germany, undoubtedly the most considerable in the two centuries following the death of Luther. Like Luther, of whom in some respects he reminds us, he was a man rooted fast in German soil, sprung from sturdy peasant stock, endowed with the sterling piety and steadfastness of moral purpose which had long been traditional in the Teutonic character. His culture was at its basis purely German. He never went abroad to seek the elegancies which his nation lacked. He did not despise them, but he let them come to him to be absorbed into the massive substance of his national education, in order that this education might become in the deepest sense liberal and human. He interpreted what was permanent and hereditary in German culture, not what was ephemeral and exotic. He ignored the opera, although it was the reigning form in every country in Europe. He planted himself squarely on German church music, particularly the essentially German art of organ playing, and on that foundation, supplemented with what was best of Italian and French device, he built up a massive edifice which bears in plan, outline, and every decorative detail the stamp of a German craftsman.

The most musical family known to history was that of the Bachs. In six generations (Sebastian belonging to the fifth) we find marked musical ability, which in a number of instances before Sebastian appeared amounted almost to genius. As many as thirty-seven of the name are known to have held important musical positions. A large number during the seventeenth and eighteenth centuries were members of the town bands and choruses, which sustained almost the entire musical culture among the common people of Germany during that period. These organizations, combining the public practice of religious and secular music, were effective in nourishing both the artistic and the religious spirit of the time. In Germany in the seventeenth century there was as yet no opera and concert system to concentrate musical activity in the theatre and public hall. The Church was the nursery of musical culture, and this culture was in no sense artificial or borrowed, — it was based on types long known and beloved by the common people as their peculiar national inheritance, and associated with much that was stirring and honorable in their history.

Thuringia was one of the most musical districts in Germany in the seventeenth century, and was also a stronghold of the reformed religion. From this and its neighboring districts the Bachs never wandered. Eminent as they were in music, hardly one of them ever visited Italy or received instruction from a foreign master. They kept aloof from the courts, the hot-beds of foreign musical growths, and submitted themselves to the service of the Protestant Church. They were peasants and small farmers, well to do and everywhere respected. Their stern self-mastery held them uncontaminated by the wide-spread demoralization that followed the Thirty Years' War. They appear as admirable types of that undemonstrative, patient, downright, and tenacious quality which has always saved Germany from social decline or disintegration in critical periods.

Into such a legacy of intelligence, thrift, and pro-
bity came Johann Sebastian Bach. All the most
admirable traits of his ancestry shine out again in him,
reinforced by a creative gift which seems the accumulation of all the several talents of his house. He was
born at Eisenach, March 21, 1685. His training as a
boy was mainly received in choir schools at Ohrdruf
and Lüneburg, attaining mastership as organist and
contrapuntist at the age of eighteen. He held official
positions at Arnstadt, Mühlhausen, Weimar, and Anhalt-
Cöthen, and was finally called to Leipsic as cantor of
the Thomas school and director of music at the Thomas
and Nicolai churches, where he labored from 1723 until
his death in 1750. His life story presents no incidents
of romantic interest. But little is known of his temperament or habits. In every place in which he labored
his circumstances were much the same. He was a
church organist and choir director from the beginning
to the end of his career. He became the greatest
organist of his time and the most accomplished master
of musical science. His declared aim in life was to
reform and perfect German church music. The means
to achieve this were always afforded him, so far as the
scanty musical facilities of the churches of that period
would permit. His church compositions were a part of
his official routine duties. His recognized abilities
always procured him positions remunerative enough
to protect him from anxiety. He was never subject to
interruptions or serious discouragements. From first
to last the path in life which he was especially qualified
to pursue was clearly marked out before him. His

genius, his immense physical and mental energy, and his high sense of duty to God and his employers did the rest. Nowhere is there the record of a life more simple, straightforward, symmetrical, and complete.

In spite of the intellectual and spiritual apathy prevailing in many sections of Germany, conditions were not altogether unfavorable for the special task which Bach assigned to himself. His desire to build up church music did not involve an effort to restore to congregational singing its pristine zeal, or to revive an antiquarian taste for the historic choir anthem. Bach was a man of the new time; he threw himself into the current of musical progress, seized upon the forms which were still in process of development, giving them technical completeness and bringing to light latent possibilities which lesser men had been unable to discern.

The material for his purpose was already within his reach. The religious folk-song, freighted with a precious store of memories, was still an essential factor in public and private worship. The art of organ playing had developed a vigorous and pregnant national style in the choral prelude, the fugue, and a host of freer forms. The Passion music and the cantata had recently shown signs of brilliant promise. The Italian solo song was rejoicing in its first flush of conquest on German soil. No one, however, could foresee what might be done with these materials until Bach arose. He gathered them all in his hand, remoulded, blended, enlarged them, touched them with the fire of his genius and his religious passion, and thus produced works of art which, intended for German evangelicalism, are now being adopted by the world as the most, comprehensive symbols in music of the essential Christian faith.[1]

Bach was one of those supreme artists who concentrate in themselves the spirit and the experiments of an epoch. In order, therefore, to know how the persistent religious consciousness of Germany strove to attain self-recognition through those art agencies which finally became fully operative in the eighteenth century, we need only study the works of this great representative musician, passing by the productions of the organists and cantors who shared, although in feebler measure, his illumination. For Bach was no isolated phenomenon of his time. He created no new styles; he gave art no new direction. He was one out of many poorly paid and overworked church musicians, performing the duties that were traditionally attached to his office, improvising fugues and preludes, and accompanying choir and congregation at certain moments in the service, composing motets, cantatas, and occasionally a larger work for the regular order of the day, providing special music for a church festival, a public funeral, the inauguration of a town council, or the installation of a pastor. What distinguished Bach was simply the superiority of his work on these time-honored lines, the amazing variety of sentiment which he extracted from these conventional forms, the scientific learning which

[1] The performance of Bach's cantatas by the Catholic Schola Cantorum of Paris is one of many testimonies to the universality of the art of this son of Lutheranism.

puts him among the greatest technicians in the whole range of art, the prodigality of ideas, depth of feeling, and a sort of introspective mystical quality which he was able to impart to the involved and severe diction of his age.

Bach's devotion to the Lutheran Church was almost as absorbed as Palestrina's to the Catholic. His was a sort of cloistered seclusion. Like every one who has made his mark upon church music he reverenced the Church as a historic institution. Her government, ceremonial, and traditions impressed his imagination, and kindled a blind, instinctive loyalty. He felt that he attained to his true self only under her admonitions. Her service was to him perfect freedom. His opportunity to contribute to the glory of the Church was one that dwarfed every other privilege, and his official duty, his personal pleasure, and his highest ambition ran like a single current, fed by many streams, in one and the same channel. To measure the full strength of the mighty tide of feeling which runs through Bach's church music we must recognize this element of conviction, of moral necessity. Given Bach's inherited character, his education and his environment, add the personal factor — imagination and reverence — and you have Bach's music, spontaneous yet inevitable, like a product of nature. Only out of such single-minded devotion to the interests of the Church, both as a spiritual nursery and as a venerated institution, has great church art ever sprung or can it spring.

Bach's productions for the Church are divided into two general classes, *viz.*, organ music and vocal music

19

The organ music is better known to the world at large, and on account of its greater availability may outlive the vocal works in actual practice. For many reasons more or less obvious Bach's organ works are constantly heard in connection with public worship, both Catholic and Protestant, in Europe and America, and their use is steadily increasing; while the choral compositions have almost entirely fallen out of the stated religious ceremony, even in Germany, and have been relegated to the concert hall. In course of time the organ solo had grown into a constituent feature of the public act of worship in the German Protestant Church. In the Catholic Church solo organ playing is less intrinsic; in fact it has no real historic or liturgic authorization and gives the impression rather of an embellishment, like elaborately carved choir-screens and rose windows, very ornamental and impressive, but not indispensable. But in the German system organ playing had become established by a sort of logic, first as an accompaniment to the people's hymn — a function it assumed about 1600 — and afterwards in the practice of extemporization upon choral themes. Out of this latter custom a style of organ composition grew up in the seventeenth century which, through association and a more or less definite correspondence with the spirit and order of the prescribed service, came to be looked upon as distinctively a church style. This German organ music was strictly church music according to the only adequate definition of church music that has ever been given, for it had grown up within the Church itself, and through its very liturgic connections had come to make its appeal to the worshipers, not as an artistic decoration, but as an agency directly adapted to aid in promoting those ends which the church ceremony had in view. Furthermore, the dignity and severe intellectuality of this German organ style, combined with its majesty of sound and strength of movement, seemed to add distinctly to the biblical flavor of the liturgy, the uncompromising dogmatism of the authoritative teaching, and the intense moral earnestness which prevailed in the Church of Luther in its best estate. It was a form of art which was native to the organ, implied in the very tone and mechanism of the instrument; it was absolutely untouched by the lighter tendencies already active in secular music. The notion of making the organ play pretty tunes and tickle the ear with the imitative sound of fancy stops never entered the heads of the German church musicians. The gravity and disciplined intelligence proper to the exercise of an ecclesiastical office must pervade every contribution of the organist. This conception was equally a matter of course to the mass of the people, and so the taste of the congregation and the conviction of the clerical authorities supported the organists in their adherence to the traditions of their strict and complex art. This lordly style was no less worthy of reverence in the eyes of all concerned because it was to all intents a German art, virtually unknown in other countries, except partially in the sister land of Holland, and therefore hedged about with the sanctions of patriotism as well as the universally admitted canons of religious musical expression.

This form of music was evolved originally under the suggestion of the mediæval vocal polyphony, — counter point redistributed and systematized in accordance with the modern development of rhythm, tonality, and sectional structure. Its birthplace was Italy; the canzona of Frescobaldi and his compeers was the parent of the fugue. The task of developing this Italian germ was given to the Dutch and Germans. The instrumental instinct and constructive genius of such men as Swelinck, Scheidt, Buxtehude, Froberger, and Pachelbel carried the movement so far as to reveal its full possibilities, and Bach brought these possibilities to complete realization.

As an organ player and composer it would seem that Bach stands at the summit of human achievement. His whole art as a player is to be found in his fugues, preludes, fantasies, toccatas, sonatas, and choral variations. In his fugues he shows perhaps most convincingly that supreme mastery of design and splendor of invention and fancy which have given him the place he holds by universal consent among the greatest artists of all time. In these compositions there is a variety and individuality which, without such examples, one could hardly suppose that this arbitrary form of construction would admit. With Bach the fugue is no dry intellectual exercise. So far as the absolutism of its laws permits, Bach's imagination moved as freely in the fugue as Beethoven's in the sonata or Schubert's in the lied. Its peculiar idiom was as native to him as his rugged Teuton speech. A German student's musical education in that day began with counterpoint, as at the present time it begins with figured bass harmony; the ability to write every species of polyphony with ease

292

was a matter of course with every musical apprentice. But with Bach, the master, the fugue was not merely the sign of technical facility; it was a means of expression, a supreme manifestation of style. By the telling force of his subjects, the amazing dexterity and rich fancy displayed in their treatment, the ability to cover the widest range of emotional suggestion, his fugues appeal to a far deeper sense than wonder at technical cleverness. Considering that it lies in the very essence of the contrapuntal style that it should be governed by certain very rigid laws of design and procedure, we may apply to Bach's organ works in general a term that has been given to architecture, and say that they are "construction beautified." By this is meant that every feature, however beautiful in itself, finds its final charm and justification only as a necessary component in the comprehensive plan. Each detail helps to push onward the systematic unfolding of the design, it falls into its place by virtue of the laws of fitness and proportion; logical and organic, but at the same time decorative and satisfactory to the æsthetic sense. There is indeed something almost architectonic in these masterpieces of the great Sebastian. In their superb rolling harmonies, their dense involutions, their subtle and inevitable unfoldings, their long-drawn cadences, and their thrilling climaxes, they seem to possess a fit relation to the vaulted, reverberating ceilings, the massive pillars, and the half-lighted recesses of the sombre old buildings in which they had their birth. In both the architecture and the music we seem to apprehend a religious earnestness which drew its nourishment from the most hidden depths of the soul, and which, even in its moments of exultation, would not appear to disregard those stern convictions in which it believed that it found the essentials of its faith.

A form of instrumental music existed in the German Protestant Church which was peculiar to that institution, and which was exceedingly significant as forming a connecting link between organ solo playing and the congregational worship. We have seen that the choral, at the very establishment of the new order by Luther, became a characteristic feature of the office of devotion, entering into the very framework of the liturgy by virtue of the official appointment of particular hymns (Hauptlieder) on certain days. As soon as the art of organ playing set out upon its independent career early in the seventeenth century, the organists began to take up the choral melodies as subjects for extempore performance. These tunes were especially adapted to this purpose by reason of their stately movement and breadth of style, which gave opportunity for the display of that mastery of florid harmonization in which the essence of the organist's art consisted. The organist never played the printed compositions of others, or even his own, for voluntaries. He would no more think of doing so than a clergyman would preach another man's sermon, or even read one of his own from manuscript. To this day German unwritten law is rigorous on both these matters. The organist's method was always to improvise in the strict style upon themes invented by himself or borrowed from other sources. Nothing was more natural than that he should use the choral tunes as his

quarry, not only on account of their technical suitable-
ness, but still more from the interest that would be
aroused in the congregation, and the unity that would
be established between the office of the organist and
that of the people. The chorals that were appointed
for the day would commonly furnish the player with
his raw material, and the song of the people would
appear again soaring above their heads, adorned by effective tonal combinations. This method could also
be employed to a more moderate extent in accompanying the congregation as they sang the hymn in unison;
interludes between the stanzas and even flourishes at
the ends of the lines would give scope to the organist to
exhibit his knowledge and fancy. The long-winded
interlude at last became an abuse, and was reduced or
suppressed; but the free organ prelude on the entire
choral melody grew in favor, and before Bach's day
ability in this line was the chief test of a player's
competence. In Bach's early days choral preludes by
famous masters had found their way into print in large
numbers, and were the objects of his assiduous study.
His own productions in this class surpassed all his
models, and as a free improviser on choral themes he ex-
celled all his contemporaries. " I had supposed," said
the famous Reinken, who at the age of ninety-seven
heard Bach extemporize on "An Wasserflüssen Babylon" at Hamburg, — " I had supposed that this art was
dead, but I see that it still lives in you." In this species
of playing, the hymn melody is given out with one hand
or upon the pedals, while around it is woven a network
of freely moving parts. The prelude may be brief,

included within the space limits of the original melody, or it may be indefinitely extended by increasing the length of the choral notes and working out interludes between the lines. The one hundred and thirty choral preludes which have come down to us from Bach's pen are samples of the kind of thing that he was extemporizing Sunday after Sunday. In these pieces the accompaniment is sometimes fashioned on the basis of a definite melodic figure which is carried, with modulations and subtle modifications, all through the stanza, sometimes on figures whose pattern changes with every line; while beneath or within the sounding arabesques are heard the long sonorous notes of the choral, holding the hearer firmly to the ground idea which the player's art is striving to impress and beautify. This form of music is something very different from the " theme and variations," which has played so conspicuous a part in the modern instrumental school from Haydn down to the present. In the choral prelude there is no modification of the theme itself; the subject in single notes forms a *cantus firmus*, on the same principle that appears in the mediæval vocal polyphony, around which the freely invented parts, moving laterally, are entwined. Although these compositions vary greatly in length, a single presentation of the decorated choral tune suffices with Bach except in rare instances, such as the prelude on " O Lamm Gottes unschuldig," in which the melody is given out three times, with a different scheme of ornament at each repetition.

That Bach always restricts his choral elaboration to the end of illustrating the sentiment of the words with which the theme is illustrated would be saying too much. Certainly he often does so, as in such beautiful examples as " O Mensch, bewein' dein' Sünde gross," " Schmücke dich, meine liebe Seele," and that touching setting of " Wenn wir in höchsten Nöthen sein " which Bach dictated upon his deathbed. But the purpose of the choral prelude in the church worship was not necessarily to reflect and emphasize the thought of the hymn. This usage having become conventional, and the organist being allowed much latitude in his treatment, his pride in his science would lead him to dilate and elaborate according to a musical rather than a poetic impulse, thinking less of appropriateness to a precise mood (an idea which, indeed, had hardly became lodged in instrumental music in Bach's time) than of producing an abstract work of art contrived in accordance with the formal prescriptions of German musical science. The majority of Bach's works in this form are, it must be said, conventional and scholastic, some even dry and pedantic. Efforts at popularizing them at the present day have but slight success; but in not a few Bach's craving for expression crops out, and some of his most gracious inspirations are to be found in these incidental and apparently fugitive productions.

In order to win the clue to Bach's vocal as well as his instrumental style, we must constantly refer back to his works for the organ. As Händel's genius in oratorio was shaped under the influence of the Italian aria, direct or derived, and as certain modern composers, such as Berlioz, seize their first conceptions already clothed in orchestral garb, so Bach seemed to think in

297

terms of the organ. Examine one of his contrapuntal choruses, or even one of his ariás with its obligato accompaniment, and you are instantly reminded of the mode of facture of his organ pieces. His education rested upon organ music, and he only yielded to one of the most potent influences of his time when he made the organ the dominant factor in his musical expression. The instrumental genius of Germany had already come to self-consciousness at the end of the seventeenth century, and was as plainly revealing itself in organ music as it did a century later in the sonata and symphony. The virtuoso spirit — the just pride in technical skill — always keeps pace with the development of style; in the nature of things these two are mutually dependent elements in progress. In Bach the love of exercising his skill as an executant was a part of his very birthright as a musician. The organ was to him very much what the pianoforte was to Liszt, and in each the virtuoso instinct was a fire which must burst forth, or it would consume the very soul of its possessor. And so we find among the fugues, fantasies, and toccatas of Bach compositions whose dazzling magnificence is not exceeded by the most sensational effusions of the modern pianoforte and orchestral schools. In all the realm of music there is nothing more superb than those Niagaras of impetuous sound which roll through such works as the F major and D minor toccatas and the G major fantasie, — to select examples out of scores of equally apt illustrations. But sound and fury are by no means their aim; Bach's invention and science are never more resourceful than when apparently driven by the demon of unrest. In

order to give the freest sweep to his fancy Bach, the
supreme lord of form, often broke through form's con-
ventionalisms, so that even his fugues sometimes became, as they have been called, fantasies in the form of
fugues, just as Beethoven, under a similar impulse,
wrote *sonate quasi fantasie*. Witness the E minor fugue
with the " wedge theme." In Bach's day and country
there was no concert stage ; the instrumental virtuoso
was the organist. It is not necessary to suppose, therefore, that pieces so exciting to the nerves as those to
which I have alluded were all composed strictly for the
ordinary church worship. There were many occasions,
such as the " opening " of a new organ or a civic festival, when the organist could " let himself go " without
incurring the charge of introducing a profane or alien
element. And yet, even as church music, these
pieces were not altogether incongruous. We must
always keep in mind that the question of appropriateness in church music depends very much upon association and custom. A style that would be execrated as
blasphemous in a Calvinist assembly would be received
as perfectly becoming in a Catholic or Lutheran ceremony. A style of music that has grown up in the very
heart of a certain Church, identified for generations with
the peculiar ritual and history of that Church, is proper
ecclesiastical music so far as that particular institution is
concerned. Those who condemn Bach's music — organ
works, cantatas, and Passions — as unchurchly ignore
this vital point. Moreover, the conception of the function of music in the service of the German Evangelical
Church was never so austere that brilliancy and grandeur

were deemed incompatible with the theory of religious ceremony. It may be said that Bach's grandest organ pieces are conceived as the expression of what may be called the religious passion — the rapture which may not unworthily come upon the believer when his soul opens to the reception of ideas the most penetrating and sublime.

Certainly no other religious institution has come so near the solution of the problem of the proper use of the instrumental solo in public worship. Through the connection of the organ music with the people's hymn in the choral prelude, and the conformity of its style to that of the choir music in motet and cantata, it became vitally blended with the whole office of praise and prayer; its effect was to gather up and merge all individual emotions into the projection of the mood of aspiration that was common to all.

The work performed by Bach for the church cantata was somewhat similar in nature to his service to the choral prelude, and was carried out with a far more lavish expenditure of creative power. The cantata, now no longer a constituent of the German Evangelical worship, in the eighteenth century held a place in the ritual analogous to that occupied by the anthem in the morning and evening prayer of the Church of England. It is always of larger scale than the anthem, and its size was one cause of its exclusion in the arbitrary and irregular reductions which the Evangelical liturgies have undergone in the last century and a half. There is nothing in its florid character to justify this procedure, for it may be, and in Bach usually is, more closely related to the ritual framework than the English anthem, in consequence of the manner in which it has been made to absorb strictly liturgic forms into its substance. Bach, in his cantatas, kept the notion of liturgic unity clearly in mind. He effected this unity largely by his use of the choral as a conspicuous element in the cantata, often as its very foundation. He checked the Italianizing process by working the arioso recitative, the aria for one or more voices, and the chorus into one grand musical scheme, in which his intricate organ style served both as fabric and decoration. By the unexampled prominence which he gave the choral as a mine of thematic material, he gave the cantata not only a striking originality, but also an air of unmistakable fitness to the character and special expression of the confession which it served. By these means, which are concerned with its form, and still more by the astonishing variety, truth, and beauty with which he was able to meet the needs of each occasion for which a work of this kind was appointed, he endowed his Church and nation with a treasure of religious song compared with which, for magnitude, diversity, and power, the creative work of any other church musician that may be named — Palestrina, Gabrieli, or whoever he may be — sinks into insignificance.

Bach wrote five series of cantatas for the Sundays and festal days of the church year — in all two hundred and ninety-five. Of these two hundred and sixty-six were written at Leipsic. They vary greatly in length, the shortest occupying twenty minutes or so in performance, the longest an hour or more. Taken together, they afford such an astonishing display of versatility that any proper characterization of them in a single chapter would be quite out of the question. A considerable number are available for study in Peters's cheap edition, and the majority are analyzed with respect to their salient features in Spitta's encyclopedic Bach biography. Among the great diversity of interesting qualities which they exhibit, the employment of the choral must be especially emphasized as affording the clue, already indicated, to Bach's whole conception of the cantata as a species of religious art. The choral, especially that appointed for a particular day (Hauptlied), is often used as the guiding thread which weaves the work into the texture of the whole daily office. In such cases the chosen choral will appear in the different numbers of the work in fragments or motives, sometimes as subject for voice parts, or woven into the accompaniment as theme or in obligato fashion. It is more common for entire lines of the choral to be treated as *canti firmi*, forming the subjects on which elaborate contrapuntal choruses are constructed, following precisely the same principle of design that I have described in the case of the organ choral preludes. In multitudes of cantata movements lines or verses from two or more chorals are introduced. There are cantatas, such as " Wer nur den lieben Gott," in which each number, whether recitative, aria, or chorus, takes its thematic material, intact or modified, from a choral. The famous "Ein' feste Burg" is a notable example of a cantata in which Bach adheres to a hymn-tune in every number, treating it line by line, deriving from it the pervading tone of the work as well as its constructional plan. The

ways in which Bach applies the store of popular religious melody to the higher uses of art are legion. A cantata of Bach usually ends with a choral in its complete
ordinary form, plainly but richly harmonized in note-for-
note four-part setting as though for congregational singing. It was not the custom, however, in Bach's day for
the congregation to join in this closing choral. There
are cantatas, such as the renowned " Ich hatte viel Be-
kümmerniss," in which the choral melody nowhere appears. Such cantatas are rare, and the use of the choral
became more prominent and systematic in Bach's work
as time went on.

The devotional ideal of the Protestant Church as
compared with the Catholic gives far more liberal
recognition to the private religious consciousness of
the individual. The believer does not so completely
surrender his personality; in his mental reactions to
the ministrations of the clergy he still remains aware
of that inner world of experience which is his world,
not merged and lost in the universalized life of a religious community. The Church is his inspirer and
guide, not his absolute master. The foundation of the
German choral was a religious declaration of independence. The German hymns were each the testimony of
a thinker to his own private conception of religious
truth. The tone and feeling of each hymn were suggested and colored by the general doctrine of the
Church, but not dictated. The adoption of these
utterances of independent feeling into the liturgy was
a recognition on the part of authority of individual
right. It was not a concession; it was the legal ac-

knowledgment of a fundamental principle. Parallel to this significant privilege was the admission of music of the largest variety and penetrated at will with subjective feeling. This conception was carried out consistently in the cantata as established by Bach, most liberally, of course, in the arias. The words of the cantata consisted of Bible texts, stanzas of church hymns, and religious poems, the whole illustrating some Scripture theme or referring to some especial commemoration. The hard and fast metrical schemes of the German hymns were unsuited to the structure and rhythm of the aria, and so a form of verse known as the madrigal, derived from Italy, was used when rhythmical flexibility was an object. For all these reasons we have in Bach's arias the widest license of expression admissible in the school of art which he represented. The Hamburg composers, in their shallow aims, had boldly transferred the Italian concert aria as it stood into the Church, as a sign of their complete defiance of ecclesiastical prescription. Not so Bach; the ancient churchly ideal was to him a thing to be reverenced, even when he departed from it. He, therefore, took a middle course. The Italian notion of an aria — buoyant, tuneful, the voice part sufficient unto itself — had no place in Bach's method. A melody to him was usually a detail in a contrapuntal scheme. And so he wove the voice part into the accompaniment, a single instrument — a violin, perhaps, or oboe — often raised into relief, vying with the voice on equal terms, often soaring above it and carrying the principal theme, while the voice part serves as an obligato. This method, hardly consistent with a pure vocal system, often results with Bach, it must be confessed, in something very mechanical and monotonous to modern ears. The artifice is apparent; the author seems more bent on working out a sort of algebraic formula than interpreting the text to the sensibility. From the traditional point of view this method is not in itself *mal à propos*, for such a treatment raises the sentiment into that calm region of abstraction which is the proper refuge of the devotional mood. But here, as in the organ pieces, Bach is no slave to his technic. There are many arias in his cantatas in which the musical expression is not only beautiful and touching in the highest degree, but also yields with wonderful truth to every mutation of feeling in the text. Still more impressively is this mastery of expression shown in the arioso recitatives. In their depth and beauty they are unique in religious music. Only in very rare moments can Händel pretend to rival them. Mendelssohn reflects them in his oratorios and psalms, — as the moon reflects the sun.

The choruses of Bach's cantatas would furnish a field for endless study. Nowhere else is his genius more grandly displayed. The only work entitled to be compared with these choruses is found in Händel's oratorios. In drawing such a parallel, and observing the greater variety of style in Händel, we must remember that Bach's cantatas are church music. Händel's oratorios are not. Bach's cantata texts are not only confined to a single sphere of thought, *viz.*, the devotional, but they are also strictly lyric. The church cantata does not admit any suggestion of action or external picture. The oratorio, on the other hand, is practically unlimited in scope, and in Händel's choruses the style and treatment are given almost unrestrained license in the way of dramatic and epic suggestion. Within the restrictions imposed upon him, however, Bach expends upon his choruses a wealth of invention in design and expression not less wonderful than that exhibited in his organ works. The motet form, the free fantasia and the choral fantasia forms are all employed, and every device known to his art is applied for the illustration of the text. Grace and tenderness, when the cheering assurances of the Gospel are the theme, crushing burdens of gloom when the author's thought turns to the mysteries of death and judgment, mournfulness in view of sin, the pleading accents of contrition, — every manifestation of emotion which a rigid creed, allied to a racial mysticism which evades positive conceptions, can call forth is projected in tones whose strength and fervor were never attained before in religious music. It is Bach's organ style which is here in evidence, imparting to the chorus its close-knit structure and majesty of sound, humanized by a melody drawn from the choral and from what was most refined in Italian art.

"One peculiar trait in Bach's nature," says Kretzschmar, "is revealed in the cantatas in grand, half-distinct outlines, and this is the longing for death and life with the Lord. This theme is struck in the cantatas more frequently than almost any other. We know him as a giant nature in all situations; great and grandiose is also his joy and cheerfulness. But never, we believe, does his art work with fuller energy and abandonment than when his texts express earth-weariness and the longing for the last hour. The fervor which then displays itself in ever-varying registers, in both calm and stormy regions, has in it something almost demonic."[1]

The work that has most contributed to make the name of Bach familiar to the educated world at large is the Passion according to St. Matthew. Bach wrote five Passions, of which only two — the St. John and the St. Matthew — have come down to us. The former has a rugged force like one of Michael Angelo's unpolished statues, but it cannot fairly be compared to the St. Matthew in largeness of conception or beauty of detail. In Bach's treatment of the Passion story we have the culmination of the artistic development of the early liturgic practice whose progress has already been sketched. Bach completed the process of fusing the Italian aria and recitative with the German chorus, hymn-tune, and organ and orchestral music, interspersing the Gospel narrative with lyric sections in the form of airs, arioso recitatives, and choruses, in which the feelings proper to a believer meditating on the sufferings of Christ in behalf of mankind are portrayed with all the poignancy of pathos of which Bach was master.

Injudicious critics have sometimes attempted to set t o a comparison between the St. Matthew Passion and Händel's "Messiah," questioning which is the greater. But such captious rivalry is derogatory to both, for they are not to be gauged by the same standard. To

[1] Kretzschmar, *Führer durch den Concertsaul; Kirchliche Werke.*

say nothing of the radical differences in style, origin, and artistic conception, — the one a piece of Lutheran church music, the other an English concert oratorio of Italian ancestry, — they are utterly unlike also in poetic intention. Bach's work deals only with the human in Christ; it is the narrative of his last interviews with his disciples, his arrest, trial, and death, together with comments by imagined personalities contemplating these events, both in their immediate action upon the sensibilities and in their doctrinal bearing. It is, therefore, a work so mixed in style that it is difficult to classify it, for it is both epic and implicitly dramatic, while in all its lyric features it is set firmly into the Evangelical liturgic scheme. The text and musical construction of the " Messiah " have no connection with any liturgy; it is concert music of a universal religious character, almost devoid of narrative, and with no dramatic suggestion whatever. Each is a triumph of genius, but of genius working with quite different intentions.

In the formal arrangement of the St. Matthew Passion Bach had no option; he must perforce comply with church tradition. The narrative of the evangelist, taken without change from St. Matthew's Gospel and sung in recitative by a tenor, is the thread upon which the successive divisions are strung. The words of Jesus, Peter, the high priest, and Pilate · are given to a bass, and are also in recitative. The Jews and the disciples are represented by choruses. The " Protestant con- gregation " forms another group, singing appropriate chorals. A third element comprises the company of believers and the "daughter of Zion," singing choruses and arias in comment upon the situations as described by the evangelist. It must be remembered that these chorus factors are not indicated by any division of singers into groups. The work is performed throughout by the same company of singers, in Bach's day by the diminutive choir of the Leipsic Church, composed of boys and young men. Even in the chorals the congregation took no part. The idea of the whole is much the same as in a series of old Italian chapel frescoes. The disciple sits with Christ at the last supper, accompanies him to the garden of Gethsemane and to the procurator's hall, witnesses his mockery and condemnation, and takes his station at the foot of the cross, lamenting alternately the sufferings of his Lord and the sin which demanded such a sacrifice.

Upon this prescribed formula Bach has poured all the wealth of his experience, his imagination, and his piety. His science is not brought forward so prominently as in many of his works, and where he finds it necessary to employ it he subordinates it to the expression of feeling. Yet we cannot hear without amazement the gigantic opening movement in which the awful burden of the great tragedy is foreshadowed; where, as if organ, orchestra, and double chorus were not enough to sustain the composer's conception, a ninth part, bearing a choral melody, floats above the surging mass of sound, holding the thought of the hearer to the significance of the coming scenes. The long chorus which closes the first part, which is constructed in the form of a figured choral, is also built upon a scale which

Bach has seldom exceeded. But the structure of the work in general is comparatively open, and the expression direct and clear. An atmosphere of profoundest gloom pervades the work from beginning to end, ever growing darker as the scenes of the terrible drama advance and culminate, yet here and there relieved by gleams of divine tenderness and human pity. That Bach was able to carry a single mood, and that a depressing one, through a composition of three hours' length without falling into monotony at any point is one of the miracles of musical creation.

The meditative portions of the work in aria, recitative, and chorus are rendered with great beauty and pathos, in spite of occasional archaic stiffness. Dry and artificial some of the *da capo* arias undoubtedly are, for that quality of fluency which always accompanies genius never yet failed to beguile its possessor into by-paths of dulness. But work purely formalistic is not common in the St. Matthew Passion. Never did religious music afford anything more touching and serene than such numbers as the tenor solo and chorus, "Ich will bei meinem Jesu wachen," the bass solo, "Am Abend, da es kühle war," and the recitative and chorus, matchless in tenderness, beginning "Nun ist der Herr zur Ruh' gebracht." Especially impressive are the tones given to the words of the Saviour. These tones are distinguished from those of the other personages not only by their greater melodic beauty, but also by their accompaniment, which consists of the stringed instruments, while the other recitatives are supported by the organ alone. In Christ's despairing cry upon the cross, "Eli, Eli, lama sabachthani," this ethereal stringed accompaniment is extinguished. What Bach intended to signify by this change is not certainly known. This exclamation of Jesus, the only instance in his life when he seemed to lose his certainty of the divine coöperation, must be distinguished in some way, Bach probably thought, from all his other utterances. Additional musical means would be utterly futile, for neither music nor any other art has any expression for the mental anguish of that supreme moment. The only expedient possible was to reduce music at that point, substituting plain organ chords, and let the words of Christ stand out in bold relief in all their terrible significance.

The chorals in the St. Matthew Passion are taken bodily, both words and tunes, from the church hymn-book. Prominent among them is the famous " O Haupt voll Blut und Wunden " by Gerhardt after St. Bernard, which is used five times. These choral melodies are harmonized in simple homophonic style, but with extreme beauty. As an instance of the poetic fitness with which these chorals are introduced we may cite the last in the work, where immediately after the words "Jesus cried with a loud voice and gave up the ghost," the chorus sings a stanza beginning "When my death hour approaches forsake not me, O Lord." "This climax," says Spitta, "has always been justly regarded as one of the most thrilling of the whole work. The infinite significance of the sacrifice could not be more simply, comprehensively, and convincingly expressed than in this marvellous prayer."

This wonderful creation closes with a chorus of farewell sung beside the tomb of Jesus. It is a worthy close, for nothing more lovely and affecting was ever confided to human lips. The gloom and agony that have pervaded the scenes of temptation, trial, and death have quite vanished. The tone is indeed that of lamentation, for the Passion drama in its very aim and tradition did not admit any anticipation of the resurrection; neither in the Catholic or Lutheran ceremonies of Good Friday is there a foreshadowing of the Easter rejoicing. But the sentiment of this closing chorus is not one of hopeless grief; it expresses rather a sense of relief that suffering is past, mingled with a strain of solemn rapture, as if dimly conscious that the tomb is not the end of all.

The first performance of the St. Matthew Passion took place in the Thomas church at Leipsic, on Good Friday, April 15, 1729. It was afterwards revised and extended, and performed again in 1740. From that time it was nowhere heard until it was produced by Felix Mendelssohn in the Sing Academie at Berlin in 1829. The impression it produced was profound, and marked the beginning of the revival of the study of Bach which has been one of the most fruitful movements in nineteenth-century music.

A work equally great in a different way, although it can never become the object of such popular regard as the St. Matthew Passion, is the Mass in B minor. It may seem strange that the man who more than any other interpreted in art the genius of Protestantism should have contributed to a form of music that is identified with the Catholic ritual. It must be remembered that Luther was by no means inclined to break with all the forms and usages of the mother Church. He had no quarrel with those features of her rites which did not embody the doctrines which he disavowed, and most heartily did he recognize the beauty and edifying power of Catholic music. We have seen also that he was in favor of retaining the Latin in communities where it was understood. Hence it was that not only in Luther's day, but long after, the Evangelical Church retained many musical features that had become sacred in the practice of the ancient Church. The congregations of Leipsic were especially conservative in this respect. The entire mass in figured form, however, was not used in the Leipsic service; on certain special days a part only would be sung. The Kyrie and Gloria, known among the Lutheran musicians as the "short mass," were frequently employed. The B minor Mass was not composed for the Leipsic service, but for the chapel of the king of Saxony in Bach's honorary capacity of composer to the royal and electoral court. It was begun in 1735 and finished in 1738, but was not performed entire in Bach's lifetime. By the time it was completed it had outgrown the dimensions of a service mass, and it has probably never been sung in actual church worship. It is so difficult that its performance is an event worthy of special commemoration. Its first complete production in the United States was at Bethlehem, Pa., in the spring of 1900. It is enough to say of this work here that all Bach's powers as fabricator of intricate

313

design, and as master of all the shades of expression which the contrapuntal style admits, are forced to their furthest limit. So vast is it in scale, so majestic in its movement, so elemental in the grandeur of its climaxes, that it may well be taken as the loftiest expression in tones of the prophetic faith of Christendom, unless Beethoven's Missa Solemnis may dispute the title. It belongs not to the Catholic communion alone, nor to the Protestant, but to the Church universal, the Church visible and invisible, the Church militant and triumphant. The greatest master of the sublime in choral music, Bach in this mass sounded all the depths of his unrivalled science and his imaginative energy.

There is no loftier example in history of artistic genius devoted to the service of religion than we find in Johann Sebastian Bach. He always felt that his life was consecrated to God, to the honor of the Church and the well-being of men. Next to this fact we are impressed in studying him with his vigorous intellectuality, by which I mean his accurate estimate of the nature and extent of his own powers and his easy self-adjustment to his environment. He was never the sport of his genius but always its master, never carried away like so many others, even the greatest, into extravagancies or rash experiments. Mozart and Beethoven failed in oratorio, Schubert in opera; the Italian operas of Gluck and Händel have perished. Even in the successful work of these men there is a strange inequality. But upon all that Bach attempted — and the amount of his work is no less a marvel than its quality — he affixed the stamp of final and inimitable perfection. We know from testimony that this perfection was the result of thought and unflagging toil. The file was not the least serviceable tool in his work-shop. This intellectual restraint, operating upon a highly intellectualized form of art, often gives Bach's music an air of severity, a scholastic hardness, which repels sympathy and makes difficult the path to the treasures it contains. The musical culture of our age has been so long based on a different school that no little discipline is needed to adjust the mind to Bach's manner of presenting his profound ideas. The diffi-culty is analogous to that experienced in acquiring an appreciation of Gothic sculpture and the Floren-tine painting of the fourteenth century. We are compelled to learn a new musical language, for it is only in a qualified sense that the language of music is universal. We must put ourselves into another century, face another order of ideas than those of our own age. We must learn the temper of the Ger-man mind in the Reformation period and after, its proud self-assertion, coupled to an aggressive positive-ness of religious belief, which, after all, was but the hard shell which enclosed a rare sweetness of piety.

All through Bach we feel the well-known German mysticism which seeks the truth in the instinctive convictions of the soul, the idealism which takes the mind as the measure of existence, the romanticism which colors the outer world with the hues of per-sonal temperament. Bach's historic position required that this spirit, in many ways so modern, should take shape in forms to which still clung the tech-

315

nical methods of an earlier time. His all-encompassing organ style was Gothic — if we may use such a term for illustration's sake — not Renaissance. His style is Teutonic in the widest as well as the most literal sense. It is based on forms identified with the practice of the people in church and home. He recognized not the priestly or the aristocratic element, but the popular. His significance in the history of German Evangelical Christianity is great. Protestantism, like Catholicism, has had its supreme poet. As Dante embodied in an immortal epic the philosophic conceptions, the hopes and fears of mediæval Catholicism, so Bach, less obviously but no less truly, in his cantatas, Passions, and choral preludes, lent the illuminating power of his art to the ideas which brought forth the Reformation. It is the central demand of Protestantism, the immediate personal access of man to God, which, constituting a new motive in German national music, gave shape and direction to Bach's creative genius.

It has been reserved for recent years to discover that the title of chief representative in art of German Protestantism is, after all, not the sum of Bach's claims to honor. There is something in his art that touches the deepest chords of religious feeling in whatever communion that feeling has been nurtured. His music is not the music of a confession, but of humanity. What changes the spirit of religious progress is destined to undergo in the coming years it would be vain to predict; but it is safe to assume that the warrant of faith will not consist in authority committed to councils or synods, or altogether in a verbal revelation supposed to have been vouchsafed at certain epochs in the past, but in the intuition of the continued presence of the eternal creative spirit in the soul of man. This consciousness, of which creeds and liturgies are but partial and temporary symbols, can find no adequate artistic expression unless it be in the art of music. The more clearly this fact is recognized by the world, the more the fame of Sebastian Bach will increase, for no other musician has so amply embraced and so deeply penetrated the universal religious sentiment. It may well be said of Bach what a French critic says of Albrecht Dürer: " He was an intermediary between the Middle Age and our modern times. Typical of the former in that he was primarily a craftsman, laboring with all the sincerity and unconscious modesty of the good workman who delights in his labor, he yet felt something of the tormented spiritual unrest of the latter; and indeed so strikingly reflects what we call the 'modern spirit' that his work has to-day more influence upon our own thought and art than it had upon that of his contemporaries." [1]

The verdict of the admirers of Bach in respect to his greatness is not annulled when it is found that the power and real significance of his work were not comprehended by the mass of his countrymen during his life, and that outside of Leipsic he exerted little influence upon religious art for nearly a century after his death. He was not the less a typical German on this account. Only at certain critical moments do nations

[1] Arsène Alexandre, *Histoire populaire de la Peinture.*

seem to be true to their better selves, and it often happens that their greatest men appear in periods of general moral relaxation, apparently rebuking the unworthiness of their fellow citizens instead of exemplifying common traits of character. But later generations are able to see that, after all, these men are not detached ; their real bases, although out of sight for the time, are immovably set in nationality. Milton was no less representative of permanent elements in English character when " fallen upon evil days," when the direction of affairs seemed given over to " sons of Belial," who mocked at all he held necessary to social welfare. Michael Angelo was still a genuine son of Italy when he mourned in bitterness of soul over her degradation. And so the spirit that pervaded the life and works of Bach is a German spirit, — a spirit which Germany has often seemed to disown, but which in times of need has often reasserted itself with splendid confidence and called her back to soberness and sincerity.

When Bach had passed away, it seemed as if the mighty force he exerted had been dissipated. He had not checked the decline of church music. The art of organ playing degenerated. The choirs, never really adequate, became more and more unable to do justice to the great works that had been bequeathed to them. The public taste relaxed, and the demand for a more florid and fetching kind of song naturalized in the Church the theatrical style already predominant in France and Italy. The people lost their perception of the real merit of their old chorals and permitted them to be altered to suit the requirements of contemporary fashion, or else slighted them altogether in favor of the new "art song." No composers appeared who were able or cared to perpetuate the old traditions. This tendency was inevitable; its causes are perfectly apparent to any one who knows the conditions prevailing in religion and art in Germany in the last half of the eighteenth and the early part of the nineteenth centuries. Pietism, with all its merits, had thrown a sort of puritanic wet blanket over art in its protest against the external and formal in worship. In the orthodox church circles the enthusiasm necessary to nourish a wholesome spiritual life and a living church art at the same time had sadly abated. The inculcation of a dry utilitarian morality and the cultivation of a dogmatic pedantry had taken the place of the joyous freedom of the Gospel. Other more direct causes also entered to turn public interest away from the music of the Church. The Italian opera, with its equipment of sensuous fascinations, devoid of serious aims, was at the high tide of its popularity, patronized by the ruling classes, and giving the tone to all the musical culture of the time. A still more obvious impediment to the revival of popular interest in church music was the rapid formation throughout Germany of choral societies devoted to the performance of oratorios. Following the example of England, these societies took up the works of Händel, and the enthusiasm excited by Haydn's "Creation" in 1798 gave a still more powerful stimulus to the movement. These choral unions had no connection with the church choirs of the eighteenth century, but grew out of private musical associations. The great German music festivals date from about 1810, and they absorbed the interest of those composers whose talent turned towards works of religious content. The church choirs were already in decline when the choral societies began to raise their heads. Cantatas and Passions were no longer heard in church worship. Their place in public regard was taken by the concert oratorio. The current of instrumental music, one of the chief glories of German art in the nineteenth century, was absorbing more and more of the contributions of German genius. The whole trend of the age was toward secular music. It would appear that a truly great art of church music cannot maintain itself beside a rising enthusiasm for secular music. Either the two styles will be amalgamated, and church music be transformed to the measure of the other, as happened in the case of Catholic music, or church song will stagnate, as was the case in Protestant Germany.

After the War of Liberation, ending with the downfall of Napoleon's tyranny, and when Germany began to enter upon a period of critical self-examination, demands began to be heard for the reinstatement of church music on a worthier basis. The assertion of nationality in other branches of musical art — the symphonies of Beethoven, the songs of Schubert, the operas of Weber — was echoed in the domain of church music, not at first in the production of great works, but in performance, criticism, and appeal. It is not to be denied that a steady uplift in the department of church music has been in progress in Germany all through the nineteenth century. The transition from rationalism and infidelity to a new and higher phase of evangelical religion effected under the lead of Schleiermacher, the renewed interest in church history, the effort to bring the forms of worship into coöperation with a quickened spiritual life, the revival of the study of the great works of German art as related to national intellectual development, — these influences and many more have strongly stirred the cause of church music both in composition and performance. Choirs have been enlarged and strengthened; the soprano and alto parts are still exclusively sung by boys, but the tenor and bass parts are taken by mature and thoroughly trained men, instead of by raw youths, as in Bach's time and after. In such choirs as those of the Berlin cathedral and the Leipsic Thomas church, artistic singing attains a richness of tone and finish of style hardly to be surpassed.

The most wholesome result of these movements has been to bring about a clearer distinction in the minds of churchmen between a proper church style in music and the concert style. Church-music associations (evangelische Kirchengesang-Vereine), analogous to the Catholic St. Cecilia Society, have taken in hand the question of the establishment of church music on a more strict and efficient basis. Such masters as Mendelssohn, Richter, Hauptmann, Kiel, and Grell have produced works of great beauty, and at the same time admirably suited to the ideal requirements of public worship.

In spite of the present more healthful condition of German Evangelical music as compared with the feebleness and indefiniteness of the early part of the nineteenth century, there is little assurance of the restoration of this branch of art to the position which it held in the national life two hundred years ago. In the strict sense writers of the school of Spitta are correct in asserting that a Protestant church music no longer exists. " It must be denied that an independent branch of the tonal art is to be found which has its home only in the Church, which contains life and the capacity for development in itself, and in whose sphere the creative artist seeks his ideals." [1]

On the other hand, a hopeful sign has appeared in recent German musical history in the foundation of the New Bach Society, with headquarters at Leipsic, in 1900. The task assumed by this society, which includes a large number of the most eminent musicians of Germany, is that of making Bach's choral works better known, and especially of reintroducing them into their old place in the worship of the Evangelical churches. The success of such an effort would doubtless be fraught with important consequences, and perhaps inaugurate a new era in the history of German church music.

[1] Spitta, *Zur Musik: Wiederbelebung protestantischer Kirchenmusik auf geschichtlicher Grundlage.*

CHAPTER X

THE MUSICAL SYSTEM OF THE CHURCH OF ENGLAND

THE musical productions that have emanated from the Church of England possess no such independent interest as works of art as those which so richly adorn the Catholic and the German Evangelical systems. With the exception of the naturalized Händel (whose few occasional anthems, Te Deums, and miscellaneous church pieces give him an incidental place in the roll of English ecclesiastical musicians), there is no name to be found in connection with the English cathedral service that compares in lustre with those that give such renown to the religious song of Italy and Germany. Yet in spite of this mediocrity of achievement, the music of the Anglican Church has won an honorable historic position, not only by reason of the creditable average of excellence which it has maintained for three hundred years, but still more through its close identification with those fierce conflicts over dogma, ritual, polity, and the relation of the Church to the individual which have given such a singular interest to English ecclesiastical history. Methods of musical expression have been almost as hotly contested as vital matters of doctrine and authority, and the result has been that the English people look upon their national religious song with a respect such as, perhaps, no other school of church music receives in its own home. The value and purpose of music in worship, and the manner of performance most conducive to edification, have been for centuries the subjects of such serious discussion that the problems propounded by the history of English church music are of perennial interest. The dignity, orderliness, tranquillity, and graciousness in outward form and inward spirit which have come to distinguish the Anglican Establishment are reflected in its anthems and " services," its chants and hymns ; while the simplicity and sturdy, aggressive sincerity of the non-conformist sects may be felt in the accents of their psalmody. The clash of liturgic and non-liturgic opinions, conformity and independence, Anglicanism and Puritanism, may be plainly heard in the church musical history of the sixteenth, seventeenth, and eighteenth centuries, and even to-day the contest has not everywhere been settled by conciliation and fraternal sympathy.

The study of English church music, therefore, is the study of musical forms and practices more than of works of art as such. We are met at the outset by a spectacle not paralleled in other Protestant countries, *viz.*, the cleavage of the reformed Church into two violently hostile divisions ; and we find the struggle for supremacy between Anglicans and Puritans fought out in the sphere of art and ritual as well as on the battlefield and the arena of theological polemic. Consequently we are obliged to trace two distinct lines of development — the ritual music of the Establishment and the psalmody of the dissenting bodies — trying to discover how these contending principles acted upon each other, and what instruction can be drawn from their collision and their final compromise.

The Reformation in England took in many respects a very different course from that upon the continent. In Germany, France, Switzerland, and the Netherlands the revolt against Rome was initiated by men who sprung from the ranks of the people. Notwithstanding the complication of motives which drew princes and commoners, ecclesiastics and laymen, into the rebellion, the movement was primarily religious, first a protest against abuses, next the demand for free privileges in the Gospel, followed by restatements of belief and the establishment of new forms of worship. Political changes followed in the train of the religious revolution, because in most instances there was such close alliance between the secular powers and the papacy that allegiance to the former was not compatible with resistance to the latter.

In England this process was reversed; political separation preceded the religious changes; it was the alliance between the government and the papacy that was first to break. The emancipation from the supremacy of Rome was accomplished at a single stroke by the crown itself, and that not upon moral grounds or doctrinal disagreement, but solely for political advantage. In spite of tokens of spiritual unrest, there was no sign of a disposition on the part of any considerable number of the English people to sever their fealty to the Church of Rome when, in 1534, Henry VIII. issued a royal edict repudiating the papal authority, and a submissive Parliament decreed that "the king, our sovereign lord, his neirs and successors, kings of this realm, shall be taken, accepted, and reputed the only supreme head in earth of the Church of England." The English Church became in a day what it had often shown a desire to become — a national Church, free from the arbitrary authority of an Italian overlordship, the king instead of the pope at its head, with supreme power in all matters of appointment and discipline, possessing even the prerogative of deciding what should be the religious belief and manner of worship in the realm. No doctrinal change was involved in this proceeding ; there was no implied admission of freedom of conscience or religious toleration. The mediæval conception of the necessity of religious unanimity among all the subjects of the state — one single state Church maintained in every precept and ordinance by the power of the throne — was rigorously reasserted. The English Church had simply exchanged one master for another, and had gained a spiritual tyranny to which were attached no conceptions of right drawn from ancestral association or historic tradition.

The immediate occasion for this action on the part of Henry VIII. was, as all know, his exasperation against Clement VII. on account of that pope's refusal to sanction the king's iniquitous scheme of a divorce from his faithful wife Catherine and a marriage with Anne Boleyn. This grievance was doubtless a mere pretext, for a temper so imperious as that of Henry could not permanently brook a divided loyalty in his kingdom. But since Henry took occasion to proclaim anew the fundamental dogmas of the Catholic Church, with the old bloody penalties against heresy, it would not be proper to speak of him as the originator of the Reformation in England. That event properly dates from the reign of his successor, Edward VI.

It was not possible, however, that in breaking the ties of hierarchical authority which had endured for a thousand years the English Church should not undergo further change. England had always been a more or less refractory child of the Roman Church, and more than once the conception of royal prerogative and national right had come into conflict with the pretensions of the papacy, and the latter had not always emerged victorious from the struggle. The old Germanic spirit of liberty and individual determination, always especially strong in England, was certain to assert itself when the great European intellectual awakening of the fourteenth and fifteenth centuries had taken hold of the mass of the people ; and it might have been foreseen after Luther's revolt that England would soon throw herself into the arms of the Reformation. The teachings of Wiclif and the Lollards were still cherished at many English firesides. Humanistic studies had begun to flourish under the auspices of such men as Erasmus, Colet, and More, and humanism, as the natural foe of superstition and obscurantism, was instinctively set against ecclesiastical assumption. Lastly, the trumpet blast of Luther had found an echo in many stout British hearts. The initiative of the crown, however, forestalled events and changed their course, and instead of a general rising of the people, the overthrow of every vestige of Romanism, and the creation of a universal Calvinistic system, the conservatism and moderation of Edward VI. and Elizabeth and their advisers retained so much of external form and ceremony in the interest of dignity, and fixed so firmly the pillars of episcopacy in the interest of stability and order, that the kingdom found itself divided into two parties, and the brief conflict between nationalism and Romanism was succeeded by the long struggle between the Establishment, protected by the throne, and rampant, all-levelling Puritanism.

With the passage of the Act of Supremacy the Catholic and Protestant parties began to align themselves for conflict. Henry VIII. at first showed himself favorable to the Protestants, inclining to the acceptance of the Bible as final authority instead of the decrees and traditions of the Church. After the Catholic rebellion of 1536, however, the king changed his policy, and with the passage of the Six Articles, which decreed the doctrine of transubstantiation, the celibacy of the clergy, the value of private masses, and the necessity of auricular confession, he began a bloody persecution which ended only with his death.

The boy king, Edward VI., who reigned from 1547 to 1553, had been won over to Protestantism by Archbishop Cranmer, and with his accession reforms in doctrine and ritual went on rapidly. Parliament was again subservient, and a modified Lutheranism took possession of the English Church. The people were taught from the English Bible, the Book of Common Prayer took the place of Missal and Breviary; the Mass, compulsory celibacy of the clergy, and worship of images were abolished, and invocation of saints forbidden. We must observe that these changes, like those effected by Henry VIII., were not brought about by popular pressure under the leadership of great tribunes, but were decreed by the rulers of the state, ratified by Parliament under due process of law, and enforced by the crown under sanction of the Act of Supremacy. The revolution was regular, peaceful, and legal, and none of the savage conflicts between Catholics and Protestants which tore Germany, France, and the Netherlands in pieces and drenched their soil with blood, ever occurred in England. Amid such conditions reaction was easy. Under Mary (1553–1558) the old religion and forms were reënacted, and a persecution, memorable for the martyrdoms of Cranmer, Ridley, Latimer, Hooper, and other leaders of the Protestant party, was carried on with ruthless severity, but without weakening the cause of the reformed faith. Elizabeth (1558–1603) had no pronounced religious convictions, but under the stress of European political conditions she became of necessity a protector of the Protestant cause. The reformed service was restored, and from Elizabeth's day the Church of England has rested securely upon the constitutions of Edward VI.

With the purification and restatement of doctrine according to Protestant principles was involved the question of the liturgy. There was no thought on the part of the English reformers of complete separation from the ancient communion and the establishment of a national Church upon an entirely new theory. They held firmly to the conception of historic Christianity; the episcopal succession extending back to the early ages of the Church was not broken, the administration of the sacraments never ceased. The Anglican Church was conceived as the successor of the universal institution which, through her apostasy from the pure doctrine of the apostles, had abrogated her claims upon the allegiance of the faithful. Anglicanism contained in itself a continuation of the tradition delivered to the fathers, with an open Bible, and the emancipation of the reason; it was legitimate heir to what was noblest and purest in Catholicism. This conception is strikingly manifest in the liturgy of the Church of England, which is partly composed of materials furnished by the office-books of the ancient Church, and in the beginning associated with music in no way to be distinguished in style from the Catholic. The prominence given to vestments, and to ceremonies calculated to impress the senses, also points unmistakably to the conservative spirit which forbade that the reform should in any way take on the guise of revolution.

The ritual of the Church of England is contained in a single volume, *viz*., the Book of Common Prayer. It is divided into matins and evensong, the office of Holy Communion, offices of confirmation and ordination, and occasional offices. But little of this liturgy is entirely original; the matins and evensong are compiled from the Catholic Breviary, the Holy Communion with collects, epistles, and gospels from the Missal, occasional offices from the Ritual, and the confirmation and ordination offices from the Pontifical. All these offices, as compared with the Catholic sources, are greatly modified and simplified. A vast amount of legendary and unhistoric matter found in the Breviary has disappeared, litanies to and invocations of the saints and the Virgin

Mary have been omitted. The offices proper to saints' days have disappeared, the seven canonical hours are compressed to two, the space given to selections from Holy Scripture greatly extended, and the English language takes the place of Latin.

In this dependence upon the offices of the mother Church for the ritual of the new worship the English reformers, like Martin Luther, testified to their conviction that they were purifiers and renovators of the ancient faith and ceremony, not violent destroyers, seeking to win the sympathies of their countrymen by deferring to old associations and inherited prejudices, so far as consistent with reason and conscience. Their sense of historic continuity is further shown in the fact that the Breviaries which they consulted were those specially employed from early times in England, particularly the use known as the "Sarum use," drawn up and promulgated about 1085 by Osmund, bishop of Salisbury, and generally adopted in the south of England, and which deviated in certain details from the use of Rome.

Propositions looking to the amendment of the service-books were brought forward before the end of the reign of Henry VIII., and a beginning was made by introducing the reading of small portions of the Scripture in English. The Litany was the first of the prayers to be altered and set in English, which was done by Cranmer, who had before him the old litanies of the English Church, besides the "Consultation" of Hermann, archbishop of Cologne (1543).

With the accession of Edward VI. in 1547 the revolution in worship was thoroughly confirmed, and in 1549 the complete Book of Common Prayer, essentially in its modern form, was issued. A second and modified edition was published in 1552 and ordered to be adopted in all the churches of the kingdom. The old Catholic office-books were called in and destroyed, the images were taken from the houses of worship, the altars removed and replaced by communion tables, the vestments of the clergy were simplified, and the whole conception of the service, as well as its ceremonies, completely transformed. Owing to the accession of Mary in 1553 there was no time for the Prayer Book of 1552 to come into general use. A third edition, somewhat modified, published in 1559, was one of the earliest results of the accession of Elizabeth. Another revision followed in 1604 under James I.; additions and alterations were made under Charles II. in 1661–2. Since that date only very slight changes have been made.

The liturgy of the Church of England is composed, like the Catholic liturgy, of both constant and variable offices, the latter, however, being in a small minority. It is notable for the large space given to reading from Holy Scripture, the entire Psalter being read through every month, the New Testament three times a year, and the Old Testament once a year. It includes a large variety of prayers, special psalms to be sung, certain psalm-like hymns called canticles, the hymns comprising the chief constant choral members of the Latin Mass, *viz.*, Kyrie, Gloria, Credo, and Sanctus — the Te Deum, the ten commandments, a litany, besides short sentences and responses known as versicles. In addition to the regular morning and evening worship there are special series of offices for Holy Communion and for particular occasions, such as ordinations, confirmations, the burial service, etc.

Although there is but one ritual common to all the congregations of the established Church, one form of prayer and praise which ascends from cathedral, chapel, and parish church alike, this service differs in respect to the manner of rendering. The Anglican Church retained the conception of the Catholic that the service is a musical service, that the prayers, as well as the psalms, canticles, and hymns, are properly to be given not in the manner of ordinary speech, but in musical tone. It was soon found, however, that a full musical service, designed for the more conservative and wealthy establishments, was not practicable in small country parishes, and so in process of time three modes of performing the service were authorized, *viz.*, the choral or cathedral mode, the parochial, and the mixed.

The choral service is that used in the cathedrals, royal and college chapels, and certain parish churches whose resources permit the adoption of the same practice. In this mode everything except the lessons is rendered in musical tone, from the monotoned prayers of the priest to the figured chorus music of "service" and anthem. The essential parts of the choral service, as classified by Dr. Jebb,[1] are as follows:

1. The chanting by the minister of the sentences, exhortations, prayers, and collects throughout the lit-

[1] Jebb, *Choral Service of the United Church of England and Ireland.*

urgy in a monotone, slightly varied by occasional modulations.

2. The alternate chant of the versicles and responses by minister and choir.

3. The alternate chant, by the two divisions of the choir, of the daily psalms and of such as occur in the various offices of the Church.

4. The singing of all the canticles and hymns, in the morning and evening service, either to an alternated chant or to songs of a more intricate style, resembling anthems in their construction, and which are technically styled "services."

5. The singing of the anthem after the third collect in both morning and evening prayer.

6. The alternate chanting of the litany by the minister and choir.

7. The singing of the responses after the commandments in the Communion service.

8. The singing of the creed, Gloria in excelsis, and Sanctus in the Communion service anthem-wise. [The Sanctus has in recent years been superseded by a short anthem or hymn.]

9. The chanting or singing of those parts in the occasional offices which are rubrically permitted to be sung.

In this manner of worship the Church of England conforms to the general usage of liturgic churches throughout the world in ancient and modern times, by implication honoring that conception of the intimate union of word and tone in formal authorized worship which has been expounded in the chapters on the

Catholic music and ritual. Since services are held on week days as well as on Sundays in the cathedrals, and since there are two full choral services, each involving an almost unbroken current of song from clergy and choir, this usage involves a large and thoroughly trained establishment, which is made possible by the endowments of the English cathedrals.

The parochial service is that used in the smaller churches where it is not possible to maintain an endowed choir. "According to this mode the accessories of divine service necessary towards its due performance are but few and simple." "As to the ministers, the stated requirements of each parochial church usually contemplate but one, the assistant clergy and members of choirs being rarely objects of permanent endowment." "As to the mode of performing divine service, the strict parochial mode consists in reciting all parts of the liturgy in the speaking tone of the voice unaccompanied by music. According to this mode no chant, or canticle, or anthem, properly so called, is employed; but metrical versions of the psalms are sung at certain intervals between the various offices." (Jebb.)

This mode is not older than 1549, for until the Reformation the Plain Chant was used in parish churches. The singing of metrical psalms dates from the reign of Elizabeth.

The mixed mode is less simple than the parochial; parts of the service are sung by a choir, but the prayers, creeds, litany, and responses are recited in speaking voice. It may be said, however, that the parochial and

335

the mixed modes are optional and permitted as matters of convenience. There is no law that forbids any congregation to adopt any portion or even the whole of the choral mode. In these variations, to which we find nothing similar in the Catholic Church, may be seen the readiness of the fathers of the Anglican Church to compromise with Puritan tendencies and guard against those reactions which, as later history shows, are constantly urging sections of the English Church back to extreme ritualistic practices.

The music of the Anglican Church follows the three divisions into which church music in general may be separated, *viz.*, the chant, the figured music of the choir, and the congregational hymn.

The history of the Anglican chant may also be taken to symbolize the submerging of the ancient priestly idea in the representative conception of the clerical office, for the chant has proved itself a very flexible form of expression, both in structure and usage, endeavoring to connect itself sometimes with the anthem-like choir song and again with the congregational hymn. In the beginning, however, the method of chanting exactly followed the Catholic form. Two kinds of chant were employed, — the simple unaccompanied Plain Song of the minister, which is almost monotone; and the accompanied chant, more melodious and florid, employed in the singing of the psalms, canticles, litany, etc., by the choir or by the minister and choir.

The substitution of English for Latin and the sweeping modification of the liturgy did not in the least alter the system and principle of musical rendering which had existed in the Catholic Church. The litany, the oldest portion of the Book of Common Prayer, compiled by Cranmer and published in 1544, was set for singing note for note from the ancient Plain Song. In 1550 a musical setting was given to all parts of the Prayer Book by John Marbecke, a well-known musician of that period. He, like Cranmer, adapted portions of the old Gregorian chant, using only the plainer forms. In Marbecke's book we find the simplest style, consisting of monotone, employed for the prayers and the Apostles' Creed, a larger use of modulation in the recitation of the psalms, and a still more song-like manner in the canticles and those portions, such as the Kyrie and Gloria, taken from the mass. To how great an extent this music of Marbecke was employed in the Anglican Church in the sixteenth century is not certainly known. Certain parts of it gave way to the growing fondness for harmonized and figured music in all parts of the service, but so far as Plain Chant has been retained in the cathedral service the setting of Marbecke has established the essential form down to the present day.[1]

The most marked distinction between the choral mode of performing the service, and those divergent usages which have often been conceived as a protest against it, consists in the practice of singing or monotoning the prayers by the minister. The notion of impersonality which underlies the liturgic conception of worship everywhere, the merging of the individual

---

[1] An edition of Marbecke's Book of Common Prayer with Notes edited by Rimbault, was published by Novello, London, in 1845.

in an abstract, idealized, comprehensive entity — the Church — is symbolized in this custom. Notwithstanding the fact that the large majority of congregational hymns are really prayers, and that in this case the offering of prayer in metrical form and in musical strains has always been admitted by all ranks of Christians as perfectly appropriate, yet there has always seemed to a large number of English Protestants something artificial and even irreverent in the delivery of prayer in an unchanging musical note, in which expression is lost in the abandonment of the natural inflections of speech. Here is probably the cause of the repugnant impression, — not because the utterance is musical in tone, but because it is monotonous and unexpressive.

It is of interest to note the reasons for this practice as given by representative English churchmen, since the motive for the usage touches the very spirit and significance of a ritualistic form of worship.

Dr. Bisse, in his *Rationale on Cathedral Worship*, justifies the practice on the ground (1) of necessity, since the great size of the cathedral churches obliges the minister to use a kind of tone that can be heard throughout the building; (2) of uniformity, in order that the voices of the congregation may not jostle and confuse each other; and (3) of the advantage in preventing imperfections and inequalities of pronunciation on the part of both minister and people. Other reasons which are more mystical, and probably on that account still more cogent to the mind of the ritualist, are also given by this writer. "It is emblematic," he says, "of the delight which Christians have in the law of God. It bespeaks the cheerfulness of our Christian profes- sion, as contrasted with that of the Gentiles. It gives to divine worship a greater dignity by separating it more from all actions and interlocutions that are com- mon and familiar. It is more efficacious to awaken the attention, to stir up the affections, and to edify the understanding than plain reading." And Dr. Jebb puts the case still more definitely when he says: "In the Church of England the lessons are not chanted,· but read. The instinctive good taste of the revisers of the liturgy taught them that the lessons, being nar- ratives, orations, records of appeals to men, or writings of an epistolary character, require that method of reading which should be, within due bounds, imitative. But with the prayers the case is far different. These are uttered by the minister of God, not as an indi- vidual, but as the instrument and channel of petitions which are of perpetual obligation, supplications for all those gifts of God's grace which are needful for all mankind while this frame of things shall last. The prayers are not, like the psalms and canticles, the ex- pression, the imitation, or the record of the hopes and fears, of the varying sentiments, of the impassioned thanksgivings, of the meditative musings of inspired individuals, or of holy companies of men or angels; they are the unchangeable voice of the Church of God, seeking through one eternal Redeemer gifts that shall be for everlasting. And hence the uniformity of tone in which she seeks them is significant of the unity of spirit which teaches the Church universal so to pray, of the unity of means by which her prayers are made available, of the perfect unity with God her Father which shall be her destiny in the world to come."

The word "chant" as used in the English Church (to be in strictness distinguished from the priestly mono-toning) signifies the short melodies which are sung to the psalms and canticles. The origin of the Anglican chant system is to be found in the ancient Gregorian chant, of which it is only a slight modification. It is a sort of musically delivered speech, the punctuation and rate of movement being theoretically the same as in spoken discourse. Of all the forms of religious music the chant is least susceptible to change and progress, and the modern Anglican chant bears the plainest marks of its mediæval origin. The modifications which distinguish the new from the old may easily be seen upon comparing a modern English chant-book with an office-book of the Catholic Church. In place of the rhythmic freedom of the Gregorian, with its frequent florid passages upon a single syllable, we find in the Anglican a much greater simplicity and strictness, and also, it must be admitted, a much greater melodic monotony and dryness. The English chant is almost entirely syllabic, even two notes to a syllable are rare, while there is nothing remotely corresponding to the melismas of the Catholic liturgic song. The bar lines, unknown in the Roman chant, give the English form much greater steadiness of movement. The intonation of the Gregorian chant has been dropped, the remaining four divisions — recitation, mediation, second recitation, and ending — retained. The Anglican chant is of two kinds, single and double. A single chant comprises one verse of a psalm; it consists of two melodic strains, the first including three measures, the second four. A double chant is twice the length of a single chant, and includes two verses of a psalm, the first ending being an incomplete cadence. The double chant is an English invention; it is unknown in the Gregorian system. The objections to it are obvious, since the two verses of a psalm which may be comprised in the chant often differ in sentiment.

The manner of fitting the words to the notes of the chant is called "pointing." There is no authoritative method of pointing in the Church of England, and there is great disagreement and controversy on the subject in the large number of chant-books that are used in England and America. In the cathedral service the chants are sung antiphonally, the two divisions of the chorus answering each other from opposite sides of the choir.

There are large numbers of so-called chants which are more properly to be called hymns or anthems in chant style, such as the melodies sometimes sung to the Te Deum and the Gloria in excelsis. These compositions may consist of any number of divisions, each comprising the three-measure and four-measure members found in the single chant.

The modern Anglican chant form is not so old as commonly supposed. The ancient Gregorian chants for the psalms and canticles were in universal use as late as the middle of the seventeenth century. The modern chant was of course a gradual development, and was the inevitable result of the harmonization of the old chant melodies according to the new system with its corresponding balancing points of tonic and dominant. A few of the Anglican chants sung at the present day go back to the time of the Restoration, that is, soon after 1660; the larger number date from the eighteenth and nineteenth centuries. The modern chant, however, has never been able entirely to supplant the ancient Plain Song melody. The "Gregorian" movement in the Church of England, one of the results of the ritualistic reaction inaugurated by the Oxford Tractarian agitation, although bitterly opposed both on musical grounds and perhaps still more through alarm over the tendencies which it symbolizes, has apparently become firmly established; and even in quarters where there is little sympathy with the ritualistic movement, musical and ecclesiastical conservatism unites with a natural reverence for the historic past to preserve in constant use the venerated relics of early days. Sir John Stainer voiced the sentiment of many leading English musical churchmen when he said: "I feel very strongly that the beautiful Plain Song versicles, responses, inflections, and prefaces to our prayers and liturgy should not be lightly thrown aside. These simple and grand specimens of Plain Song, so suited to their purpose, so reverent in their subdued emotion, appeal to us for their protection. The Plain Song of the prefaces of our liturgy as sung now in St. Paul's cathedral are note for note the same that rang at least eight hundred years ago through the vaulted roof of that ancient cathedral which crowned the summit of the fortified hill of old Salisbury. Not a stone remains of wall or shrine, but the old Sarum office-books have survived, from which we can draw ancient hymns and Plain Song as from a pure fount. Those devout monks recorded all their beautiful offices and the music of these offices, because they were even then venerable and venerated. Shall we throw them into the fire to make room for neat and appropriate excogitations, fresh from the blotting-pad of Mr. A, or Dr. B, or the Reverend C, or Miss D?"

It must be acknowledged, however, that the Gregorian chant melodies undergo decided modification in spirit and impression when set to English words. In their pure state their strains are thoroughly conformed to the structure and flow of the Latin texts from which they grew. There is something besides tradition and association that makes them appear somewhat forced and ill at ease when wedded to a modern language. As Curwen says: "In its true form the Gregorian chant has no bars or measures; the time and the accent are verbal, not musical. Each note of the mediation or the ending is emphatic or non-emphatic, according to the word or syllable to which it happens to be sung. The endings which follow the recitation do not fall into musical measures, but are as unrhythmical as the reciting tone itself. Modern music, and the instinctive observance of rhythm which is an essential part of it, have modified the old chant and given it accent and time. The reason why the attempt to adapt the Gregorian tones to the English language has resulted in their modification is not far to seek. The non-accented sys·

tem suits Latin and French, but not English. Aside
from the instinct for time, and the desire to make a
'tune' of the chant, which is a part of human nature,
it is a feature of the English language that in speaking
we pass from accent to accent and elide the intervening
syllables. The first attempts to adapt the Gregorian
tones to English use proceeded strictly upon the plan
of one syllable to a note. Of however many notes the
mediation or cadence of the chant consisted, that number of syllables was marked off from the end of each
half-verse, and the recitation ended when they were
reached." [1] The attempt to sing in this fashion,
Curwen goes on to show, resulted in the greatest
violence to English pronunciation. In order to avoid
this, slurs, which are no part of the Gregorian system
proper, were employed to bring the accented syllables
upon the first of the measure.

Doubtless the fundamental and certainly praise-
worthy motive of those who strongly desire to reintro-
duce the Gregorian melodies into the Anglican service
is to establish once for all a body of liturgic tones
which are pure, noble, and eminently fitting in character,
endowed at the same time with venerable ecclesiastical
associations which shall become fixed and authoritative,
and thus an insurmountable barrier against the intrusion of the ephemeral novelties of "the Reverend C and
Miss D." Every intelligent student of religious art
may well say Amen to such a desire. As the case now
stands there is no law or custom that prevents any
minister or cantor from introducing into the service

[1] Curwen, *Studies in Worship Music.*

any chant-tune which he chooses to invent or adopt. Neither is there any authority that has the right to select any system or body of liturgic song and compel its introduction. The Gregorian movement is an attempt to remedy this palpable defect in the Anglican musical system. It is evident that this particular solution of the difficulty can never generally prevail. Any effort, however, which tends to restrict the number of chants in use, and establish once for all a store of liturgic melodies which is preëminently worthy of the historic associations and the conservative aims cf the Anglican Church, should receive the hearty support of English musicians and churchmen.

If Marbecke's unison chants were intended as a complete scheme for the musical service, they were at any rate quickly swallowed up by the universal demand for harmonized music, and the choral service of the Church of England very soon settled into the twofold classification which now prevails, *viz.*, the harmonized chant and the more elaborate figured setting of "service" and anthem. The former dates from 1560, when John Day's psalter was published, containing three and four-part settings of old Plain Song melodies, contributed by Tallis, Shepherd, and other prominent musicians of the time. From the very outset of the adoption of the vernacular in all parts of the service, that is to say from the reign of Edward VI., certain selected psalms and canticles, technically known as "services," were sung anthem-wise in the developed choral style of the highest musical science of the day. The components of the "service" are to be distinguished from the daily psalms which are always sung in antiphonal chant form, and may be said to correspond to the choral unvarying portions of the Catholic Mass. The "service" in its fullest form includes the Venite (Ps. xcv.), Te Deum, Benedicite (Song of the Three Children, from the Greek continuation of the book of Daniel), Benedictus (Song of Zacharias), Jubilate (Ps. c.), Kyrie eleison, Nicene Creed, Sanctus, Gloria in excelsis, Magnificat (Song of Mary), Cantate Domino (Ps. xcviii.), Nunc dimittis (Song of Simeon), and the Deus Misereatur (Ps. lxvii). Of these the Venite, Benedicite, and the Sanctus have in recent times fallen out. These psalms and canticles are divided between the morning and evening worship, and not all of them are obligatory.

The "service," in respect to musical style, has moved step by step with the anthem, from the strict contrapuntal style of the sixteenth century, to that of the present with all its splendor of harmony and orchestral color. It has engaged the constant attention of the multitude of English church composers, and it has more than rivalled the anthem in the zealous regard of the most eminent musicians, from the time of Tallis and Gibbons to the present day.

The anthem, although an almost exact parallel to the "service" in musical construction, stands apart, liturgically, from the rest of the service in the Church of England, in that while all the other portions are laid down in the Book of Common Prayer, the words of the anthem are not prescribed. The Prayer Book merely says after the third collect, " In quires and places where they sing here followeth the anthem." What the anthem shall be at any particular service is left to the determination of the choir master, but it is commonly understood, and in some dioceses is so decreed, that the words of the anthem shall be taken from the Scripture or the Book of Common Prayer. This precept, how· ever, is frequently transgressed, and many anthems have been written to words of metrical hymns. The restriction of the anthem texts to selections from the Bible or the liturgy is designed to exclude words that are unfamiliar to the people or unauthorized by ecclesiastical authority. Even with these limitations the freedom of choice on the part of the musical director serves to withdraw the anthem from that vital organic connection with the liturgy held by the " service," and it is not infrequently omitted from the daily office altogether. The object of the fathers of the Church of England in admitting so exceptional a musical composition into the service was undoubtedly to give the worship more variety, and to relieve the fatigue that would otherwise result from a long unbroken series of prayers.

The anthem, although the legitimate successor of the Latin motet, has taken in England a special and peculiar form. According to its derivation (from ant-hymn, responsive or alternate song) the word anthem was at first synonymous with antiphony. The modern form, succeeding the ancient choral motet, dates from about the time of Henry Purcell (1658–1695). The style was confirmed by Händel, who in his celebrated Chandos anthems first brought the English anthem into European recognition. The anthem in its present shape is a sort of mixture of the ancient motet and the German cantata.

From the motet it derives its broad and artistically constructed choruses, while the influence of the cantata is
seen in its solos and instrumental accompaniment. As
the modern anthem is free and ornate, giving practically
unlimited scope for musical invention, it has been cultivated with peculiar ardor by the English church composers, and the number of anthems of varying degrees
of merit or demerit which have been produced in England would baffle the wildest estimate. This style of
music has been largely adopted in the churches of
America, and American composers have imitated it,
often with brilliant success.

The form of anthem in which the entire body of
singers is employed from beginning to end is technically known as the " full " anthem. In another form,
called the " verse " anthem, portions are sung by selected voices. A " solo " anthem contains passages for
a single voice.

The anthem of the Church of England has been more
or less affected by the currents of secular music, but to
a much slighter extent than the Catholic mass. The
opera has never taken the commanding position in England which it has held in the Catholic countries, and
only in rare cases have the English church composers,
at any rate since the time of Händel, felt their allegiance divided between the claims of religion and the
attractions of the stage. In periods of religious depres-
sion or social frivolity the church anthem has sometimes become weak and shallow, but the ancient austere
traditions have never been quite abrogated. The natural conservatism of the English people, especially in

matters of churchly usage, and their tenacious grasp upon the proper distinction between religious and profane art, while acting to the benefit of the anthem and "service" on the side of dignity and appropriateness in style, have had a correspondingly unfavorable influence so far as progress and sheer musical quality are concerned. One who reads through large numbers of English church compositions cannot fail to be impressed by their marked similarity in style and the rarity of features that indicate any striking originality. This monotony and predominance of conventional commonplace must be largely attributed, of course, to the absence of real creative force in English music; but it is also true that even if such creative genius existed, it would hardly feel free to take liberties with those strict canons of taste which have become embedded in the unwritten laws of Anglican musical procedure. In spite of these limitations English church music does not wholly deserve the obloquy that has been cast upon it by certain impatient critics. That it has not rivalled the Catholic mass, nor adopted the methods that have transformed secular music in the modern era is not altogether to its discredit. Leaving out the wonderful productions of Sebastian Bach (which, by the way, are no longer heard in church service in Germany), the music of the Church of England is amply worthy of comparison with that of the German Evangelical Church; and in abundance, musical value, and conformity to the ideals which have always governed public worship in its noblest estate, it is entitled to be ranked as one of the four great historic schools of Christian worship music.

349

England had not been lacking in eminent composers for the Church before the Reformation, but their work was in the style which then prevailed all over Europe. Some of these writers could hold their own with the Netherlanders in point of learning. England held an independent position during " the age of the Netherlanders " in that the official musical posts in the schools and chapels were held by native Englishmen, and not, as was so largely the case on the continent, by men of Northern France and Flanders or their pupils. This fact speaks much for the inherent force of English music, but the conditions of musical culture at that time did not encourage any originality of style or new efforts after expression.

The continental development of the polyphonic school to its perfection in the sixteenth century was paralleled in England; and since the English Reformation was contemporary with this musical apogee, the newly founded national Church possessed in such men as Tallis, Byrd, Tye, Gibbons, and others only less conspicuous, a group of composers not unworthy to stand beside Palestrina and Lassus. It is indeed good fortune for the Church of England that its musical traditions have been founded by such men. Thomas Tallis, the most eminent of the circle, who died in 1585, devoted his talents almost entirely to the Church. In science he was not inferior to his continental compeers, and his music is pre-eminently stately and solid. Besides the large number of motets, "services," etc., which he contributed to the Church, he is now best remembered by the harmonies added by him to the Plain Song of the old régime.

Tallis must therefore be regarded as the chief of the founders of the English harmonized chant. His tunes arranged for Day's psalter give him an honorable place also in the history of English psalmody.

Notwithstanding the revolutions in the authorized ceremony of the Church of England during the stormy Reformation period, from the revised constitutions of Henry VIII. and Edward VI. to the restored Catholicism of Mary, and back to Protestantism again under Elizabeth, the salaried musicians of the Church retained their places while their very seats seemed often to rock beneath them, writing alternately for the Catholic and Protestant services with equal facility, and with equal satisfaction to themselves and their patrons. It was a time when no one could tell at any moment to what doctrine or discipline he might be commanded to subscribe, and many held themselves ready loyally to accept the faith of the sovereign as their own. Such were the ideas of the age that the claims of uniformity could honestly be held as paramount to those of individual judgment. Only those who combined advanced thinking with fearless independence of character were able to free themselves from the prevailing sophistry on this matter of conformity *vs.* freedom. Even a large number of the clergy took the attitude of compliance to authority, and it is often a matter of wonder to readers of the history of this period to see how comparatively few changes were made in the incumbencies of ecclesiastical livings in the shifting triumphs of the hostile confessions. If this were the case with the clergy it is not surprising that the church musicians should have been still more complaisant. The style of music performed in the new worship, we must remember, hardly differed in any respect from that in use under the old system. The organists and choir masters were not called upon to mingle in theological controversies, and they had probably learned discretion from the experience of John Marbecke, who came near to being burned at the stake for his sympathy with Calvinism. As in Germany, there was no necessary conflict between the musical practices of Catholics and Protestants. The real animosity on the point of liturgies and music was not between Anglicans and Catholics, but between Anglicans and Puritans.

The old polyphonic school came to an end with Orlando Gibbons in 1625. No conspicuous name appears in the annals of English church music until we meet that of Henry Purcell, who was born in 1658 and died in 1695. We have made a long leap from the Elizabethan period, for the first half of the seventeenth century was a time of utter barrenness in the neglected fields of art. The distracted state of the kingdom during the reign of Charles I., the Great Rebellion, and the ascendency of the Puritans under Cromwell made progress in the arts impossible, and at one time their very existence seemed threatened. A more hopeful era began with the restoration of the Stuarts in 1660. Charles II. had spent some years in France after the ruin of his father's cause, and upon his triumphant return he encouraged those light French styles in art and literature which were so congenial to his character. He was a devotee of music after his fashion; he warmly encouraged it in the Royal Chapel, and a number of skilful musicians came from the boy choirs of this establishment.

The earliest anthems of the Anglican Church were, like the Catholic motet, unaccompanied. The use of the organ and orchestral instruments followed soon after the middle of the seventeenth century. No such school of organ playing arose in England as that which gave such glory to Germany in the same period. The organ remained simply a support to the voices, and attained no distinction as a solo instrument. Even in Händel's day and long after, few organs in England had a complete pedal board; many had none at all. The English anthem has always thrown greater proportionate weight upon the vocal element as compared with the Catholic mass and the German cantata. In the Restoration period the orchestra came prominently forward in the church worship, and not only were elaborate accompaniments employed for the anthem, but performances of orchestral instruments were given at certain places in the service. King Charles II., who, to use the words of Dr. Tudway, was " a brisk and airy prince," did not find the severe solemnity of the *a capella* style of Tallis and Gibbons at all to his liking. Under the patronage of "the merry monarch," the brilliant style, then in fashion on the continent, flourished apace. Henry Purcell, the most gifted of this school, probably the most highly endowed musical genius that has ever sprung from English soil, was a man of his time, preëminent likewise in opera, and much of his church music betrays the influence of the gay atmosphere which he breathed. But his profound musicianship prevented him from degrading

23   353

his art to the level of the prevailing taste of the royal court, and much of his religious music is reckoned even at the present day among the choicest treasures of English art. As a chorus writer he is one of the first of the moderns, and one who would trace Händel's oratorio style to its sources must take large account of the church works of Henry Purcell.

With the opening of the eighteenth century the characteristics of the English anthem of the present day were virtually fixed. The full, the verse, and the solo anthem were all in use, and the accompanied style had once for all taken the place of the *a capella*. During the eighteenth and early part of the nineteenth centuries English choir music offers nothing especially noteworthy, unless we except the Te Deums and so-called anthems of Händel, whose style is, however, that of the oratorio rather than church music in the proper sense.

The works of Hayes, Attwood, Boyce, Greene, Battishill, Crotch, and others belonging to the period between the middle of the eighteenth and the middle of the nineteenth centuries are solid and respectable, but as a rule dry and perfunctory. A new era began with the passing of the first third of the nineteenth century, when a higher inspiration seized English church music. The work of the English cathedral school of the second half of the nineteenth century is highly honorable to the English Church and people. A vast amount of it is certainly the barrenest and most unpromising of routine manufacture, for every incumbent of an organist's post throughout the kingdom, however obscure, feels that his dignity requires him to contribute his quota to the enormously swollen accumulation of anthems and " services." But in this numerous company we find the names of such men as Goss, Bennett, Hopkins, Monk, Barnby, Sullivan, Smart, Tours, Stainer, Garrett, Martin, Bridge, Stanford, Mackenzie, and others not less worthy, who have endowed the choral service with richer color and more varied and appealing expression. This brilliant advance may be connected with the revival of spirituality and zeal in the English Church which early in the nineteenth century succeeded to the drowsy indifference of the eighteenth ; but we must not push such coincidences too far. The church musician must always draw some of his inspiration from within the institution which he serves, but we have seen that while the religious folksong is stimulated only by deep and widespread enthusiasm, the artistic music of the Church is dependent rather upon the condition of music at large. The later progress in English church music is identified with the forward movement in all European music which began with the symphonies of Beethoven, the operas of Weber and the French masters, and the songs of Schubert, and which was continued in Berlioz, Wagner, Schumann, Mendelssohn, Chopin, and the still more recent national schools. England has shared this uplift of taste and creative activity ; her composers are also men of the new time. English cathedral music enters the world-current which sets towards a more intense and personal expression. The austere traditions of the Anglican Church restrain efforts after the brilliant and emotional within distinctly marked boundaries. Its music can never, as the Catholic mass has often done, relapse into the tawdry and sensational; but the English church composers have recognized that the Church and its art exist for the people, and that the changing standards of beauty as they arise in the popular mind must be considered, while at the same time the serene and elevated tone which makes church music truly churchly must be reverently preserved. This, as I understand it, is the motive, more or less conscious, which actuates the Church of England composers, organists, and directors of the present day. They have not yet succeeded in bringing forth works of decided genius, but they have certainly laid a foundation so broad, and so compounded of durable elements, that if the English race is capable of producing a master of the first rank in religious music he will not be compelled to take any radical departure, nor to create the taste by which he will be appreciated.

English church music has never been in a more satisfactory condition than it is to-day. There is no other country in which religious music is so highly honored, so much the basis of the musical life of the people. The organists and choir masters connected with the cathedrals and the university and royal chapels are men whose character and intellectual attainments would make them ornaments to any walk of life. The deep-rooted religious reverence which enters into the substance of English society, the admiration for intellect and honesty, the healthful conservatism, the courtliness of speech, the solidity of culture which comes from inherited wealth largely devoted to learning and the embellishment of public and private life, — have all permeated ecclesiastical art and ceremony, and have imparted to them an ideal dignity which is as free from superstition as it is from vulgarity. The music of the Church of England, like all church music, must be considered in connection with its history and its liturgic attachments. It is inseparably associated with a ritual of singular stateliness and beauty, and with an architecture in cathedral and chapel in which the recollections of a heroic and fading past unite with a grandeur of structure and beauty of detail to weave an overmastering spell upon the mind. Church music, I must constantly repeat, is never intended to produce its impression alone. Before we ever allow ourselves to call any phase of it dry and uninteresting let us hear it actually or in imagination amid its native surroundings. As we mentally connect the Gregorian chant and the Italian choral music of the sixteenth century with all the impressive framework of their ritual, hearing within them the echoes of the prayers of fifteen hundred years; as the music of Bach and his contemporaries stands forth in only moderate relief from the background of a Protestantism in which scholasticism and mysticism are strangely blended, — so the Anglican chant and anthem are venerable with the associations of three centuries of conflict and holy endeavor. Complex and solemnizing are the suggestions which strike across the mind of the student of church history as he hears in a venerable English cathedral the lofty strains which might elsewhere seem commonplace, but which in their ancestral home are felt to be the natural speech of an institution which has found in such structures its **fitting** habitation.

CHAPTER XI

THE revised liturgy and musical service of the Church of England had not been long in operation when they encountered adversaries far more bitter and formidable than the Catholics. The Puritans, who strove to effect a radical overturning in ecclesiastical affairs, to reduce worship to a prosaic simplicity, and also to set up a more democratic form of church government, violently assailed the established Church as half papist. The contest between the antagonistic principles, Ritualism *vs.* Puritanism, Anglicanism *vs.* Presbyterianism, broke out under Elizabeth, but was repressed by her strong hand only to increase under the weaker James I., and to culminate with the overthrow of Charles I. and the temporary triumph of Puritanism.

The antipathy of the Puritan party to everything formal, ceremonial, and artistic in worship was powerfully promoted, if not originally instigated by John Calvin, the chief fountain-head of the Puritan doctrine and polity. The extraordinary personal ascendency of Calvin was shown not only in the adoption of his theological system by so large a section of the Protestant world, but also in the fact that his opinions concerning the ideal and method of public worship were treated with almost equal reverence, and in many localities have held sway down to the present time. Conscious, perhaps to excess, of certain harmful tendencies in ritualism, he proclaimed that everything formal and artistic in worship was an offence to God; he clung to this belief with characteristic tenacity and enforced it upon all the congregations under his rule. Instruments of music and trained choirs were to him abomination, and the only musical observance permitted in the sanctuary was the singing by the congregation of metrical translations of the psalms.

The Geneva psalter had a very singular origin. In 1538 Clement Marot, a notable poet at the court of Francis I. of France, began for his amusement to make translations of the psalms into French verse, and had them set to popular tunes. Marot was not exactly in the odor of sanctity. The popularization of the Hebrew lyrics was a somewhat remarkable whim on the part of a writer in whose poetry is reflected the levity of his time much more than its virtues. As Van Laun says, he was " at once a pedant and a vagabond, a scholar and a merry-andrew. He translated the penitential psalms and Ovid's Metamorphoses; he wrote the praises of St. Christina and sang the triumphs of Cupid." His psalms attained extraordinary favor at the dissolute court. Each of the royal family and the courtiers chose a psalm. Prince Henry, who was fond of hunting, selected " Like as the hart desireth the water brooks." The king's mistress, Diana of Poitiers, chose the 130th psalm, " Out of the depths have I cried to thee, O Lord." This fashion was, however, short-lived, for the theological doctors of the Sorbonne, those keen heresy hunters, became suspicious that there was some mysterious connection between Marot's psalms and the detestable Protestant doctrines, and in 1543 the unfortunate poet fled for safety to Calvin's religious commonwealth at Geneva. Calvin had already the year before adopted thirty-five of Marot's psalms for the use of his congregation. Marot, after his arrival at Geneva, translated twenty more, which were characteristically dedicated to the ladies of France. Marot died in 1544, and the task of translating the remaining psalms was committed by Calvin to Theodore de Beza (or Bèze), a man of a different stamp from Marot, who had become a convert to the reformed doctrines and had been appointed professor of Greek in the new university at Lusanne. In the year 1552 Beza's work was finished, and the Geneva psalter, now complete, was set to old French tunes which were taken, like many of the German chorals, from popular secular songs. The attribution of certain of these melodies, adopted into modern hymn-books, to Guillaume Franc and Louis Bourgeois is entirely unauthorized. The most celebrated of these anonymous tunes is the doxology in long metre, known in England and America as the Old Hundredth, although it is set in the Marot-Beza psalter not to the 100th psalm but to the 134th. These psalms were at first sung in unison, unharmonized, but between 1562 and 1565 the melodies were set in four-part counterpoint, the melody in the tenor according to the custom of the day. This was the work of Claude Goudimel, a Netherlander, one of the foremost musicians of his time, who, coming under suspicion of sympathy with the Huguenot party, perished in the massacre on St. Bartholomew's night in 1572.

A visitor to Geneva in 1557 wrote as follows: " A most interesting sight is offered in the city on the week days, when the hour for the sermon approaches. As soon as the first sound of the bell is heard all shops are closed, all conversation ceases, all business is broken off, and from all sides the people hasten into the nearest meeting-house. There each one draws from his pocket a small book which contains the psalms with notes, and out of full hearts, in the native speech, the congregation sings before and after the sermon. Everyone testifies to me how great consolation and edification is derived from this custom."

Such was the origin of the Calvinistic psalmody, which holds so prominent a place in the history of religious culture, not from any artistic value in its products, but as the chosen and exclusive form of praise employed for the greater part of two centuries by the Reformed Churches of Switzerland, France, and the Netherlands, and the Puritan congregations of England, Scotland, and America. On the poetic side it sufficed for Calvin, for he said that the psalms are the anatomy of the human heart, a mirror in which every pious mood of the soul is reflected.

It is a somewhat singular anomaly that the large liberty given to the Lutheran Christians to express their religious convictions and impulses in hymns of their own spontaneous production or choosing was denied to the followers of Calvin. Our magnificent heritage of English hymns was not founded amid the Reformation struggles, and thus we have no lyrics freighted with the priceless historic associations which consecrate in the mind of a German the songs of a Luther and a Gerhardt. Efficacious as the Calvinistic psalmody has been in many respects, the repression of a free poetic impulse in the Protestant Churches of Great Britain and America for so long a period undoubtedly tended to narrow the religious sympathies, and must be given a certain share of responsibility for the hardness of temper fostered by the Calvinistic system. The reason given for the prohibition, viz., that only "inspired" words should be used in the service of praise, betrayed a strange obtuseness to the most urgent demands of the Christian heart in forbidding the very mention of Christ and the Gospel message in the song of his Church. In spite of this almost unaccountable self-denial, if such it was, we may, in the light of subsequent history, ascribe an appropriateness to the metrical versions of the psalms of which even Calvin could hardly have been aware. It was given to Calvinism to furnish a militia which, actuated by a different principle than the Lutheran repugnance to physical resistance, could meet political Catholicism in the open field and maintain its rights amid the shock of arms. In this fleshly warfare it doubtless drew much of its martial courage from those psalms which were ascribed to a bard who was himself a military chieftain and an avenger of blood upon his enemies.

The unemotional unison tunes to which these rhymed psalms were set also satisfied the stern demands of those rigid zealots, who looked upon every appeal to the æsthetic sensibility in worship as an enticement to compromise with popery. Before condemning such a position as this we should take into account the natural effect upon a conscientious and high-spirited people of the fierce persecution to which they were subjected, and the hatred which they would inevitably feel toward everything associated with what was to them corruption and tyranny.

We must, therefore, recognize certain conditions of the time working in alliance with the authority of Calvin to bring into vogue a conception and method of public worship absolutely in contradiction to the almost universal usage of mankind, and nullifying the general conviction, we might almost say the instinct, in favor of the employment in devotion of those artistic agencies by which the religious emotion is ordinarily so strongly moved. For the first time in the history of the Christian Church, at any rate for the first time upon a conspicuous or extensive scale, we find a party of religionists abjuring on conscientious grounds all employment of art in the sanctuary. Beginning in an inevitable and salutary reaction against the excessive development of the sensuous and formal, the hostility to everything that may excite the spirit to a spontaneous joy in beautiful shape and color and sound was exalted into a universally binding principle. With no reverence for the conception of historic development and Christian tradition, the supposed simplicity of the apostolic practice was assumed to be a constraining law upon all later generations. The Scriptures were taken not only as a rule of faith and conduct, but also as a law of universal obligation in the matter of church government and discipline. The expulsion of organs and the prohibition of choirs was in no way due to a hostility to music in itself, but was simply a detail of that sweeping revolution which, in the attempt to level all artificial distinctions and restore the offices of worship to a simplicity such that they could be understood and administered by the common people, abolished the good of the ancient system together with the bad, and stripped religion of those fair adornments which have been found in the long run efficient to bring her into sympathy with the inherent human demand for beauty and order.

With regard to the matter of art and established form in public worship Calvinism was at one with itself, whether in Geneva or Great Britain. A large number of active Protestants had fled from England at the beginning of the persecution of Mary, and had taken refuge at Geneva. Here they came under the direct influence of Calvin, and imbibed his principles in fullest measure. At the death of Mary these exiles returned, many of them to become leaders in that section of the Protestant party which clamored for a complete eradication of ancient habits and observances. No inspiration was really needed from Calvin, for his democratic and anti-ritualistic views were in complete accord with the temper of English Puritanism. The attack was delivered all along the line, and not the least violent was the outcry against the liturgic music of the established Church. The notion held by the Puritans concerning a proper worship music was that of plain unison psalmody. They vigorously denounced what was known as "curious music," by which was meant scientific, artistic music, and also the practice of antiphonal chanting and the use of organs. Just why organs were looked upon with especial detestation is not obvious. They had played but a very incidental part in the Catholic service, and it would seem that their efficiency as an aid to psalm singing should have commended them to Puritan favor. But such was not the case. Even early in Elizabeth's reign, among certain articles tending to the further alteration of the liturgy which were presented to the lower house of Convocation, was one requiring the removal of organs from the churches, which was lost by only a single vote. It was a considerable time, however, before the opposition again mustered such force. Elizabeth never wavered in her determination to maintain the solemn musical service of her Church. Even this was severe enough as compared with its later expansion, for the multiplication of harmonized chants and florid anthems belongs to a later date, and the ancient Plain Song still included a large part of the service. Neither was Puritanism in the early stages of the movement by any means an uncompromising enemy to the graces of art and culture. The Renaissance delight in what is fair and joyous, its satisfaction in the good things of this world, lingered long even in Puritan households. The young John Milton, gallant, accomplished, keenly alive to the charms of poetry and music, was no less a representative Puritan than when in later years, "fallen on evil days," he fulminated against the levities of the time. It was the stress of party strife, the hardening of the mental and moral fibre that often follows the denial of the reasonable demands of the conscience, that drove the Puritan into bigotry and intolerance. Gradually episcopacy and ritualism became to his mind the mark of the beast. Intent upon knowing the divine will, he exalted his conception of the dictates of that will above all human ordinances, until at last his own interpretations of Scripture, which he made his sole guide in every public and private relation of life, seemed to him guaranteed by the highest of all sanctions. He thus became capable of trampling with a serene conscience upon the rights of those who maintained opinions different from his own. Fair and just in matters in which questions of doctrine or polity were not involved, in affairs of religion the Puritan became the type and embodiment of all that is unyielding and fanatical. Opposition to the use of the surplice, the sign of the cross in baptism, the posture of kneeling at the Lord's Supper, and antiphonal chanting, expanded into uncompromising condemnation of the whole ritual. Puritanism and Presbyterianism became amalgamated, and it only wanted the time and opportunity to pull down episcopacy and liturgy in a common overthrow. The antipathy of the Puritans to artistic music and official choirs was, therefore, less a matter of personal feeling than it was with Calvin. His thought was more that of the purely religious effect upon the individual heart; with the Puritan, hatred of cultured church music was simply a detail in the general animosity which he felt toward an offensive institution.

The most conspicuous of the agitators during the

reign of Elizabeth was Thomas Cartwright, Margaret Professor of Divinity in the University of Cambridge, who first gained notoriety by means of public lectures read in 1570 against the doctrine and discipline of the established Church. The coarseness and violence of this man drew upon him the royal censure, and he was deprived of his fellowship and expelled from the University. His antipathy was especially aroused by the musical practice of the established Church, particularly the antiphonal chanting, "tossing the psalms from one side to the other," to use one of his favorite expressions. "The devil hath gone about to get it authority," said Cartwright. "As for organs and curious singing, though they be proper to popish dens, I mean to cathedral churches, yet some others also must have them. The queen's chapel and these churches (which should be spectacles of Christian reformation) are rather patterns to the people of all superstition."

The attack of Cartwright upon the rites and discipline of the Church of England, since it expressed the feeling of a strong section of the Puritan party, could not be left unanswered. The defence was undertaken by Whitgift and afterward by Richard Hooker, the latter bringing to the debate such learning, dignity, eloquence, and logic that we may be truly grateful to the unlovely Cartwright that his diatribe was the occasion of the enrichment of English literature with so masterly an exposition of the principles of the Anglican system as the *Laws of Ecclesiastical Polity.*

As regards artistic and liturgic music Hooker's argument is so clear, persuasive, and complete that all

later contestants upon the ritualistic side have derived
their weapons, more or less consciously, from his armory.
After an eloquent eulogy of the power of music over
the heart, Hooker passes on to prove the antiquity of
antiphonal chanting by means of citations from the
early Christian fathers, and then proceeds: "But who-
soever were the author, whatsoever the time, whenceso-
ever the example of beginning this custom in the
Church of Christ; sith we are wont to suspect things
only before trial, and afterward either to approve them
as good, or if we find them evil, accordingly to judge
of them; their counsel must needs seem very unseason-
able, who advise men now to suspect that wherewith
the world hath had by their own account twelve hundred years' acquaintance and upwards, enough to take
away suspicion and jealousy. Men know by this time,
if ever they will know, whether it be good or evil
which hath been so long retained." The argument of
Cartwright, that all the people have the right to praise
God in the singing of psalms, Hooker does not find a
sufficient reason for the abolition of the choir; he denies
the assertion that the people cannot understand what is
being sung after the antiphonal manner, and then con-
cludes: "Shall this enforce us to banish a thing which
all Christian churches in the world have received; a
thing which so many ages have held; a thing which
always heretofore the best men and wisest governors
of God's people did think they could never commend
enough; a thing which filleth the mind with comfort
and heavenly delight, stirreth up flagrant desires and
affections correspondent unto that which the words

contain, allayeth all kind of base and earthly cogita-
tions, banisheth and driveth away those evil secret
suggestions which our invisible enemy is always apt to
minister, watereth the heart to the end it may fructify,
maketh the virtuous in trouble full of magnanimity and
courage, serveth as a most approved remedy against all
doleful and heavy accidents which befall men in this
present life; to conclude, so fitly accordeth with the
apostle's own exhortation, ' Speak to yourselves in
psalms and hymns and spiritual songs, making melody,
and singing to the Lord in your hearts,' that surely
there is more cause to fear lest the want thereof be a
maim, than the use a blemish to the service of God." [1]

The just arguments and fervent appeals of Hooker
produced no effect upon the fanatical opponents of the
established Church. Under the exasperating conditions which produced the Great Rebellion and the substitution of the Commonwealth for the monarchy, the
hatred against everything identified with ecclesiastical
and political oppression became tenfold confirmed; and
upon the triumph of the most extreme democratic and
non-conformist faction, as represented by the army of
Cromwell and the "Rump" Parliament, nothing stood
in the way of carrying the iconoclastic purpose into
effect. In 1644 the House of Lords, under the pressure of the already triumphant opposition, passed an
ordinance that the Prayer Book should no longer be
used in any place of public worship. In lieu of the
liturgy a new form of worship was decreed, in which
the congregational singing of metrical psalms was all the

[1] *Laws of Ecclesiastical Polity,* book v., secs. 38 and 39.

music allowed. "It is the duty of Christians," so the new rule declares, "to praise God publicly by singing of psalms, together in the congregation and also privately in the family. In singing of psalms the voice is to be tunably and gravely ordered; but the chief care is to sing with understanding and with grace in the heart, making melody unto the Lord. That the whole congregation may join herein, every one that can read is to have a psalm-book, and all others not disabled by age or otherwise are to be exhorted to learn to read. But for the present, where many in the congregation cannot read, it is convenient that the minister, or some fit person appointed by him and the other ruling officers, do read the psalm line by line before the singing thereof." [1]

The rules framed by the commission left the matter of instrumental music untouched. Perhaps it was considered a work of supererogation to proscribe it, for if there was anything which the Puritan conscience supremely abhorred it was an organ. Sir Edward Deering, in his bill for the abolition of episcopacy, expressed the opinion of the zealots of his party in the assertion that "one groan in the Spirit is worth the diapason of all the church music in the world."

As far back as 1586 a pamphlet which had a wide circulation prays that "all cathedral churches may be put down, where the service of God is grievously abused by piping with organs, singing, ringing, and

[1] It appears from this injunction that the grotesque custom of "lining out" or "deaconing" the psalm was not original in New England, but was borrowed, like most of the musical customs of our Puritan forefathers, from England.

370

trowling of psalms from one side of the choir to the other, with the squeaking of chanting choristers, disguised in white surplices; some in corner caps and silly copes, imitating the fashion and manner of Antichrist the Pope, that man of sin and child of perdition, with his other rabble of miscreants and shavelings."

Such diatribes as this were no mere idle vaporing. As soon as the Puritan army felt its victory secure, these threats were carried out with a ruthless violence which reminds one of the havoc of the image breakers of Antwerp in 1566, who, with striking coincidence of temper, preluded their ravages by the singing of psalms. All reverence for sacred association, all respect for works of skill and beauty, were lost in the indiscriminate rage of bigotry. The ancient sanctuaries were invaded by a vulgar horde, the stained glass windows were broken, ornaments torn down, sepulchral monuments defaced, libraries were ransacked for ancient service-books which, when found, were mutilated or burned, organs were demolished and their fragments scattered. These barbarous excesses had in fact been directly enjoined by act of Parliament in 1644, and it is not surprising that the rude soldiery carried out the desires of their superiors with wantonness and indignity. A few organs, however, escaped the general destruction, one being rescued by Cromwell, who was a lover of religious music, and not at all in sympathy with the vandalism of his followers. Choirs were likewise dispersed, organists, singers, and composers of the highest ability were deprived of their means of livelihood, and in many cases reduced to the extreme of destitution. The beautiful service of the Anglican Church, thus swept away in a single day, found no successor but the dull droning psalmody of the Puritan congregations, and only in a private circle in Oxford, indirectly protected by Cromwell, was the feeble spark of artistic religious music kept alive.

The reëstablishment of the liturgy and the musical service of the Church of England upon the restoration of the Stuarts in 1660 has already been described. The Puritan congregations clung with tenacity to their peculiar tenets and usages, prominent among which was their invincible repugnance to artistic music. Although such opinions could probably not prevail so extensively among a really musical people, yet this was not the first nor the last time in history that the art which seems peculiarly adapted to the promotion of pure devotional feeling has been disowned as a temptation and a distraction. We find similar instances among some of the more zealous German Protestants of Luther's time, and the German Pietists of the seventeenth and eighteenth centuries. At many periods of the Middle Age there were protests against the lengths to which artistic music had gone in the Church and a demand for the reduction of the musical service to the simplest elements. Still further back, among the early Christians, the horror at the abominations of paganism issued in denunciation of all artistic tendencies in the worship of the Church. St. Jerome may not inaccurately be called the first great Puritan. Even St. Augustine was at one time inclined to believe that his love for the moving songs of the Church was a snare, until, by analysis, he persuaded himself that it was the sacred words, and not merely the musical tones, which softened his heart and filled his eyes with tears. As in all these cases, including that of the Puritans, the sacrifice of æsthetic pleasure in worship was not merely a reactionary protest against the excess of ceremonialism and artistic enjoyment. The Puritan was a precisian. The love of a highly developed and sensuously beautiful music in worship always implies a certain infusion of mysticism. The Puritan was no mystic. He demanded hard distinct definition in his pious expression as he did in his argumentation. The vagueness of musical utterance, its appeal to indefinable emotion, its effect of submerging the mind and bearing it away upon a tide of ecstasy were all in exact contradiction to the Puritan's conviction as to the nature of genuine edification. These raptures could not harmonize with his gloomy views of sin, righteousness, and judgment to come. And so we find the most spiritual of the arts denied admittance to the sanctuary by those who actually cherished music as a beloved social and domestic companion.

More difficult to understand is the Puritan prohibition of all hymns except rhymed paraphrases of the psalms. Metrical versions were substituted for chanted prose versions for the reason, no doubt, that a congregation, as a rule, cannot sing in perfect unity of coöperation except in metre and in musical forms in which one note is set to one syllable. But why the psalms alone? Why suppress the free utterance of the believers in hymns of faith and hope? In the view of that day the psalms were directly inspired by the Holy Spirit and contemporary hymns could not be. We know that a characteristic of the Puritan mind was an intense, an impassioned reverence for the Holy Scripture, so that all other forms of human speech seemed trivial and unworthy in comparison. The fact that the psalms, as the product of the ante-Christian dispensation, could have no reference to the Christian scheme except by far-fetched interpretation as symbolic and prophetic, did not escape the Puritans, but they consoled themselves for the loss in the thought that the earliest churches, in which they found, or thought they found their ideal and standard, were confined to a poetic expression similar to their own. And how far did they feel this to be a loss? Was not the temper of the typical Puritan, after all, thoroughly impregnated with Hebraism? The real nature of the spiritual deprivation which this restriction involved is apparent enough now, for it barred out a gracious influence which might have corrected some grave faults in the Puritan character, faults from which their religious descendants to this day continue to suffer.

The rise of an English hymnody corresponding to that of Germany was, therefore, delayed for more than one hundred and fifty years. English religious song-books were exclusively psalm-books down to the eighteenth century. Poetic activity among the non-conformists consisted in translations of the psalms in metre, or rather versions of the existing translations in the English Bible, for these sectaries, as a rule, were not strong in Hebrew. The singular passion in that period for putting everything into rhyme and metre, which produced such grotesque results as turning an act of Parliament into couplets, and paraphrasing "Paradise Lost" in rhymed stanzas in order, as the writer said, "to make Mr. Milton plain," gave aid and comfort to the peculiar Puritan views. The first complete metrical version of the psalms was the celebrated edition of Sternhold and Hopkins, the former a gentleman of the privy chamber to Edward VI., the latter a clergyman and schoolmaster in Suffolk. This version, published in 1562, was received with universal satisfaction and adopted into all the Puritan congregations, maintaining its credit for full two hundred and thirty years, until it came at last to be considered as almost equally inspired with the original Hebrew text. So far as poetic merit is concerned, the term is hardly applicable to the lucubrations of these honest and prosaic men. As Fuller said, "their piety was better than their poetry, and they had drunk more of Jordan than of Helicon." In fact the same comment would apply to all the subsequent versifiers of the psalms. It would seem that the very nature of such work precludes all real literary success. The sublime thought and irregular, vivid diction of the Hebrew poets do not permit themselves to be parcelled out in the cut and dried patterns of conventional metres. Once only does Sternhold rise into grandeur — in the two stanzas which James Russell Lowell so much admired :

> The Lord descended from above,
>   And bowed the heavens most high,
> And underneath his feet he cast
>   The darkness of the sky.

On cherub and on cherubim
  Full royally he rode;
And on the wings of all the winds
  Came flying all abroad.

The graces of style, however, were not greatly prized by the Puritan mind. Sternhold and Hopkins held the suffrages of their co-religionists so long on account of their strict fidelity to the thought of the original, the ruggedness and genuine force of their expression, and their employment of the simple homely phraseology of the common people. The enlightened criticism of the present day sees worth in these qualities, and assigns to the work of Sternhold and Hopkins higher credit than to many smoother and more finished versions.

Sternhold and Hopkins partially yielded to Tate and Brady in 1696, and were still more urgently pushed aside by the version of Watts in 1719. The numerous versions which have since appeared from time to time were written purely for literary purposes, or else in a few cases (as, for example, the psalms of Ainsworth, brought to America by the Pilgrim Fathers) were granted a temporary and local use in the churches. Glass, in his *Story of the Psalter*, enumerates one hundred and twenty-three complete versions, the last being that of Wrangham in 1885. This long list includes but one author — John Keble — who has attained fame as a poet outside the annals of hymnology. No other version ever approached in popularity that of Sternhold and Hopkins, whose work passed through six hundred and one editions.

Social hymn singing, unlike liturgic choir music, is

entirely independent of contemporary art movements.
It flourishes only in periods of popular religious awakening, and declines when religious enthusiasm ebbs, no
matter what may be going on in professional musical
circles. Psalm singing in the English Reformation
period, whatever its æsthetic shortcomings, was a powerful promoter of zeal in moments of triumph, and an unfailing source of consolation in adversity. As in the
case of the Lutheran choral, each psalm had its " proper "
tune. Many of the melodies were already associated
with tender experiences of home life, and they became
doubly endeared through religious suggestion. " The
metrical psalms," says Curwen, " were Protestant in their
origin, and in their use they exemplified the Protestant
principle of allowing every worshiper to understand
and participate in the service. As years went on, the
rude numbers of Sternhold and Hopkins passed into the
language of spiritual experience in a degree only less
than the authorized version of the Bible. They were a
liturgy to those who rejected liturgies." [1] It was their
one outlet of poetic religious feeling, and dry and
prosaic as both words and music seem to us now, we
must believe, since human nature is everywhere moved
by much the same impulses, that these psalms and tunes
were not to those who used them barren and formal
things, and that in the singing of them there was an
undercurrent of rapture which to our minds it seems
almost impossible that they could produce. In every
form of popular expression there is always this invisible
aura, like the supposed imperceptible fluid around an

[1] Curwen, *Studies in Worship Music.*

electrified body. There are what we may call emotion-alized reactions, stimulated by social, domestic, or ancestral associations, producing effects for which the unsympathetic critic cannot otherwise account.

Even this inspiration at last seemed to fade away. When the one hundred years' conflict, of alternate ascendency and persecution, came to an end with the Restoration in 1660, zeal abated with the fires of conflict, and apathy, formalism, and dulness, the counterparts of lukewarmness and Pharisaical routine in the established Church, settled down over the dissenting sects. In the eighteenth century the psalmody of the Presbyterians, Independents, and Separatists, which had also been adopted long before in the parochial services of the established Church, declined into the most contracted and unemotional routine that can be found in the history of religious song. The practice of "lining out" destroyed every vestige of musical charm that might otherwise have remained; the number of tunes in common use grew less and less, in some congregations being reduced to a bare half-dozen. The conception of individualism, which was the source of congregational singing in the first place, was carried to such absurd extremes that the notion extensively prevailed that every person was privileged to sing the melody in any key or tempo and with any grotesque embellishment that might be pleasing to himself. These fantastic abuses especially prevailed in the New England congregations in the last half of the seventeenth and the first half of the eighteenth centuries, but they were only the ultimate consequences of ideas and practices which prevailed in the mother country. The early Baptists forbade singing altogether. The Brownists tried for a short time to act upon the notion that singing in worship, like prayer, should be extempore. The practical results may easily be imagined. About the year 1700 it seemed as though the fair genius of sacred song had abandoned the English and American non-liturgic sects in despair.

Like a sun-burst, opening a brighter era, came the Wesleyan movement, and in the same period the hymns of Dr. Isaac Watts. Whatever the effect of the exuberant singing of the Methodist assemblies may have had upon a cultivated ear, it is certain that the enthusiastic welcome accorded by the Wesleys to popular music as a proselyting agent, and the latitude permitted to free invention and adoption of hymns and tunes, gave an impulse to a purer and nobler style of congregational song which has never been lost. The sweet and fervent lyrics of Charles and John Wesley struck a staggering blow at the prestige of the "inspired" psalmody. Historians of this movement remind us that hymns, heartily sung by a whole congregation, were unknown as an element in public worship at the time when the work of the Wesleys and Whitefield began. Watts's hymns were already written, but had as yet taken no hold upon either dissenters or churchmen. The example of the Methodists was a revelation of the power that lies in popular song when inspired by conviction, and as was said of the early Lutheran choral, so it might be said of the Methodist hymns, that they won more souls than even the preaching of the evangelists. John Wesley, in

his published directions concerning congregational singing, enjoined accuracy in notes and time, heartiness,
moderation, unanimity, and spirituality as with the aim of
pleasing God rather than one's self. He strove to bring
the new hymns and tunes within the means of the poor,
and yet took pains that the music should be of high
quality, and that nothing vulgar or sensational should
obtain currency.

The truly beneficent achievement of the Wesleys in
summoning the aid of the unconfined spirit of poesy in
the revival of spiritual life found a worthy reinforcement in the songs of Isaac Watts (1674–1748). Although his deficiencies in the matter of poetical technic
and his frequent dry, scholastic, and dogmatic treatment
have rendered much the greater part of his work obsolete, yet a true spiritual and poetic fire burns in many of
his lyrics, and with all necessary abatement his fame seems
secure. Such poems as " High in the Heavens, eternal
God," " Before Jehovah's awful throne," and " When
I survey the wondrous cross " are pearls which can
never lose their place in the chaplet of English evangelical hymnody. The relaxing prejudice against " unin-
spired " hymns in church worship yielded to the fervent
zeal, the loving faith, the forceful natural utterance of
the lyrics of Watts. In his psalms also, uniting as they
did the characteristic modes of feeling of both the Hebrew
and the Christian conceptions, he made the transition
easy, and in both he showed the true path along which
the reviving poetic inspiration of the time must proceed.

What has come of the impulse imparted by Watts
and the Wesleys every student of Christian literature

knows. To give any adequate account of the movement which has enriched the multitude of modern hymn-books and sacred anthologies would require a large volume.[1] No more profitable task could be suggested to one who deems it his highest duty to expand and deepen his spiritual nature, than to possess his mind of the jewels of devotional insight and chastened expression which are scattered through the writings of such poets as Charles Wesley, Cowper, Newton, Faber, Newman, Lyte, Heber, Bonar, Milman, Keble, Ellerton, Montgomery, Ray Palmer, Coxe, Whittier, Holmes, the Cary sisters, and others equal or hardly inferior to these, who have performed immortal service to the divine cause which they revered by disclosing to the world the infinite beauty and consolation of the Christian faith. No other nation, not even the German, can show any parallel to the treasure embedded in English and American popular religious poetry. This fact is certainly not known to the majority of church members. The average church-goer never looks into a hymn-book except when he stands up to sing in the congregation, and this performance, whatever else it may do for the worshiper, gives him very little information in regard to the artistic, or even the spiritual value of the book which he holds in his hand. Let him read his hymn-book in private, as he reads his Tennyson; and although he will not be inclined to compare it in point of literary quality with Palgrave's *Golden Treasury* or Stedman's

---

[1] This has been done by several writers, but by no other in such admirable fashion as by Horder in his delightful book, *The Hymn Lover* (London, Curwen, 1889).

Victorian Anthology, yet he will probably be surprised at the number of lyrics whose delicacy, fervor, and pathos will be to him a revelation of the gracious elements that pervade the minor religious poetry of the English tongue.

Parallel with the progress of hymnody, and undoubtedly stimulated by it, has been the development of the hymn-tune and the gradual rise of public taste in this branch of religious art. The history of the English and American hymn-tune may easily be traced, for its line is unbroken. Its sources also are well known, except that the origins of the first settings of the psalms of Sternhold and Hopkins are in many cases obscure. Those who first fitted tunes to the metrical psalms borrowed some of their melodies (the "Old Hundredth" is a conspicuous instance) from the Huguenot psalter of Marot and Beza, and others probably from English folk-songs. There were eminent composers in England in the Reformation period, many of whom lent their services in harmonizing the tunes found in the early psalters, and also contributed original melodies. All these ancient tunes were syllabic and diatonic, dignified and stately in movement, often sombre in coloring, in all these particulars bearing a striking resemblance to the German choral. Some of the strongest tunes in the modern hymnals, for example, "Dundee," are derived from the Scotch and English psalters of the sixteenth and seventeenth centuries, and efforts are being made in some quarters to bring others of the same source and type into favor with present-day congregations. This severe diatonic school was succeeded in the eighteenth century by a taste for the florid and ornate which, in spite of some contributions of a very beautiful and expressive character, on the whole marked a decline in favor of the tawdry and sensational. If this tendency was an indication of an experimenting spirit, its result was not altogether evil. Earnest and dignified as the old psalm-tunes were, the Church could not live by them alone. The lighter style was a transition, and the purer modern school is the outcome of a process which strives to unite the breadth and dignity of the ancient tunes with the warmth and color of those of the second period. Together with the cultivation of the florid style we note a wider range of selection. Many tunes were taken from secular sources (not in itself a fault, since, as we have seen, many of the best melodies in the Lutheran and Calvinistic song-books had a similar origin); and the introduction of Catholic tunes, such as the peerless " Adeste Fideles " and the " Sicilian hymn," together with some of the finest German chorals, greatly enriched the English tune-books.

In comparatively recent times a new phase of progress has manifested itself in the presence in the later hymnals of a large number of musical compositions of novel form and coloring, entirely the product of our own period. These tunes are representative of the present school of Church of England composers, such as Dykes, Barnby, Smart, Sullivan, Monk, Hopkins, and many others equally well known, who have contributed a large quantity of melodies of exceeding beauty, supported by varied and often striking harmonies, quite unlike the congregational songs of any other nation. Composed for the noble ceremony of the Anglican Church, these tunes have made their way into many of the non-liturgic sects, and the value of their influence in inspiring a love for that which is purest and most salutary in worship music has been incalculable. Much has been written in praise of these new Anglican tunes, and a good deal also in depreciation. Many of them are, it must be confessed, over-sophisticated for the use of the average congregation, carrying refinements of harmony and rhythm to such a point that they are more suitable for the choir than for the congregation. Their real value, taken collectively, can best be estimated by those who, having once used them, should imagine themselves deprived of them. The tunes that served the needs of former generations will not satisfy ours. Dr. Hanslick remarks that there is music of which it may correctly be said that it once was beautiful. It is doubtless so with hymn-tunes. Church art can never be kept unaffected by the secular currents of the time, and those who, in opera house and concert hall, are thrilled by the impassioned strains of the modern romantic composers, will inevitably long for something at least remotely analogous in the songs of the sanctuary. That is to say, the congregational tune must be appealing, stirring, emotional, as the old music doubtless was to the people of the old time, but certainly is no longer. This logical demand the English musicians of the present day and their American followers assume to gratify — that is, so far as the canons of pure art and ecclesiastical propriety will allow — and, in spite of the cavils of purists and reactionaries, their melodies seem to have taken a permanent place in the affections of the Protestant English-speaking world. The success of these melodies is due not merely to their abstract musical beauty, but perhaps still more to the subtle sympathy which their style exhibits with the present-day tendencies in theology and devotional experience, which are reflected in the peculiarly joyous and confiding note of recent hymnody. So far as music has the power to suggest definite conceptions, there seems to be an apt correspondence between this fervent, soaring, touching music and the hymns of the faith by which these melodies were in most instances directly inspired.

So far as there are movements in progress bringing into shape a body of congregational song which contains features that are likely to prove a permanent enrichment of the religious anthology, they are more or less plainly indicated in the hymnals which have been compiled in this country during the past ten or twelve years. Not that we may look forward to any sudden outburst of hymn-singing enthusiasm parallel to that which attended the Lutheran and Wesleyan revivals, for such a musical impulse is always the accompaniment of some mighty religious awakening, of which there is now no sign. The significance of these recent hymnals lies rather in the evidence they give of the growth of higher standards of taste in religious verse and music, and also of certain changes in progress in our churches in the prevailing modes of religious thought. The evident tendency of hymnology, as indicated by the new books, is to throw less emphasis upon those more mechanical conceptions which gave such a hard precision to a large

25   385

portion of the older hymnody. A finer poetic afflatus has joined with a more penetrating and intimate vision of the relationship between the divine and the human; and this mental attitude is reflected in the loving trust, the emotional fervor, and the more delicate and inward poetic expression which prevail in the new hymnody. It is inevitable that the theological readjustment, which is so palpable to every intelligent observer, should color and deflect those forms of poetic and musical expression which are instinctively chosen as the utterance of the worshiping people. Every one at all familiar with the history of religious experience is aware how sensitive popular song has been as an index of popular feeling. Nowhere is the power of psychologic suggestion upon the masses more evident than in the domain of song. Hardly does a revolutionary religious idea, struck from the brains of a few leading thinkers and reformers, effect a lodgment in the hearts of any considerable section of the common people, than it is immediately projected in hymns and melodies. So far as it is no mere scholastic formula, but possesses the power to kindle an active life in the soul, it will quickly clothe itself in figurative speech and musical cadence, and in many cases it will filter itself through this medium until all that is crude, formal, and speculative is drained away, and what is essential and fruitful is retained as a permanent spiritual possession.

If we were able to view the present movement in popular religious verse from a sufficient distance, we should doubtless again find illustration of this general law. Far less obviously, of course, than in the cases of the Hussite, Lutheran, and Wesleyan movements, for the changes of our day are more gradual and placid. I would not imply that the hymns that seem so much the natural voice of the new tendencies are altogether, or even in the majority of cases, recent productions. Many of them certainly come from Watts and Cowper and Newton, and other eighteenth-century men, whose theology contained many gloomy and obsolete tenets, but whose hearts often denied their creeds and spontaneously uttered themselves in strains which every shade of religious conviction may claim as its own. It is not, therefore, that the new hymnals have been mainly supplied by new schools of poetry, but the compilers, being men quick to sense the new devotional demands and also in complete sympathy with them, have made their selections and expurgations from a somewhat modified motive, repressing certain phases of thought and emphasizing others, so that their collections take a wider range, a loftier sweep, and a more joyful, truly evangelical tone than those of a generation ago. It is more the inner life of faith which these books so beautifully present, less that of doctrinal assent and outer conformity.

These recent contributions to the service of praise are not only interesting in themselves, but even more so, perhaps, as the latest terms in that long series of popular religious song-books which began with the independence of the English Church. *The Plymouth Hymnal* and *In Excelsis* are the ripened issue of that movement whose first official outcome was the quaint psalter of Sternhold and Hopkins; and the contrast between the old and the new is a striking evidence of the changes which three and a half centuries have effected in culture and spiritual emphasis as revealed in popular song. The early lyrics were prepared as a sort of testimony against formalism and the use of human inventions in the office of worship; they were the outcome of a striving after apostolic simplicity, while in their emotional aspects they served for consolation in trial and persecution, and as a means of stiffening the resolution in times of conflict. The first true hymns, as distinct from versified psalms, were designed still more to quicken joy and hope, and yet at the same time a powerful motive on the part of their authors was to give instruction in the doctrines of the faith by a means more direct and persuasive than sermons, and to reinforce the exhortations of evangelists by an instrument that should be effective in awaking the consciences of the unregenerate. It is very evident that the hymnals of our day are pervaded by an intention somewhat different from this, or at least supplementary to it The Church, having become stable, and having a somewhat different mission to perform under the changed conditions of the time, employs its hymns and tunes not so much as revival machinery, or as a means for inculcating dogma, as for spiritual nurture. Hymns have become more subjective, melodies and harmonies more refined and alluring; the tone has become less stern and militant; the ideas are more universal and tender, less mechanical and precise; appeal is made more to the sensibility than to the intellect, and the chief stress is laid upon the joy and peace that come from believing. It is impossible to avoid vagueness in attempting so broad a generalization. But one who studies the new hymn-books, reads the prefaces of their editors, and notes the character of the hymns that are most used in our churches, will realize that now, as it has always been in the history of the Church, the guiding thought and feeling of the time may be traced in popular song, more faintly but not less inevitably than in the instructions of the pulpit. When viewed in historic sequence one observes the growing prominence of the mystical and subjective elements, the fading away of the early fondness for scholastic definition. Lyric poetry is in its nature mystical and intuitive, and the hymnody of the future, following the present tendency in theology to direct the thought to the personal, historic Christ, and to appropriate his example and message in accordance with the light which advancing knowledge obtains concerning man's nature, needs, and destiny, will aim more than ever before to purify and quicken the higher emotional faculties, and will find a still larger field in those fundamental convictions which transcend the bounds of creeds, and which affirm the brotherhood of all sincere seekers after God.

CHAPTER XII

In the foregoing sketch of the rise and growth of music in the Western Church no account was taken of a history of church music in America. If by art history we mean a record of progressive changes, significant of a persistent impulse which issues in distinctive styles and schools, the chronicles of ecclesiastical song in this country hardly come within the scope of history. No new forms or methods have arisen on this side of the Atlantic. The styles of composition and the systems of practice which have existed among us have simply been transferred from the older countries across the sea. Every form of church music known in Europe flourishes in America, but there is no native school of religious music, just as there is no American school of secular music. The Puritan colonists brought with them a few meagre volumes of metrical psalms, and a dozen or so of tunes wherewith to sing 'them in the uncouth fashion which already prevailed in England. They brought also the rigid Calvinistic hostility to everything that is studied and uniform in religious ceremony, and for a century or more they seemed to glory in the distinction of maintaining church song in the most barbarous condition that

390

this art has ever suffered since the founding of Christianity. It was not possible that this state of affairs could endure in a community that was constantly advancing in education and in the embellishments of life, and a bitter conflict arose between puritanic tradition and the growing perception of the claims of fitness and beauty. One who would amuse himself with the grotesque controversies which raged around this question among the pious New England colonists, the acrid disputes between the adherents of the " usual way " and the " rulable way " of singing psalmody, the stern resistance to choirs and to organs, and the quaint annals of the country singing-school, may find rich gratification in some of the books of Mrs. Earle, especially *The Sabbath in Puritan New England.* The work of such reformers as William Billings in the eighteenth century and Lowell Mason in the nineteenth, the first concerts of the Handel and Haydn Society, the influx of the German culture shifting all American music upon new foundations, are all landmarks which show how rapid and thorough has been our advance in musical scholarship and taste, but which also remind us how little of our achievement has been really indigenous.

In spite of the poverty of original invention which forbids us to claim that American church music has in any way contributed to the evolution of the art, there is no epoch in this art's history which possesses a more vital interest to the American churchman of the present day. We have found amid all the fluctuations of ecclesiastical music, mediæval and modern,

Catholic and Protestant, one ever-recurring problem, which is no sooner apparently settled than new conditions arise which force it once more upon the attention of minister and layman. The choice of a style of music which shall most completely answer the needs of worship as the conceptions and methods of public worship vary among different communities and in different epochs, and which at the same time shall not be unworthy of the claims of music as a fine art, — this is the historic dilemma which is still, as ever, a fruitful source of perplexity and discord. The Catholic and Episcopal Churches are less disturbed by this spectre than their non-liturgic brethren. An authoritative ritual carries its laws over upon music also; tradition, thus fortified, holds firm against innovation, and the liturgic and clerical conception of music gives a stability to musical usages which no aberrations of taste can quite unsettle. But in the non-liturgic churches of America one sees only a confusion of purposes, a lack of agreement, an absence of every shade of recognized authority. The only tradition is that of complete freedom of choice. There is no admitted standard of taste; the whole musical service is experimental, subject to the preferences, more or less capricious, of choir-master or music committee. There is no system in the separate societies that may not be overthrown by a change of administration. The choir music is eclectic, drawn indiscriminately from Catholic, German, and English sources; or if it is of American composition it is merely an obvious imitation of one of these three. The congregational music ranges from the German choral to the "Gospel song," or it may be an alternation of these two incongruous styles. The choir is sometimes a chorus, sometimes a solo quartet; the latter mainly forced to choose its material from "arrangements," or from works written for chorus. Anon the choir is dismissed and the congregation, led by a precentor with voice or cornet, assumes the whole burden of the office of song. These conditions are sufficient to explain why a distinct school of American church music does not exist and never can exist. The great principle of self-determination in doctrine and ecclesiastical government, which has brought into existence such a multitude of sects, may well be a necessity in a composite and democratic nation, but it is no less certainly a hindrance to the development of a uniform type of religious music.

There would be a much nearer approach to a reconcilement of all these differences, and the cause of church music would be in a far more promising condition, if there were a closer sympathy between the standard of music within the Church and that prevailing in educated society outside. There is certainly a diversity of purpose between church music and secular music, and corresponding distinctions must be preserved in respect to form and expression. A secularized style of church music means decadence. But the vitality of ecclesiastical art has always seemed to depend upon retaining a conscious touch with the large art movements of the world, and church music has certainly never thrived when, in consequence of neglect or complacency, it has been suffered to become inferior to its rival. In America there is no such stimulating interaction between the music of the Church and that of the concert hall and the social circle as there has been for centuries in Germany and England. The Church is not the leader in musical culture. We are rapidly becoming a musical nation. When one sees what is going on in the opera houses, concert halls, colleges, conservatories, public schools, and private instruction rooms, contrasting the present situation with that of fifty years ago, the outcome can easily be predicted. But the music of the Church, in spite of gratifying efforts here and there, is not keeping pace with this progress, and the Church must inevitably suffer in certain very important interests if this gap is permitted continually to widen.

There are many causes for this state of affairs, some incidental and avoidable, others lying in the very nature of music itself and the special service which the Church requires of it. Perhaps the chief difficulty in the way of a high artistic development of religious music is the opinion, which prevails widely among the most devout, that music when allied to worship must forego what seems the natural right of all art to produce pleasure as an end in itself, and that it must subordinate itself to the sacred text and employ its persuasive powers solely to enforce divine truth upon the heart, — meaning by divine truth some particular form of religious confession. Whether this view is true or false, whenever it is consistently acted upon, it seems to me, music declines.

Now it is evident that music is less willing than any

394

other art to assume this inferior station. Architecture serves a utilitarian purpose, the pleasure of the eye being supplementary; painting and sculpture may easily become didactic or reduced to the secondary function of ornament. But of all the arts music is the most sensuous (I use the word in its technical psychologic sense), direct, and penetrating in its operation. Music acts with such immediateness and intensity that it seems as though it were impossible for her to be anything but supreme when she puts forth all her energies. We may force her to be dull and commonplace, but that does not meet the difficulty. For it is the very beauty and glory of music which the Church wishes to use, but how shall this be prevented from asserting itself to such an extent that devotion is swept away upon the wings of nervous excitement? Let any one study his sensations when a trained choir pours over him a flood of rapturous harmony, and he will perhaps find it difficult to decide whether it is a devotional uplift or an æsthetic afflatus that has seized him. Is there actually any essential difference between his mental state at this moment and that, for instance, at the close of " Tristan und Isolde "? Any one who tries this experiment upon himself will know at once what is this problem of music in the Church which has puzzled pious men for centuries, and which has entered into every historic movement of church extension or reform.

A little clear thinking on this subject, it seems to me, will convince any one that music alone, in and of itself, never makes people religious. There is no such thing as religious music *per se.* When music in religious ceremony inspires a distinctly prayerful mood, it does so mainly through associations and accessories. And if this mood is not induced by other causes, music alone can never be relied upon to create it. Music, even the noblest and purest, is not always or necessarily an aid to devotion, and there may even be a snare in what seems at first a devoted ally. The analogy that exists between religious emotion and musical rapture is, after all, only an analogy; æsthetic delight, though it be the most refined, is not worship; the melting tenderness that often follows a sublime instrumental or choral strain is not contrition. Those who speak of all good music as religious do not understand the meaning of the terms they use. For devotion is not a mere vague feeling of longing or transport. It must involve a positive recognition of an object of worship, a reaching up, not to something unknown or inaccessible, but to a God who reveals himself to us, and whom we believe to be cognizant of the sincerity of the worship offered him; it must involve also a sense of humility before an almighty power, a penitence for sin, a desire for pardon and reconciliation, a consciousness of need and dependence, and an active exercise of faith and love. Into such convictions music may come, lending her aid to deepen them, to give them tangible expression, and to enhance the sense of joy and peace which may be their consequence; but to create them is beyond her power.

The office of music is not to suggest concrete images, or even to arouse definite namable sentiments, but rather to intensify ideas and feelings already existing,

396

or to release the mind and put it into that sensitive, expectant state in which conceptions that appeal to the emotion may act unhampered. The more generalized function of music in the sanctuary is to take possession of the prepared and chastened mood which is the antecedent of worship, to separate it from other moods and reminiscences which are not in perfect accord with it, and to establish it in a more complete self-consciousness and a more permanent attitude. This antecedent sense of need and longing for divine communion cannot be aroused by music alone; the enjoyment of abstract musical beauty, however refined and elevating, is not worship, and a musical impression disconnected from any other cannot conduce to the spirit of prayer. It is only when the prayerful impulse already exists as a more or less conscious tendency of the mind, induced by a sense of love and duty, by the associations of the time and place, by the administration of the other portions of the service, or by any agencies which incline the heart of the believer in longing toward the Mercy Seat, — it is only in alliance with such an anticipatory state of mind and the causes that produce it that music fulfils its true office in public worship. It is not enough to depend upon the influence of the words to which the music is set, for they, being simultaneous with the music, do not have time or opportunity to act with full force upon the understanding; since the action of music upon the emotion is more immediate and vivid than that of words upon the intellect, the latter is often unregarded in the stress of musical excitement. However it may be in solo singing, it is not possible or even desirable that the words of a chorus should be so distinct as to make the prime impression. Those who demand distinct articulation, as though the religious effect of church song hung solely upon that, do not listen musically. At any rate they see but a little way into the problem, which is concerned not with the effect of words but of tones. The text and music reinforce each other when the words are known to the hearer before the singing begins, aiding thus to bring about the expectancy of which I have spoken, and producing that satisfaction which is felt when musical expression is perceived to be appropriate to its poetic subject.

The spirit of worship, therefore, must be aroused by favoring conditions and means auxiliary to music, — it is then the province of music to direct this spirit toward a more vivid consciousness of its end. The case is with music as Professor Shairp says it is with nature: "If nature is to be the symbol of something higher than itself, to convey intimations of him from whom both nature and the world proceed, man must come to the spectacle with the thought of God already in his heart. He will not get a religion out of the mere sight of nature. If beauty is to lead the soul upward, man must come to the contemplation of it with his moral convictions clear and firm, and with faith in these as connecting him directly with God. Neither morality nor religion will he get out of beauty taken by itself."

The soundest writers on art maintain that art, taken abstractly, is neither moral nor immoral. It occupies a sphere apart from that of religion or ethics. It may lend its aid to make religious and moral ideas more persuasive; it may, through the touch of pure beauty, overbear material and prosaic interests and help to produce an atmosphere in which spiritual ideas may range without friction, but the mind must first have been made morally sensitive by other than purely artistic means. It is the peculiar gift of music that it affords a speedier and more immediate means of fusion between ideas of sensuous beauty and those of devotional experience than any other of the art sisterhood. It is the indefiniteness of music as compared with painting and sculpture, the intensity of its action as compared with the beauty of architecture and decoration, which gives to it its peculiar power. To this searching force of music, its freedom from reminiscences of actual life or individual experience, is due the prominence that has been assigned to music in the observances of religion in all times and nations. Piety falls into the category of the most profound and absorbing of human emotions — together with such sentiments as patriotism and love of persons — which instinctively utter themselves not in prose but in poetry, not in ordinary unimpassioned speech, but in rhythmic tone. Music is the art most competent to enter into such an ardent and mobile state of mind. The ecstasy aroused in the lover of music by the magic of his art is more nearly analogous than any other producible by art to that mystic rapture described by religious enthusiasts. Worship is disconnected from all the concerns of physical life; it raises the subject into a super-earthly region; it has for the moment nothing to do with

399

temporal activities; it is largely spontaneous and unreflective. The absorption of the mind in contemplation, the sense of inward peace which accompanies emancipation from the disturbances of ordinary life, those joyous stirrings of the soul when it seems to catch glimpses of eternal blessedness, have a striking resemblance to phases of musical satisfaction where the analytical faculties are not called into exercise. Hence the readiness with which music combines with these higher experiences. Music in its mystic, indefinable action seems to make the mood of prayer more active, to interpret it to itself, and by something that seems celestial in the harmony to make the mood deeper, stronger, more satisfying than it would be if shut up within the soul and deprived of this means of deliverance. Music also, by virtue of its universal and impersonal quality, furnishes the most efficient means of communication among all the individuals engaged in a common act; the separate personalities are, we might say, dissolved in the general tide of rapture symbolized by the music, and the common sentiment is again enhanced by the consciousness of sympathy between mind and mind to which the music testifies, and which it is so efficient to promote.

The substance of this whole discussion, therefore, is that those who have any dealing with music in the Church must take into account the inherent laws of musical effect. Music is not a representative art; it bears with it an order of impressions untranslatable into those of poetry or painting. To use Walter Pater's phrase, "it presents no matter of sentiment

or thought separable from the special form in which
it is conveyed to us." It may, through its peculiar
power of stimulating the sensibility and conveying
ideas of beauty in the purest, most abstract guise, help
to make the mind receptive to serious impressions;
but in order to excite a specifically religious feeling
it must coöperate with other impressions which act
more definitely upon the understanding. The words
to which the music is sung, being submerged in the
mind of a music-lover by the tide of enchanting sound,
are not sufficient for this purpose unless they are
known and dwelt upon in advance; and even then they
too need reinforcement out of the environment in
which the musical service is placed. The singing of
the choir must be contrived and felt as a part of the
office of prayer. The spirit and direction of the whole
service for the day must be unified; the music must be
a vital and organic element in this unit. All parts of
the service must be controlled by the desire for beauty
and fitness. Music, however beautiful, loses something
of its effect if its accompaniments are not in harmony
with it. This desideratum is doubtless most easily
attained in a liturgic service. One great advantage
of an ancient and prescribed form is that its components
work easily to a common impression, and in course of
time the ritual tends to become venerable as well as
dignified and beautiful. The non-liturgic method
may without difficulty borrow this conception of harmony and elevation, applying it so far as its own
customs and rules of public worship allow. How this
unity of action in the several factors of a non-liturgic

401

service may best be effected is outside the purpose of this book to discuss. The problem is not a difficult one when minister, choir leader, and church members are agreed upon the principle. In every church there are sanctities of time and place; there are common habits of mind induced by a common faith; there are historic traditions, — all contributing to a unity of feeling in the congregation. These may all be cultivated and enhanced by a skilfully contrived service, devised and moulded in recognition of the psychologic law that an art form acts with full power only when the mind is prepared by anticipation and congenial accessories.

This conclusion is, however, very far from being the end of the matter. The most devout intention will not make the church music effective for its ideal end if the æsthetic element is disregarded. There seems to be in many quarters a strange distrust of beauty and skill in musical performance, as if artistic qualities were in some way hostile to devotion. This distrust is a survival of the old Calvinistic fear of everything studied, formal, and externally beautiful in public worship. In other communities the church music is simply neglected, as one of the results of the excessive predominance given to the sermon in the development of Protestantism. It is often deemed sufficient, also, if the church musicians are devout men and women, in forgetfulness of the fact that a musical performance that is irritating to the nerves can never be a help to devotion. These enemies to artistic church music — hostility, indifference, and ignorance — are especially injurious in a country where, as in America, the general knowledge and taste in music are rapidly growing. Those churches which, for any reason whatever, keep their musical standard below the level of that which prevails in the educated society around them are not acting for their own advantage, materially or spiritually. President Faunce was right when he told one of the churches of his denomination: " Your music must be kept noble and good. If your children hear Wagner and the other great masters in their schools, they will not be satisfied with ' Pull for the shore ' in the church." Those churches, for example, which rely mainly upon the " Gospel Songs " should soberly consider if it is profitable in the long run to maintain a standard of religious melody and verse far below that which prevails in secular music and literature. " The Church is the art school of the common man," says Professor Riehl; and while it may be answered that it is not the business of the Church to teach art, yet the Church cannot afford to keep its spiritual culture out of harmony with the higher intellectual movements of the age. One whose taste is fed by the poetry of such masters as Milton and Tennyson, by the music of such as Händel and Beethoven, and whose appreciations are sharpened by the best examples of performance in the modern concert hall, cannot drop his taste and critical habit when he enters the church door. The same is true in a modified degree in respect to those who have had less educational advantages. It is a fallacy to assert that the masses of the people are responsive only to that which is trivial and sensational. In any case, what shall be said of a church that is satisfied to leave its votaries upon the same intellectual and spiritual level upon which it finds them?

In all this discussion I have had in mind the steady and more normal work of the Church. Forms of song which, to the musician, lie outside the pale of art may have a legitimate place in seasons of special religious quickening. No one who is acquainted with the history of religious propagation in America will despise the revival hymn, or deny the necessity of the part it has played. But these seasons of spiritual upheaval are temporary and exceptional; they are properly the beginning not the end of the Church's effort. The revival hymn may be effective in soul-winning, it is inadequate when treated as an element in the larger task of spiritual development.

There is another reason for insistence upon beauty and perfection in all those features of public worship into which art enters — to a devout mind the most imperative of all reasons. This is so forcibly stated by the great Richard Hooker that it will be sufficient to quote his words and leave the matter there. Speaking of the value of noble architecture and adornment in connection with public acts of religion, he goes on to say: " We do thereby give unto God a testimony of our cheerful affection which thinketh nothing too dear to be bestowed about the furniture of his service; as also because it serveth to the world for a witness of his almightiness, whom we outwardly honor with the chiefest of outward things, as being of all things himself incomparably the greatest. To set forth the majesty of kings, his vicegerents in this world, the most gorgeous and rare treasures which the world hath, are procured. We think belike that he will accept what the meanest of them would disdain." [1]

In urging onward the effort after beauty and perfection in church music I have no wish to set up any single style as a model, — in fact, a style competent to serve as a universal model does not exist. There can be no general agreement, for varied conditions demand diverse methods. The Catholic music reformer points to the ancient Gregorian chant and the masterpieces of choral art of the sixteenth century as embodying the ideal which he wishes to assert. The Episcopalian has the Anglican chant and anthem, noble and appropriate in themselves, and consecrated by the associations of three eventful centuries. But the only hereditary possession of the Congregationalists, Presbyterians, and other non-liturgic bodies is the crude psalmody of the early Calvinists and Puritans which, unlike the Lutheran choral, has none of the musical potencies out of which a church art can be developed. In these societies there is no common demand or opportunity which, in the absence of a common musical heritage, can call forth any new and distinctive form of ecclesiastical song. They must be borrowers and adapters, not creators. The problem of these churches is the application of existing forms to new conditions — directing the proved powers of music along still higher lines of service in the epoch of promise which is now opening before them.

In this era just upon us, in which new opportunities demand of the Church in America new methods through

[1] Hooker, *Laws of Ecclesiastical Polity*, book **v.** chap. **15.**

out the whole range of its action, music will have a
larger part to play than even heretofore. It is of great
importance that her service should be employed intelli-
gently. Both ministers and choir leaders should be
aware of the nature of the problems which ecclesiastic
music presents. They should know something of the
experience of the Church in its historic dealings with
this question, of the special qualities of the chief forms
of church song which have so greatly figured in the
past, and of the nature of the effect of music upon the
mind both by itself alone and in collusion with other
religious influences. How many ministers and choir-
masters are well versed in these matters? What are the
theological seminaries and musical conservatories doing
to disseminate knowledge and conviction on this subject?
In the seminaries lectures are given on liturgiology and
hymnology; but what are hymns and liturgies without
music? And how many candidates for the ministry are
prepared to second the efforts of church musicians in
musical improvement and reform? I am, of course,
aware that in a few of the seminaries of the non-liturgic
denominations work in this department of ecclesiology
has been effectively begun. In the conservatories organ
playing and singing, both solo and chorus, are taught,
but usually from the technical side, — the adaptation of
music to the spiritual demands of the Church is rarely
considered. Every denomination needs a St. Cecilia
Society to convince the churches of the spiritual quickening that lies in genuine church music and the mis-
chief in the false, to arouse church members to an
understanding of the injury that attends an obvious

incongruity between the character of the music and the spirit of prayer which it is the purpose of the established offices of worship to create, and to show how all portions of the service may act in harmony.

The general growth in musical culture, which is so marked a feature of our time, should everywhere be made to contribute to the benefit of the Church. The teaching of music in the public schools should be a means of supplying the churches with efficient chorus singers. The Church must also offer larger inducements to musicians and musical students. Here we touch upon a most vital point. If the Church wants music that is worthy of her dignity, and which will help her to maintain the place she seeks to occupy in modern life, she must pay for it. The reason why so few students of talent are preparing themselves for work in the Church as organists and choir leaders is that the prospect of remuneration is too small to make this special study worth their while. The musical service of the Church is, therefore, in the vast majority of cases, in the hands either of amateurs or of musicians who are devoting themselves through the entire week to work which has nothing to do with the Church. A man who is trained wholly or chiefly as a pianist, and who gives his strength and time for six days to piano study and teaching, or a singer whose energy is mainly expended in private vocal instruction, can contribute little to the higher needs of Church music. It is not his fault; he must seek his income where he can find it. The service of the Church is a side issue, and receives the benefit which any cause must expect when it is given only the remnants of interest and energy that are left over from a week's hard labor. There is a host of young musicians to whom church work is exceedingly attractive. Let the Church magnify the importance of its musical service, and raise its salaries in proportion, and an abundant measure of the rising musical talent and enthusiasm will be ready at its call.

The musical problem of the non-liturgic Church in America is, therefore, not one of creation, but of administration. Whatever the mission of the Church is to be in our national life, the opportunities of its music are not to be less than of old, but greater. It is evident that the notion of conviction of sin and sudden conversion is gradually losing the place which it formerly held in ecclesiastical theory, and is being supplemented, if not supplanted, by the notion of spiritual nurture. The Church is finding its permanent and comprehensive task in alliance with those forces that make for social regeneration; no longer to separate souls from the world and prepare them for a future state of existence, but to work to establish the kingdom of God here on earth; not denying the rights of the wholesome human instincts, but disciplining and refining them for fraternal service. In this broader sphere art, especially music, will be newly commissioned and her benign powers utilized with ever-increasing intelligence. The Church can never recover the old musical leadership which was wrested from her in the seventeenth and eighteenth centuries by the opera, the choral society, and the concert system, but in the twentieth she will find means of coöperating with these institutions for the general welfare.

The council of Carthage in the fourth century laid this injunction upon church singers : " See that what thou singest with thy lips thou believest in thy heart; and what thou believest in thy heart thou dost exemplify in thy life." This admonition can never lose its authority ; back of true church music there must be faith. There comes, however, to supplement this ancient warning, the behest from modern culture that the music of the sanctuary shall adapt itself to the complex and changing conditions of modern life, and while it submits to the pure spirit of worship it shall grow continually in those qualities which make it worthy to be honored by the highest artistic taste. For among the venerable traditions of the Church, sanctioned by the wisdom of her rulers from the time of the fathers until now, is one which bids her cherish the genius of her children, and use the appliances of imagination and skill to add strength and grace to her habitations, beauty, dignity, and fitness to her ordinances of worship.

BIBLIOGRAPHY

List of books that are of especial value to the student of church music, not including works on church history. Books that the author deems of most importance are marked by a star.

* Ambros. Geschichte der Musik, 5 vols. and index. Leipzig, Leuckart, 1880–1887.

* Archer and Reed (editors). The Choral Service Book. Philadelphia, General Council Publication Board, 1901.

* Bacon and Allen (editors). The Hymns of Martin Luther set to their Original Melodies, with an English Version. New York, Scribner, 1883.

Bäumker. Das Katholische-deutsche Kirchenlied. Freiburg, Herder, 1886.

Burney. General History of Music, 4 vols. London, 1776.

* Cæcilien Kalendar, 5 vols.; Haberl, editor. Regensburg, 1876–1885.

Clément. Histoire générale de la musique religieuse. Paris, Adrien le Clere, 1861.

Chappell. History of Music from the Earliest Records to the Fall of the Roman Empire. London, Chappell.

Chrysander. Georg Friedrich Haendel, 3 vols. (unfinished). Leipzig, Breitkopf & Haertel, 1856–1867.

* Coussemaker. Histoire de l'harmonie au Moyen Age. Paris, Didron, 1852.

* Curwen. Studies in Worship Music, 2 vols. London, Curwen.

Davey. History of English Music. London, Curwen, 1895.

* Dommer. Elemente der Musik. Leipzig, Weigl, 1862.

411

* Dommer. Handbuch der Musikgeschichte. Leipzig, Grunow, 1878.

Duen. Clement Marot et la psautier huguenot, 2 vols. Paris, 1878.

Duffield. English Hymns. New York, Funk, 1888.

Duffield. Latin Hymn Writers and their Hymns. New York, Funk, 1889.

Earle. The Sabbath in Puritan New England. New York, Scribner, 1891.

Engel. Musical Instruments (South Kensington Museum Art Handbooks). London, Chapman & Hall.

* Engel. The Music of the Most Ancient Nations. London, Murray, 1864.

Fetis. Biographie universelle des Musiciens, 8 vols. with 2 supplementary vols. by Pougin. Paris, Didot.

* Gevaert. La Mélopée antique dans le Chant de l'Église latine. Gand, Hoste, 1895.

* Gevaert. Les Origines du Chant liturgique de l'Église latine. Gand, Hoste, 1890.

Glass. The Story of the Psalter. London, Paul, 1888.

Gould. Church Music in America. Boston, Gould, 1853.

* Grove. Dictionary of Music and Musicians, 4 vols. London, Macmillan, 1879–1890.

* Haberl. Magister Choralis, tr. by Donnelly. Regensburg and New York, Pustet, 1892.

Häuser. Geschichte des Christlichen Kirchengesanges und der Kirchenmusik. Quedlinburg, Basse, 1834.

Hawkins. General History of the Science and Practice of Music, 3 vols. London, 1853.

* Helmore. Plain Song (Novello's Music Primers). London, Novello.

Hoffman von Fallersleben. Geschichte des deutschen Kirchenliedes bis auf Luther's Zeit. Hannover, Rümpler, 1861.

Hope. Mediæval Music. London, Stock, 1894.

* Horder. The Hymn Lover. London, Curwen, 1889.

Hughes. Contemporary American Composers. Boston, Page, 1900.

* Jakob. Die Kunst im Dienste der Kirche. Landshut, Thomann, 1885.

*Jebb. The Choral Service of the United Church of England and Ireland. London, Parker, 1843.

*Julian. Dictionary of Hymnology. London, Murray, 1892.

Kaiser and Sparger. A Collection of the Principal Melodies of the Synagogue. Chicago, Rubovits, 1893.

* Kirchenmusikalisches Jahrbuch; Haberl, editor. Regensburg, begun in 1886.

Koch. Geschichte des Kirchenliedes und Kirchengesanges, 8 vols. Stuttgart, Belser, 1866.

* Köstlin. Geschichte des Christlichen Gottesdienstes. Freiburg, Mohr, 1887.

* Kretzschmar. Führer durch den Concertsaal : Kirchliche Werke. Leipzig, Liebeskind, 1888.

* Kümmerle. Encyclopëdie der evangelischen Kirchenmusik, 4 vols. Gütersloh, Bertelsmann, 1888-1895.

Langhans. Geschichte der Musik des 17, 18 und 19 Jahrhunderts, 2 vols. Leipzig, Leuckart, 1887.

La Trobe. The Music of the Church. London, Seeley, 1831.

Liliencron. Deutsches Leben im Volkslied um 1530. Stuttgart, Spemann, 1884.

Malim. English Hymn Tunes from the Sixteenth Century to the Present Time. London, Reeves.

* Marbecke. The Book of Common Prayer with Musical Notes; Rimbault, editor. · London, Novello, 1845.

Maskell. Ancient Liturgy of the Church of England.

McClintock and Strong. Cyclopædia of Biblical, Theological, and Ecclesiastical Literature. New York, Harper, 1867-1885.

* Mees. Choirs and Choral Music. New York, Scribner, 1901.

Mendel-Reissmann. Musikalisches Conversations-Lexikon, 11 vols. Leipzig, List & Francke.

Naumann. History of Music, tr. by Praeger, 2 vols. London, Cassell.

* Neale. Hymns of the Eastern Church. London, 1882.

* O'Brien. History of the Mass. New York, Catholic Pub. Soc., 1893.

* Oxford History of Music, 6 vols. ; Hadow, editor. Oxford, Clarendon Press, now appearing.

* Parry. Evolution of the Art of Music. New York, Appleton, 1896.

413

Perkins and Dwight. History of the Handel and Haydn Society. Boston, Mudge, 1883–1893.

Pothier. Les Melodies gregoriennes. German translation by Kienle.

* Pratt. Musical Ministries in the Church. New York, Revell, 1901. Contains valuable bibliography.

* Proctor. History of the Book of Common Prayer. London, Macmillan, 1892.

Riemann. Catechism of Musical History, 2 vols. London, Augener; New York, Schirmer.

Ritter, A. W. Zur Geschichte des Orgelspiels. Leipzig, Hesse, 1884.

Ritter, F. L. Music in America. New York, Scribner, 1890.

Ritter, F. L. Music in England. New York, Scribner, 1890.

Rousseau. Dictionnaire de Musique.

Rowbotham. History of Music, 3 vols. London, Trübner, 1885–. 1887.

Same, 1 vol.

Schelle. Die Sixtinische Kapelle. Wien, Gotthard, 1872.

Schlecht. Geschichte der Kirchenmusik. Regensburg, Coppenrath, 1879.

Schletterer. Geschichte der kirchlichen Dichtung und geistlichen Musik. Nördlingen, Beck, 1866.

Schletterer. Studien zur Geschichte der französischen Musik. Berlin, Damköhler, 1884–1885.

* Schubiger. Die Sängerschule St. Gallens. Einsiedeln, Benziger, 1858.

Spencer. Concise Explanation of the Church Modes. London, Novello.

* Spitta. Johann Sebastian Bach, 3 vols., tr. by Clara Bell and J. A. Fuller Maitland. London, Novello, 1884–1888.

Spitta. Musikgeschichtliche Aufsätze. Berlin, Paetel, 1894.

Spitta. Zur Musik. Berlin, Paetel, 1892.

* Stainer. The Music of the Bible. London, Cassell, 1882.

Stainer and Barrett. Dictionary of Musical Terms. Boston, Ditson.

Thibaut. Purity in Music, tr. by Broadhouse. London, Reeves.

* Wagner, P. Einführung in die gregorianischen Melodien. Freiburg (Schweiz), Veith, 1895.

414

Winterfeld. Das evangelische Kirchengesang, 3 vols. Leipzig, Breitkopf & Haertel, 1845.

Winterfeld. Johannes Gabrieli und sein Zeitalter, 2 vols. Berlin, Schlesinger, 1834.

* Wiseman. Lectures on the Offices and Ceremonies of Holy Week. Baltimore, Kelly, 1850.

INDEX

27

INDEX

A

Act of Supremacy, 325, 328, 329.
Agathon, pope, 110.
Agnus Dei, 90.
Ahle, 266.
Ainsworth, psalm-book of, 376.
Altenburg, 266.
Ambrose, St., 58; introduces psalm singing into Milan, 66.
Anerios, the, 133, 168.
Anthem, Anglican, 346; its different forms, 348; periods and styles, 353.
Aria, Italian, origin of, 190; its supremacy in the seventeenth and eighteenth centuries, 191; its introduction into church music in Italy, 193, 269; influence upon German church music, 267, 269, 318; adoption into the cantata, 273; into the Passion music, 276, 280.
Art, Catholic conception of religious, 70, 174; Calvinist and Puritan hostility to art in connection with worship, 363, 369, 372.
Asor, 23.
Assyrians, religious music among the, 12.
Attwood, 354.
Augustine, missionary to England, 117.
Augustine, St., quoted, 51, 67; traditional author, with St. Ambrose, of the Te Deum, 58; effect of music upon, 372.

B

Bach, Johann Sebastian, his relation to German church music, 282, 287, 289; the Bach family, 284; Bach's birth, education, and official positions, 286; condition of German music in his early days, 287; his organ music, 290, 292; fugues, 292; choral preludes, 295; cantatas, 300; style of his arias, 304; of his choruses, 305; Passion according to St. Matthew, 307; compared with Händel's "Messiah," 307; its formal arrangement and style, 308; performance by Mendelssohn, 312; the Mass in B minor, 204, 211, 312; national and individual character of Bach's genius, 314; its universality, 316; decline of his influence after his death, 317.
Bach Society, New, 322.
Bardi, 188.
Barnby, 355, 383.
Battishill, 354.
Beethoven, his Mass in D, 119, 200, 204, 210.
Behem, 229.
Benedictus, 88.
Bennett, 355.
Berlioz, his Requiem, 199, 200, 204
Beza, 360.
Bisse, quoted, 338.
Boleyn, Anne, 326.
Bonar, 381.
Boniface, 118.
Bourgeois, 360.